Unhappy Dialogue

Unhappy Dialogue
The Metropolitan Police and black Londoners in post-war Britain

James Whitfield

WILLAN
PUBLISHING

Published by

Willan Publishing
Culmcott House
Mill Street, Uffculme
Cullompton, Devon
EX15 3AT, UK
Tel: +44(0)1884 840337
Fax: +44(0)1884 840251
e-mail: info@willanpublishing.co.uk
Website: www.willanpublishing.co.uk

Published simultaneously in the USA and Canada by

Willan Publishing
c/o ISBS, 920 NE 58th Ave, Suite 300,
Portland, Oregon 97213-3786, USA
Tel: +001(0)503 287 3093
Fax: +001(0)503 280 8832
e-mail: info@isbs.com
Website: www.isbs.com

First published 2004

ISBN 1-84392-064-6

British Library Cataloguing-in-Publication Data

A catalogue record for this book is available from the British Library

Typeset by TW Typesetting, Plymouth, Devon
Project managed by Deer Park Productions, Tavistock, Devon
Printed and bound by TJ International Ltd, Trecerus Industrial Estate, Padstow, Cornwall

Contents

List of tables and figures

List of abbreviations

ACA	Assistant Commissioner 'A' Department
ACD	Assistant Commissioner 'D' Department
ACPO	Association of Chief Police Officers
BCA	British Caribbean Association
BLO	Borough Liaison Officer
BNP	British National Party
CAB	Citizens' Advice Bureaux
CARD	Campaign Against Racial Discrimination
CDRP	Crime and Disorder Reduction Partnerships
CIAC	Commonwealth Immigrants Advisory Committee
CID	Criminal Investigation Department
CLO	Community Liaison Officer
CND	Campaign for Nuclear Disarmament
CO	Colonial Office
CO	Commissioner's Office, New Scotland Yard
CPPA	Coloured People's Progressive Association
CPS	Crown Prosecution Service
CRC	Community Relations Commission
CRR (training)	Community and Race Relations Training
CSS	Council for Social Services
DAC	Deputy Assistant Commissioner
DPP	Director of Public Prosecutions
ESN	Educationally Sub-Normal
EVW	European Voluntary Worker
FLC	Foreign Labour Committee
GLA	Greater London Authority
GLC	Greater London Council
GO	General Orders (Metropolitan Police)
HAT	Human Awareness Training
HMIC	Her Majesty's Inspector of Constabulary
IB	Instruction Book (Metropolitan Police)
KCIRC	Kensington & Chelsea Inter-Racial Council
LCSS	London Council of Social Services
LEL	League of Empire Loyalists
Met (the)	Metropolitan Police

MP	Metropolitan Police
MPD	Metropolitan Police District
MPS	Metropolitan Police Service
MPSD	Metropolitan Police Solicitors' Department
NA	National Archive, Kew (formerly PRO)
NAACP	National Association for the Advancement of Colored People
NACCI	National Advisory Committee for Commonwealth Immigrants
NCCI	National Committee for Commonwealth Immigrants
NCCL	National Council for Civil Liberties
NCIS	National Criminal Intelligence Service
NSY	New Scotland Yard
NYPD	New York Police Department
OB	Occurrence Book (Metropolitan Police)
PAB	Police Advisory Board
PB	Pocket Book (Metropolitan Police)
PACE	Police and Criminal Evidence Act 1984
PCCG	Police and Community Consultative Group
PDR	Performance Development Review
PEP	Political and Economic Planning
PRO	Public Record Office, Kew
PSC	Police Service Commission
PSI	Policy Studies Institute
PTC	Police Training Council
PTDB	Police Training and Development Board
RAAS	Racial Adjustment Action Society
RAT	Racial Awareness Training
RCCP	Royal Commission on Criminal Procedure
RRB	Race Relations Board
RUC	Royal Ulster Constabulary
SB	Special Branch
SPG	Special Patrol Group
TUC	Trades Union Congress
UBP	Unit Beat Policing
NVALA	National Viewers and Listeners Association
VLC	Voluntary Liaison Committee
WIF	West Indies Federation
WISC	West Indian Standing Conference

Preface and acknowledgements

It was not uncommon in the 1950s to hear British people expressing racist views. During this period large numbers of black immigrants arrived from the Caribbean in search of regular employment and a better life. Most settled in London, and quickly discovered that officers of the Metropolitan Police shared the host community's general ignorance and intolerance of their cultures and lifestyles. This study argues that it was during the 1950s and 1960s, a period that has been largely overlooked by researchers of police relations with the Caribbean community, that the origins of the well-documented difficulties in the relationship from the 1970s to the 1990s are to be found. As such, the work fills a vital gap in our knowledge of Metropolitan Police attitudes and priorities, not only regarding black immigrants, but also in relation to the role of police in a period of rapid social change; and seeks to provide answers to the question posed by one interviewee, 'Where did it all start to go wrong?'

It is my hope that this study will provide new areas of discussion and investigation for students and others interested in issues of race and diversity and policing. However, I believe that the work has particular importance for police officers and those seeking to enter the police service. I would hope that having read the book, they will realise two important facts. Firstly, that the history of the Metropolitan Police's relations with London's Caribbean community is blighted by institutional racism; and secondly, that they are the ones who have the enormous task of putting right the acts, errors and omissions of the past and present.

As with all such projects, I have benefited from the wisdom and guidance of a great many people. The study is based upon research carried out for my PhD, for which I was supervised by Dr Martin Francis at the University of London. I am also indebted to Professor Clive Emsley for his advice, encouragement and friendship; Mr Clarence Thompson, Chairman of the West Indian Standing Conference; Miss Nadine Peppard, former Secretary of the Community Relations Commission; and to Norwell Roberts QPM, a most courageous former colleague who, like Britain in 1940, fought a lone battle against an enemy – in his case, his own racist colleagues. Each of the interviewees provided rich source material, which was often amusing, shocking or both. Thanks are also due to the staff at the National Archive, Kew; and to the library staff at the Police College, Hendon who, in spite of my critique of the Met, were always helpful. Finally, I would like to thank my partner, Zena, for her constant support, encouragement and patience.

Foreword by Sir William Macpherson

Unhappy Dialogue is an illuminating study of the relationship between the Metropolitan Police Service and the black and Asian minority communities since the early days of large-scale immigration, particularly from the West Indies, in the 1950s, to the present day.

The book sets out most thoroughly and lucidly the slow and sometimes painful transition from the plain hostility and overt discrimination of 50 years ago to the situation in 2004, when at least the majority of the public and police realise that any form of racism or discrimination is to be abhorred. Such realisation is particularly important for police officers, of all ranks, since they are daily in direct contact with the problems which discrimination can cause, and with the resentment which can arise as a result of discrimination towards those who form that part of society now known as 'the ethnics minorities'.

Great progress has been made within the police services of the United Kingdom since the 1960s, when, only forty years ago, the courageous Norwell Roberts became the first black Police Officer to join the Metropolitan Police. But, as this book strongly points out, there is still work to be done to stamp out racist attitudes both within the ranks of police services, and in the relationship between police and public, and in society generally.

Towards the end of the Stephen Lawrence Inquiry Sir Paul Condon, the Commissioner of the Metropolitan Police Service, said this:

> I believe that the way the police meet the needs of minority ethnic communities in terms of their experience of crime and harassment is of such importance that a priority is needed in order to achieve lasting change. It has become increasingly clear that nothing short of a major overhaul is required.

Thus the Commissioner himself realistically accepted that problems still existed in 1998. It is much to his credit, and to that of his successor, that they both accepted that action was necessary. A problem cannot be solved without initial acceptance that a problem does exist.

The modern degree of accountability of the police services which has evolved since the 1950s is also well charted in this book. The author deals perceptively with the changing attitudes of successive Home Secretaries and Commissioners as part of the history of those 50 years. He sets out thoughtfully and sensitively the way in which politicians and senior police officers have approached the problems which race and diversity have placed in their paths.

I am myself optimistic for the future, and both I and the author have observed positive changes in attitude towards these problems. More must be done, but credit should undoubtedly be given to those who are engaged in ensuring that such change takes place. As the author says in the last lines of his excellent book:

> Traditional responses to problems of action and reaction must now find new allies in thought, reflection and a genuine willingness to embrace change.

I commend this book both to police officers and the public as a valuable contribution to understanding the roots and history of the relationship between police and ethnic minorities, particularly the West Indian communities of London, over the last 50 and more years, and as a valuable contribution to the process of necessary change.

William Macpherson of Cluny
April 2004

Introduction

From the late 1940s increasing numbers of black – predominantly West Indian – immigrants arrived in Britain in search of regular employment. The problems and social tensions that were believed to have resulted from their presence, and the way in which the Metropolitan Police (the Met) – an inward-looking organisation that was hidebound by tradition – chose to address them, provides the starting point of our examination of relations between the Met and London's black community during the early years of large-scale black immigration to Britain.

The study focuses on the period from 1950 to 1970 and explains why it was that mistrust, resentment and suspicion developed on both sides. In doing so, it places well-documented later problems into their historical context and provides new perspectives for consideration on: the relationship between the Metropolitan Police Commissioner and the Home Secretary; the cultures and sub-cultures within the police service; the differing priorities to be found within its rank structure; the nature of racial and cultural prejudice in the Met at this time and its self-imposed alienation from the community it served; comparisons of the differing policing methods in London with those in the Caribbean, and the problems that this caused for both immigrants and Metropolitan Police officers; and the Met's lack of commitment at the highest level to the question of community and race relations. These issues are examined in the broader social context of British society in the 1950s and 1960s. As such, the Met, the physical representation of the dominant culture's authority in the nation's capital, is seen as a prism though which we can explore the broader context of race relations in Britain in the period.

Academic researchers of West Indian life in Britain in the 1950s and 1960s invariably focused on important issues of direct discrimination that adversely affected the black community in general, and were subsequently addressed – albeit in somewhat half-hearted fashion – by legislation relating to housing, employment, the 'colour bar' in places of public resort, and the provision of goods and services.[1] At the same time, they took it upon themselves to represent, and thereby deny, the voice of the black immigrant.[2] As Gilroy points out, in doing so they defined blacks as 'forever victims, objects rather than subjects, beings that feel yet lack the ability to think'.[3] Policing was only mentioned, if at all, in passing.[4] Emsley noted, that in respect of racism in the police during the period, 'the problem was scarcely perceived when Whitaker published his critical appraisal of the English police in 1964'.[5] The validity of much of the research on the subject of Caribbean immigration to Britain in the 1950s and 1960s has been questioned on the basis that those conducting it were white members of the indigenous population who lacked an in-depth knowledge of the West Indian community prior to commencing their inquiries. It has also been claimed that the reports they produced were too readily consumed by those in authority, who, in their desire to find solutions to what were seen as social difficulties, introduced legislation and policies that were detrimental to the interests of black immigrants.[6] If there is truth in the old adage that 'the namer of names is always the father of things', then it was the work of early academic researchers which helped to define and provide mutually transferable interpretations of meaning for the descriptive terms 'West Indian immigrant' and 'problem'.

More recent accounts of West Indian immigration during the period have been based on what might be described as the viewpoints of the dominant and subordinate cultures. A number of authors have approached the subject from the perspective of a British establishment that was undergoing what Chris Waters refers to as 'a crisis of self-representation in the 1950s'.[7] This has been linked with popular perceptions of the decline of Empire, the ascendancy of American cultural hegemony, and the depressing realisation in the post-Suez period that the hands on the clock had moved beyond Britain's finest hour. Kathleen Paul considered the approach of successive British governments to the questions of Empire/Commonwealth and the ongoing play on words in which Whitehall's desire to control 'coloured' immigration was invariably 'disguised as an "immigration" problem – a much more politically and socially acceptable issue'.[8] Others, such as Wendy Webster, have identified the way in which black British subjects were acceptable as long as they remained at arms length, but were seen as a threat 'when the colonial encounter was reversed through migration to the metropolis, and was no longer represented in terms of colonizers bringing civilization to the primitive, but of "immigrants" bringing physical and moral decline to the civilized'.[9]

The alternative voice has been expressed through the work of researchers who have approached West Indian immigration during the period from an entirely different perspective. This 'history from below' approach has given rise to an understandable predisposition to represent black immigrants as a generally law-abiding, honourable and oppressed minority whose legal right to take up residence in Britain, and willingness to contribute to the rebuilding of the metropolis in the post-war years, was both resented and stifled by an indigenous community that practised racial discrimination in order to deny immigrants equality of opportunity. Particular criticism has been reserved for authority's physical presence, the police service.[10] Thus, one sees the police described as the strong arm of white racism, in which:

> ... attitudes towards the Caribbean migrants within the police forces mirrored attitudes in society at large. Most policemen emerged from the social groups who most feared the black migrants, and who were most prepared to use violence to express their fears.[11]

Such representations, in which West Indian immigrants appear as victims, have much in common with the way in which police tended to describe themselves during the period. As a result, one sees that in depictions of immigrant life emphasis is placed on the honest and industrious majority of Caribbean immigrants who did their best to make a positive contribution to Britain's economic and social wellbeing in the face of adversity, while the activities of the criminal, and anti-social, minority are played down. In the same context, police always sought to emphasise their sacrifices on behalf of an unappreciative society, while claiming that those of their number who indulged in corrupt and other criminal practices were 'the occasional bad apple' in an otherwise healthy barrel.[12]

Observers of police and ethnic minority disadvantage have also tended to deal with these issues from distinct and separate standpoints, though in the majority of cases the starting point for much research is taken as the decade of the 1970s – a period in which difficulties in the police's relationship with the black community became increasingly evident. Further problems in the relationship in the 1980s proved to be a particularly fruitful area of research for sociologists, some of whom chose to focus on the internal workings of the police service, its command structure, and police interaction with ethnic minority communities as part of a more general examination of policing across a broad spectrum of duties and responsibilities. Particular studies have included Holdaway's 1983 investigation of the practices and attitudes of junior ranking police officers, and what he describes as their 'occupational culture'.[13] Reiner offers a detailed examination of the decision-making processes in the police service.[14] He provides a balanced assessment of the different forms that police discrimination can take, and the ways in which they impact on ethnic minorities and the young working class in particular.[15] However, in his historical review of policing, the decades of the 1950s and 1960s are summarised in fairly general comment. Despite its title, Holdaway's more recent work, *The Racialisation of British Policing* (1996), also makes no detailed reference to relations between immigrants and police during the period before the 1970s.[16] Bowling and Phillips's study of the policing of ethnic minority communities focuses on contemporary issues and makes only a summation of relations prior to the 1980s.[17]

In his 1999 study, Waddington noted that most research and commentary had been to locate the origin of police racism in the sub-culture of the lower ranks; and, referring to Holdaway's 1996 study, suggested that the racialisation of policing, 'is not a simple one-way process, but is instead a product of interaction in which both police and young black and Asian people (especially men) engage in mutually hostile stereotyping'.[18] This research seeks to show that police racism afflicted every level of the police service, and that not only was it not confined to the lower ranks, but that racism among the highest ranks of the Met was the principal cause of the failure of the police to develop good relations with London's black community. In addition, it suggests that the racialisation of policing can be seen in police reports of the early 1950s: a time when black and Asian people were regarded as generally law-abiding, and long before relations were blighted by mutual hostility.

Historical researchers have provided an added dimension to our knowledge of the cultural aspects of British policing. The problems of accountability and police self-perception that they have identified have parallels with the Met's failure to understand and empathise with the difficulties faced by West Indian immigrants. Victor Bailey's account of rioting in Trafalgar Square in 1886 highlights the fact that there were already those who advocated the need for transference of power over the Metropolitan Police from the Home Office to municipal control,[19] and that this view was opposed by the Home Secretary, who, along with others in the Commons, believed that 'the Commissioner should have the power to act on his own responsibility without hindrance from the Home Office'.[20] Emsley's account of police disaffection in the years leading to the creation of the Police Federation in 1919 graphically illustrates the level of introspection that has always been uppermost in the police psyche.[21] As will be seen, both of these issues: the Metropolitan Police Commissioner's *de facto* independence from political control and police introspection, were central to the way in which the Met saw its role in the 1950s and 1960s.

Tony Judge has described the Police Federation's cautionary approach to the appointment of black police officers in the 1960s, and its belief that black complainants were largely unrepresentative of the wider immigrant communities.[22] Jennifer Davis's study of race, poverty and policing in London from 1850 to 1985 is somewhat misleading for it is essentially a comparison between perceived problems caused by the Irish community in Kensington in the 1860s and 1870s, and events at Broadwater Farm in 1985. She makes no reference to relations between police and West Indian immigrants during the period from 1950 to 1970.[23] Michael O'Byrne's critique of present-day policing is important, as he is both a recently retired chief constable (Bedfordshire) and a man who spent his formative policing years (constable to chief inspector) in the Met. He charts the development of policing since the 1950s but does not discuss immigration in his review of the period, focusing instead on the development of motorised police patrols, the implications of the 1964 Police Act and the introduction of Unit Beat Policing (UBP) in the 1960s.[24]

One sees, therefore, that there has been a broad range of academic interest in West Indian immigration to Britain, though during the period under consideration, the police were largely peripheral to a debate that focused primarily on the social implications of racial discrimination. During the turbulent decades of the 1970s and 1980s a number of observers alleged that policing became more politicised and, at the same time, black people of West Indian descent began to express their discontent towards the police service. The outbreaks of public disorder involving sections of the black community that extended over a decade from the mid-1970s prompted a new wave of academic interest, but unlike the earlier period, policing was now central to the debate. The way in which relations between the police (the Met in particular) and London's West Indian community deteriorated during the crucial early years of immigration was either overlooked or taken for granted by academic researchers.

As a result, there has been a distinct lack of detailed research and analysis of the original causes of the deterioration in relations between the Met and London's West Indian community during the 1950s, when immigration from the Caribbean reached its peak; and the 1960s, when legislation was introduced to tackle racial discrimination. It is this gap in our knowledge that the present work seeks to address. As such, it provides essential new information that broadens our understanding of policing and race relations and provides a firm basis for a better appreciation of the development of the Met's relationship with the West Indian community and its descendants. The study is based upon government records, principally those relating to the Metropolitan Police, the Home Office and the Colonial Office; *Metropolitan Police Orders*;[25] interviews with one of Her Majesty's Inspectors of Constabulary (HMIC), senior staff at the Metropolitan Police Authority (MPA), serving and former police officers, politicians and senior officials at the Home Office; discussions with leading figures from the National

Committee for Commonwealth Immigrants, and its successor, the Community Relations Commission; as well as with members of the Caribbean community in London.

The Metropolitan Police is responsible, with the exception of the tiny area covered by the City of London Police, for the policing of the whole of Greater London. West Indians were the first group of black immigrants to come to Britain in large numbers after the Second World War, and well over half of those who came chose to settle in London. It followed, therefore, that the Met's involvement with this group would be considerably greater, and the range of problems more diverse, than those of any other police force. In the 1950s, West Indian immigrants arrived in Britain at a time of labour shortages. Their mother tongue was English, they came from a predominantly Christian background, their education system was based on that in the United Kingdom,[26] and most had been raised to regard Britain as their spiritual home. They found, however, that despite such apparent advantages, they encountered prejudice and discrimination among sections of the host community. They, more than any other immigrant group, were stigmatised as having the potential to corrupt traditional British values of decency and respectability, and, over time, became increasingly associated with violent criminality.

In focusing on relations between the Met and West Indian immigrants there are inevitably related topics that have not been addressed in this research. Though reference is made to the prejudice experienced by West Indians in housing, employment, social interaction and family life, such issues have been considered at length by earlier researchers and have only been referred to in this study when they have impacted on relations between Caribbean immigrants and police. Immigration to Britain from the West Indies at this time differed in terms of volume and settlement patterns to those who came from India and Pakistan. West Indian immigration was in decline when those from South Asia were arriving in increasing numbers. Studies of relations between the police and immigrants from India, Pakistan and West Africa would merit separate investigation in their own right and would undoubtedly raise issues that have not been addressed here.

Common words or expressions of the period that are no longer in daily usage appear in quotation marks. The word 'coloured', which is today considered both archaic and distasteful, was generally used at this time to describe all people of non-white appearance. When not referring to a direct quotation, the term 'black' is used throughout when discussing matters that affected West Indian, African and Asian communities generally. The terms 'West Indian' and 'Caribbean' are used interchangeably. The Metropolitan Police now refers to itself as a 'Service' (the MPS), as opposed to a 'Force'. However, many people still refer to the 'police force', and, as with references to 'policeman' and 'police officer', such words are used interchangeably. In the 1950s and 1960s, policewomen were considered to be specialists who dealt with women and prostitutes, children and young persons, and various roles within the Criminal Investigation Department (CID). They were not, until the 1970s, in the front line of officers dealing on a daily basis with the West Indian community (other than in the specialist roles described). As such, they were not a significant factor in the deterioration of relations between the Met and the West Indian community.

Structure of this book

Chapter 1 sets out the case against successive British governments in the post-war period for creating a situation in which popular resentment of West Indian immigration could occur: and, once the need to assist immigrants had been recognised in the 1960s, for giving what was seen by many in the West Indian community to be priority treatment to the needs of immigrants from India and Pakistan, while apparently over-looking those of the West Indian community. The government's desire to stop Caribbean immigration was tempered by fears of what such action might do to Commonwealth unity. While Whitehall dithered throughout the 1950s, no efforts were made by central government to encourage assimilation or integration. Accurate figures on arrivals from the West Indies were not kept until the latter half of the 1950s and the government could only provide crude and unhelpful estimates of the number of immigrants arriving. As a result, it was in no position to counter the alarmist rhetoric of Cyril Osborne, Norman Pannell and others who claimed that West Indian immigrants were 'swamping' Britain.

Chapter 2 considers the way in which West Indian immigrants were stereotyped by police, the media and society and examines the way in which police reports from the 1950s suggested that black immigrants showed little desire to associate with the host community. A closer analysis of these reports clearly indicates that white prejudice was the more likely explanation for the failure to integrate and/or assimilate. In examining the implications of the Notting Hill disturbances of 1958, the popularly held view that these events led to a downturn in relations between police and black people will be challenged. It will be argued that the disturbances were less significant in policing terms than they were as an indication of the self-delusion that Britain was ready to accept the concept of a multi-racial society. Colonial policing was important in developing attitudes, not only among West Indians towards police, but also in shaping the approach of police officers in Britain towards immigrant communities. The chapter considers the way in which differing police cultures in the Caribbean and London were a key aspect of declining relations between the Met and West Indian immigrants. Public perceptions of the police changed during the 1950s and 1960s. The chapter concludes by reviewing representations of the police on film and television and suggests that the policing of West Indian immigrants took place in an atmosphere in which deference towards the police and authority generally no longer went unquestioned or unchallenged.

Chapter 3 deals with representative groups and the Met's approach to community relations, and suggests that the Met was selective as to which representative bodies it was willing to co-operate with. Spokespersons for the West Indian community would undoubtedly have been shocked had they discovered that, in the era of the Cold War, the Met's Special Branch classified many of them as communists. The inevitable result was that the Met preferred to deal with more 'acceptable' organisations, such as the National Committee for Commonwealth Immigrants (NCCI), and later the Community Relations Commission (CRC), rather than liaising with the leaders of the West Indian Standing Conference (WISC). The Met's response to the Parliamentary Select Committee on Race Relations and Immigration in 1968 is important for what it tells us of the Met's attitude to London's West Indian community. The Met claimed that West Indians were the architects of their own misfortune, and consequently saw no need for a revision of its own policies and strategies. As far as it was concerned, in the field of race relations, it was doing a good job.

Chapter 4 focuses on the hierarchy and institutional structure of the Met, in particular, the *de facto* independence of the Commissioner and the effects of an overly conservative outlook at Scotland Yard. Possible contributory factors to police racial prejudice that are considered include the low educational standards of police recruits; the inadequacy of Home Office supervision of the Metropolitan Police Commissioner; and the modifications to policing practices in the 1960s, such as the introduction of Unit Beat Policing and its ineffectiveness in inner-city areas. The chapter also considers and contrasts the work of various home secretaries during the period and highlights the weakness of James Callaghan and the Home Office Police Department in the face of the Police Federation's opposition to the creation of a specific police discipline offence of racial discrimination: a measure that, had it been introduced, would have done much to persuade minority ethnic communities that racism in the police would not be tolerated.

Chapter 5 examines recruitment and training in the Met and considers why a police career was an unattractive option for black people in the 1950s and 1960s. It argues that there was a strong element of racism in the Met's selection procedures at this time, and suggests that the Met's recruiting policy was targeted at sections of society in which black people were least likely to be represented. In recruiting from the British

Isles as a whole, the Met acquired many new officers with no personal knowledge of immigrant communities, and whose first contact with black people was likely to be in an enforcement role. The low priority placed on race relations training and its lack of sophistication, both in the Met and other Home Office police forces, is identified as a particularly significant factor in explaining why relations with the West Indian community deteriorated.

Chapter 6 is concerned with the way in which the Met policed West Indians living in London, and suggests that the Met's heavy-handed strategies and lack of awareness of West Indian cultures was compounded by its unwillingness to accept that racial motivation was a significant aggravating factor in reported crime. Added to this was the belief of many black people that a complaint against the police was a useless exercise. The defects in the system of police complaints at the time are discussed. The police's self-perception as victims of a society that took them for granted is examined in detail and it is suggested that, at a time when the Met was seriously understaffed, many police officers believed that they had far more to complain about than did the immigrant communities. Such attitudes were compounded by the Met's alienation from the community it served and its unwillingness to accept that more needed to be done to build bridges with its community, a task that many officers believed was more properly the responsibility of social workers rather than police officers.

Chapter 7 looks at the way in which the critical issues discussed in the previous chapters have been addressed from 1970 to the present. Particular attention is paid to the development of community and race relations (CRR) training. The chapter highlights the Met's inability/ unwillingness to ensure that continuous priority was given to such training, even after the killing of Stephen Lawrence in 1993. One sees clearly that the Met failed to provide CRR training other than when forced by political expediency to do so. The chapter examines the efforts of Sir Robert Mark, Sir Kenneth Newman and Sir Peter Imbert to change the attitude of Met officers to the community they serve and considers why the efforts of these well-meaning commissioners were only partially successful. The chapter concludes with an examination of current policies in the Met on race and diversity and argues that, without cultural change and improved leadership and supervision, such policies are unlikely to succeed.

Racism, a problem for British society as a whole in the period, was unquestionably an issue in the deterioration of relations between the Metropolitan Police and the Caribbean community. It was not, however, the sole or principal reason. The evidence will suggest that the main cause of the worsening relationship was the Met's long-standing isolation from the public it served, coupled with a belief that it had nothing to learn from outsiders as to how London should be policed. As a result, those seeking to raise police awareness of race and diversity were viewed as meddlers, and community relations was seen by many in the Met as being a distraction from its real business of preventing crime, apprehending criminals and preserving the Queen's peace.

Notes

1 Race Relations Acts 1965 and 1968.
2 C. Waters, 'Dark Strangers in Our Midst: Discourses of Race and Nation in Britain', *Journal of British Studies*, 36 (1997), p.217.
3 P. Gilroy, *There Aint' No Black in the Union Jack* (1987), p.11.
4 S. Patterson, *Dark Strangers* (1963), p.88; A.H. Richmond, *Colour Prejudice in Britain* (1954), pp.88, 99, 102, 113; R. Glass, *Newcomers* (1960), pp.168–9; A. Hyndman, 'The West Indian in London' in *The West Indian Comes to England* (1960), pp.115–116. *Darks Strangers* bears many similarities in its presentation to H. Mayhew's *London Labour and the London Poor* (1985, first published in 1851–2). See particularly 'Of the Street Jews', pp.193–208.
5 C. Emsley, *The English Police* (1991), p.178; and B. Whitaker, *The Police* (1964), pp.147, 100–2.
6 See C. Mullard, *Black Britain* (1973), pp.66–72. Mullard suggests that Rose's *Colour and Citizenship* (1969), which he refers to as a 'race bible', was based on the findings of authors, all of whom were white p.70; C. Waters, *Dark Strangers*, p.208.
7 Waters, *Dark Strangers*, p.208.
8 K. Paul, *Whitewashing Britain: Race and Citizenship in the Postwar Era* (New York: 1997), p.134.
9 W. Webster, *Imagining Home: Gender, Race and National Identity, 1945–1964* (1998), p. xv.
10 See A. Sivanandan, 'From Resistance to Rebellion: Asian and Afro-Caribbean struggles in Britain', *Race & Class*, No.23, (1981–82), pp.111–70; Mullard, *Black Britain* (1973), pp.142–4,175; M. Collins, 'Pride and Prejudice: West Indian Men in Mid-Twentieth Century Britain', *Journal of British Studies*, No.40 (July 2001), pp.391–418.
11 M. Phillips and T. Phillips, *Windrush: The Irresistible Rise of Multi-Racial Britain* (1999), p.277.
12 NA STAT14/3260, Minute 28, in which reference is made to the *Challenor Inquiry Report*.
13 S. Holdaway, *Inside the British Police* (1983), p.2.
14 R. Reiner, *The Politics of the Police* (1985).
15 Ibid., pp.124–36.
16 Holdaway, *The Racialisation of British Policing* (Basingstoke: 1996), p.5.
17 B. Bowling and C. Phillips, 'Policing ethnic minority communities', in *Handbook of Policing* (2003), pp.528–55.
18 P.A.J. Waddington, 'Discretion, 'Respectability' and Institutional Police Racism', *Sociological Research Online*, 1999, 3.1 and 9.2.

19 V. Bailey, 'The Metropolitan Police, the Home Office and the Threat of Outcast London', in *Policing and Punishment in Nineteenth Century Britain* (1981), p.103. This was more than 100 years before the Home Secretary's responsibility for the Met was transferred to the Metropolitan Police Authority.

20 Ibid. See also *Parliamentary Debates (Commons)* (18 Feb. 1886), Vol.302, Cols. 594–6, 600, 603–6.

21 Emsley, *Police* (1991), pp.94–136.

22 T. Judge, *The Forces of Persuasion* (1994), pp.180, 205–6, 247–9.

23 J. Davis, 'From "Rookeries" to Communities: Race Poverty and Policing in London: 1850–1985', *History Workshop Journal*, No.27 (1989), pp.66–85.

24 M. O'Byrne, *Changing Policing: Revolution Not Evolution* (Lyme Regis: 2001) pp.5–10.

25 A twice-weekly internal publication giving information on policy and personnel matters within the Met.

26 Examinations being set by the Cambridge Examining Board.

Chapter 1

Not quite what the government had in mind: West Indian immigration in the 1950s

As Britain emerged from the Second World War, the government was faced with the realisation that additional labour was urgently needed in order to accomplish the mammoth task of rebuilding and restructuring the nation and its economy. More than a year after the end of hostilities in Europe, the country was still employing 350,000 prisoners of war, and in February 1946 the Foreign Labour Committee (FLC) was created, the aims of which were to 'examine in the light of existing manpower shortages, the possibility of making increased use of foreign labour, particularly in essential industries which are now finding special difficulty in recruiting labour'.[1]

The recruitment of workers from mainland Europe, a policy that became known as the European Voluntary Workers (EVWs) scheme, had distinct advantages from the British perspective. The large numbers of displaced persons in Europe enabled Britain to select from a vast labour resource, not only the healthiest applicants, but also those considered to be politically suitable and most likely to be an economic asset. In addition, those chosen were recruited on a contractual basis by which they were required to live and work at prescribed locations and could be deported if rules were transgressed. They could also be directed into jobs that were considered difficult to fill.[2] In order to minimise union opposition to the scheme, and to assuage traditional home-grown reserve towards foreigners, various measures were taken by the government. The Minister of Labour, George Isaacs, warned the General Secretary of the Trades Union Congress (TUC) that a failure to afford the workers equal status would, 'run a grave danger of turning the Poles [who formed a sizeable percentage of EVWs] into an underprivileged, discontented emigrant community, which would be dangerous in every way'.[3] In order to placate public opinion, and to present a positive image of EVWs, a Committee for the Education of Public Opinion on Foreign Workers was created. Viewed in the long term, the government believed that EVWs would eventually marry members of the indigenous community and would become absorbed into British society.

No such initiatives were extended to black immigrants from the West Indies who, like their European counterparts, saw the opportunity to come to Britain from the late 1940s in search of regular employment. From the British government's perspective, they were a far less attractive proposition. As British subjects they were not liable, as EVWs were, to a selection process or to health checks. Once they stepped ashore they were entitled to remain in Britain for as long as they wished, whether or not they chose to work or, as many in the indigenous population wrongly assumed, to live off the state. Unlike EVWs, the government had no power to direct them into prescribed jobs and accommodation; and their leave to enter the United Kingdom was, save for a few exceptions, unrestricted. The result was that throughout the early 1950s, when demand for labour was at its peak, the government sought to try and persuade would-be West Indian immigrants that, contrary to favourable reports that may have been received from friends already in England, life in the metropolis could be tough.

The increasing attractiveness of Britain to those in the Caribbean was, however, patently obvious. Life in the major population centres of the West Indies was blighted by unemployment, under-employment and overcrowding. Figures given in the House of Commons in 1948 had revealed that in Barbados there were more than 1,200 people per square mile, while in Jamaica the corresponding figure stood at 300.[4] Jamaica, especially, had an economy that relied on emigration to ease its large-scale unemployment problem: predominantly and traditionally to the USA, but also to Cuba, Panama and Venezuela. The McCarran-Walter Act of 1952 restricted Caribbean immigration to the USA to a trickle. With long-established routes to economic advancement closing, Britain became increasingly attractive as an escape route from the West Indies poverty trap.

On 18 February 1949, some six months after the arrival of the first group of immigrants from the West Indies on the *Empire Windrush*, the government organised an Inter-Departmental Conference at the Home Office to consider problems arising from 'coloured' immigration.[5] The conference considered what measures might be taken to help the immigrants. It was acknowledged that there was no statistical information on the numbers involved. The problem was eased somewhat in 1949, due to a reduction in shipping and an increase in travel costs; but Home Office officials acknowledged that until employment prospects in

Jamaica improved, the desire of Jamaicans to work abroad would continue. It was found that new arrivals were prone to settle in areas of existing immigrant communities, thereby aggravating already poor conditions and overcrowding. The reluctance of many indigenous property owners to rent rooms to West Indian immigrants meant that a policy of dispersal would be difficult to implement. A scheme of repatriation for colonial citizens who were, or had become, destitute and incapacitated was introduced, the cost of the scheme being met by the National Assistance Board.[6]

The government decided that the interests of the immigrants could best be served by 'action by all Departments concerned in regard to welfare, housing, employment and repatriation and also by the stimulation of voluntary interest and service on their behalf'.[7] It was agreed that the Colonial Office (CO) would liaise with colonial governments to discourage the migration of unskilled workers from the West Indies; efforts would be made with voluntary organisations and local authorities to deal with social welfare, especially in housing and social amenities; and the CO would work with the Ministry of Labour to reduce the number of unemployed colonial citizens living in areas where work was available. It is at this point that we see the government's serious underestimation of the potential for mass migration from the Caribbean. In referring to the measures outlined, the CO advised the Cabinet that: 'Apart from the settled Colonial community only some three or four thousand persons are involved and by careful and continual attention to their needs I am confident that it can be kept within bounds without resort to drastic measures.'[8] Furthermore, at a Cabinet Office meeting held on 22 March 1950, it was confidently asserted that:

> A large number of immigrants had come over from the Colonies a year or two ago because the Treasury had given instructions that troopships which carried coloured RAF contingents back to the West Indies should on their return carry as many fare-paying passengers as possible. This experience was, however, not likely to be repeated.[9]

The intention of the British Nationality Act 1948 had been to secure a common status for the people of different Commonwealth countries who would thus become 'members of the same single family under His Majesty'.[10] Such laudable aspirations masked the fact that the British government had only ever intended that the Act would be the means by which it maintained and extended its world role. In had never imagined that membership of the 'club' would bring with it a right for black colonial citizens to settle in the United Kingdom. As a result, one sees that as early as June 1950 the Prime Minister, Clement Attlee, alarmed at the prospect of large-scale black immigration, appointed an *ad hoc* committee of ministers under the chairmanship of the Home Secretary, its terms of reference being:

> To consider and report to the Cabinet what further means might be adopted to control the immigration into this country of coloured people from British colonial territories, if amending legislation were passed limiting the right of British subjects to enter and reside in the United Kingdom, and what issues of policy would be involved in making such a change in the existing law.[11]

Speaking in the Commons on 13 June 1951, the Secretary of State for the Colonies, James Griffiths, in reply to a question on what services were being provided by the British Government to assist those arriving from the Caribbean, stated that:

> I am aware that West Indians are coming here to seek work. It would hardly be in their own best interests to encourage this immigration since most of these men lack the special skills which would ensure their employment here ... I am not in favour of encouraging it (Caribbean immigration) because I do not want them to come here and find they cannot get a job and feel frustrated.[12]

Six months later the Member for Billericay, Bernard Braine, made reference to the recently ousted Labour government's claim that it had been assisting in every way to develop industry, particularly secondary industry, in the West Indies.[13] His own fact-finding research in the West Indies had revealed that, in contrast to the government's stated position, entrepreneurial investment from Britain was being stifled as a result of Treasury policy. He continued:

> There is ... a five-year tax-free holiday for pioneer industries in respect of new factories operating not from the moment that the building of a factory is started but from the moment that it goes into production. There is Customs-free entry for building materials, plant and machinery necessary to build and equip such factories.
> In response to this kind of inducement a large number of United States and Canadian firms are moving in. That is a good thing. I can see no possible objection to the investment of North American capital in Colonial Territories. I think we should encourage it. But the interesting thing which I observed was that no British firms were establishing new factories. In fact, I found plenty of evidence that British firms were being dissuaded from going in. Why was that?
> The reason was that a company operating from Great Britain in the West Indies, and presumably elsewhere in the Colonial Empire,

may be considered a pioneer enterprise and may have these tax concessions extended to it, but these advantages are nullified because the United Kingdom Government insist on collecting the full United Kingdom rate of tax on profits. As a consequence there is no inducement to a British Company to expand its operations, to go out into the Colonial Empire and develop new resources.[14]

Government efforts to dissuade Caribbean people from coming to Britain in search of regular employment had little chance of success. News filtering back to the West Indies of measures that were being taken in the metropolis to encourage employment and improve housing prospects for those colonial immigrants who had already arrived in Britain, backed up as they were by national assistance benefits and a free trip home if all else failed, must surely have acted as a clarion call to workers in the West Indies whose job prospects were bleak. It goes without saying that, in declining to make investment in the West Indies an attractive option for British entrepreneurs, the government hardly helped itself if its desired aim was to discourage economic migrants from the West Indies from playing the only ace left at their disposal by coming to Britain in search of regular employment. The resulting perennial rise in migration from the West Indies prompted a re-think in Whitehall; and the eventual recognition that unchecked Caribbean immigration would become a political hot-potato.

The approach of successive British governments to large-scale black immigration in the 1950s and early 1960s was characterised by an unwillingness to assume responsibility for the social problems that it believed might arise. Its failure to inform the indigenous population of why such migration was occurring led to growing concerns among sections of society and significantly contributed to the fear and suspicion that developed among both host community and immigrants. Whitehall finally recognised the need to tackle social problems associated with black immigration in the early 1960s, but the evidence suggests that this was largely because of the increasing level of migration from the Indian subcontinent.

Lacking a strategy: the government, the people and race relations in the 1950s

In the 1950s, Britain's imperial heritage ensured that successive governments faced immense problems in their efforts to restrict black immigration from the West Indies and other Commonwealth countries. At a time when the Commonwealth was particularly important to the nation's economic development and prestige, the government feared that general controls on immigration from all Commonwealth countries would be seen in the most favoured outposts (Australia, Canada and New Zealand) as an unwarranted restriction on the rights of their citizens to come and go as they pleased. Secondly, the government knew that controls which were intended specifically to prevent black Commonwealth citizens coming to Britain would unquestionably be seen to be based on racial prejudice alone; and would be likely to prompt India and Pakistan, along with a number of African and Caribbean colonies, to consider their position *vis-à-vis* Britain and the Commonwealth. Finally, the anomalous position of citizens of the Republic of Ireland was that, while their own country had renounced allegiance to the Crown and had left the Commonwealth, the introduction of legislation to deter black immigration would inevitably mean that Commonwealth citizens – who still owed allegiance to the sovereign – would be treated less favourably than citizens of a country that had opted to end its ties with Britain.

The result was that British governments had both a public and private face on the question of West Indian immigration. In private, they examined a range of measures that might be introduced to prevent or deter black Commonwealth citizens from coming to Britain. These included the deportation of undesirable aliens (not proceeded with because it did not solve the real problem of too many black immigrants), and a quota system (rejected as being likely to upset the more favoured Commonwealth nations). The whole dilemma was encapsulated in a note to the Lord President of the Council on 'Coloured' Immigrants:

> But what this all means . . . is that the immigration control would be deliberately designed to hit impecunious 'blacks' from the Colonies and no one else. The plain fact is that that would be the intention and it would be quite impossible to conceal it. My personal view . . . is that tackling the problem in this way would very probably be the lesser evil; but it would be criticised both by so-called 'liberals', and possibly by people who would argue that this open discrimination against subjects of the Colonial Empire was bound to weaken the cohesion of the Commonwealth.[15]

In public, successive governments maintained that it was the right of all British subjects to enter the United Kingdom freely and that there would be serious implications for Commonwealth stability if efforts to control immigration were to be introduced. They also said that the issue of immigration controls was being given careful consideration. Such a state of affairs continued throughout the 1950s.

In 1954 the Conservative government announced that it had reached its 1951 election pledge target of building 300,000 houses a year, but subsequently declared that it was ending housing subsidy to local

17

authorities, thereby forcing them to raise funds by other means. The result was a dramatic decline in the rate of new local authority houses in comparison to those erected by private builders.[16] Most West Indian immigrants were unlikely to be able to buy their own homes, and both single men and families found themselves hampered by the housing points system that required applicants for council properties to have lived locally for a number of years before they could qualify for housing. The Cabinet Committee on Colonial Immigrants considered the housing question at its meeting on 6 June 1957. A draft progress report indicated that, 'some 40,000 additional coloured people had come to this country during 1956. The figures could only be approximate as detailed statistics were not maintained.'[17] In discussion, it was noted in the minutes that:

> Most of them [black immigrants] were accommodated in very overcrowded conditions. If official notice was taken of this fact it would be necessary to provide them with housing, in preference to white people who had long been on the housing list. At present overcrowding was being officially ignored.[18]

The message from the government was clear and unambiguous. Black immigrants living in dilapidated accommodation would have to fend for themselves. The housing shortage and the priority of British people waiting to be re-housed meant that help from government or local authorities would not be forthcoming. The government's position was reaffirmed two years later when the same committee considered the scale of the housing problem and, as if to excuse its policy on overcrowding, noted that, 'Many immigrants are accustomed to living in squalid conditions and have no desire to improve their surroundings.'[19] The majority of West Indian immigrants thus had no alternative but to live in housing that was at best sub-standard. The problem was compounded by the difficulties they faced in obtaining mortgage facilities and the unwillingness of many estate agents and vendors to entertain offers from black people who were looking to purchase property in areas considered to be, and whose residents wished them to remain, exclusively white.

The government decided that the right time to introduce immigration controls would be when the economic situation was buoyant, and when full employment negated the need for further immigrant labour. However, a slight downturn in the economy occurred in 1957–58; and, as a result, the plans were placed on hold and were subsequently incorporated in the first Commonwealth Immigrants Act in 1962. The situation was not helped by the press, whose reporting of the arrival of successive immigrants from the Caribbean became increasingly alarmist. Media concerns were also expressed at the apparent lack of any government response to what were often described as the 'hordes' of

Figure 1.1 Cummings cartoon. *Daily Express*, 12 January 1955[20]

black immigrants who were arriving in Britain. Cummings' 1955 cartoon anticipated Enoch Powell's role-reversal 'whip hand' speech by more than a decade and grossly distorted the reality of what was on offer for the overwhelming number of West Indian immigrants in Britain at the time.

Exaggerated press reports led the host community to become increasingly aware of the perceived problems associated with West Indian immigration: a situation that was meat and drink to the Union Movement and other right-wing political organisations in the 1950s. White antipathy to West Indian immigrants was shaped largely by outmoded and inaccurate depictions of Empire; an alarmist media; fears for jobs, should there be a downturn in the economy; concerns over housing in those parts of London boroughs where Caribbean immigrants had settled in numbers; and the complete lack of assurance from government that it had any ideas worthy of note on how to resolve these issues. In the absence of the latter, media fantasies about black immigration continued to escalate. As late as 1968, the Ministerial and Official Committee on Immigration and Assimilation was forced to admit that:

> It is estimated that there are at present about one million Commonwealth citizens settled in this country, representing some 2% of the population. The racist lobby indulges in the wildest speculation about the likely growth of the coloured population. We ought to be better placed to counter such speculation.[21]

Allied to the man-in-the-street's fears and concerns over immigration, heightened as they were by the activities of the press and politicians, was the all-too-obvious ignorance of the general public in Britain about their fellow British subjects. This point was well made by Sheila Patterson in her research in the early 1960s. She argued that preconceptions about black people existed in all social classes in Britain and that, 'They are for the most part the left-overs of nineteenth-century colonial attitudes, perpetuated in outmoded history and geography textbooks and in much of the classical and other fiction of the last century.'[22] She added that the decline in imperial power and national prestige, coupled with the need to form new relationships with former colonial dependants, had led to a sense of 'considerable confusion and insecurity among all classes in Britain'.[23] Even by the late 1960s it was not uncommon for a person of West Indian origin to be praised for the quality of their spoken English after such a short time in Britain. Clarence Thompson, the chairman of the West Indian Standing Conference, recalled that host community nescience of colonial citizens and cultures was not confined to linguistic proficiency:

> I used to box as a youngster here in Earlsfield and when we had to change to go into the shower nobody would be in there but as soon as I took my clothes off and I went into the shower everybody dashed in. They were looking for my tail. This is what the youngsters were told. Nineteen and twenty-year olds were told that is what this guy will have, he would have a tail. He'd be hanging by his tail. They all came in to see it. I would say 'Why are you guys in here?' They'd all say 'Where is your tail?' I'd tell them that it fell off.[24]

Racial prejudice thrived on such ignorance; a typical example being a song the author remembers hearing as a boy in Liverpool in the 1950s, which was a variation on the theme of Harry Belafonte's *Island in the Sun*:

> Oh Moss Side in the Sun,
> Give to me by the Englishman,
> Me no work but me get fat,
> Eating the plenty Kit-e-Kat.[25]

Though successive British governments spoke of the need to inform intending West Indian immigrants of the pitfalls of life in the United Kingdom, principally in an effort to deter them from coming, no efforts were ever made to educate and inform the host community on the implications of the mass migration of black people to Britain. Trevor Hall, later Race Equality Advisor to the Permanent Secretary at the Home Office, was contemptuous of government failings in this area:

Nobody actually tried to educate or inform the white community about these new people coming in, and what I hope you bring out was the cruelty of politicians that actually changed people's social environment, where they lived, by importing these new people without sending them (the host community) a leaflet or a handout. Nobody actually told the majority of white people in this country what these new people were like and why they were here. I sometimes say that we need to praise the white community more than they do get for the way the majority of them absorbed this new alien force.[26]

Local authorities and the statutory and voluntary agencies were left to sort the situation out as best they could with no strategic plan or directives from the centre. However, one might argue that the failure of central government to provide a legal framework for the concept of multi-racial Britain before the mid-1960s was the logical conclusion of successive policies that were aimed at restricting, and ultimately preventing, black colonial immigration. After all, if there was to be no welcome mat for those seeking to enter Britain from the West Indies, why bother to take measures to inform the indigenous population that they must learn to live side-by-side with them?

In the first half of the 1950s, no accurate details were kept of the numbers of West Indian citizens arriving in the United Kingdom. The only figures that were recorded were of those passengers who made the direct sea crossing from the Caribbean to British ports. This meant that the very large numbers of immigrants, who chose the more circuitous but cheaper crossing on the Grimaldi Siosa shipping line to Genoa and thence across the English Channel, as well as those who increasingly came by air, were not initially recorded.[27] As a result, government figures belied what the British people – and the media – could clearly see was the case. It also meant that when more accurate figures on immigration began to be recorded, which showed the large numbers that were arriving in Britain, the determination to take drastic action, often in a capricious manner, became even more pressing; as, by now, migration from the Indian subcontinent was also rapidly increasing. Jack Howard-Drake recalled the way in which such decisions were taken on admissions to Britain in the period after the introduction of the 1962 Immigration Act:

The thing that always worried me about the immigration committee, the controls that were exercised, was that it seemed to me were entirely arbitrary. 'How many did we let in last month?' 'Oh God, that sounds a big number. We'd better cut it down next month.' I may be wrong, and you'd have to check the minutes, but I don't

Table 1.1 Britain's black population: 1939–64[30]

1939	7,000–10,000
1953	40,000
1961	300,000
1964	1,000,000

think it was based on any considered statistical information. The policy changed from 'let them all come to the motherland', then, when governments got frightened about it they started to become selective about who they let in, and only letting in people who we wanted for our own economical reasons. But in the early days my memory of it is that it was done on a pretty arbitrary basis.[29]

Indeed, as late as 1968, the government could still only give an approximate figure of the size of Britain's black population for the 25-year period from 1939 to 1964 (see Table 1.1).

By the early 1960s, after more than a decade of West Indian immigration, and when innovative government efforts – had there been any – to integrate West Indian immigrants might have begun to pay dividends, the focus of government attention shifted to the growing problem of the now numerically more significant immigrants from India and Pakistan (with the distinct possibility of many more to come from Kenya and Uganda as a result of Africanisation policies), whose differences in language, culture and religious observance were seen as a far greater potential problem than West Indians, who prided themselves on their Britishness. In short, West Indians, became of secondary importance in the overall context of the immigration debate before any real efforts had been made to find solutions to the difficulties they were still encountering in Britain. Essentially, the West Indian community was left to integrate as best it could, and this at a time when children from the Caribbean were arriving in Britain to join parents (and in many cases siblings they had never met), after several years of separation. Consequently, there was the potential not only for increased conflict with the white community because of the greater numbers of black people in specific areas of poor-quality housing and amenities, but also for resentment among West Indians toward Asian immigrants because of perceived preferential treatment.

The concentration of government attention on Indian and Pakistani immigrants may also be explained by the better organisation of the Asian communities and the wealth that a number of them brought with them: factors that would have given them more political clout than the economically poorer, and less unified, West Indians. In addition, and unlike their West Indian counterparts, it was considered that at the time they showed little initial inclination or desire to integrate with the host community other than on an economic level. An official report on the 'social and economic effects of coloured immigration' by the Home Office suggested that:

> All the evidence shows an increasing tendency of immigrants to settle in their own communities with minimal contact with the rest of the population except at their place of work. It seems more than likely that the Indian and Pakistani immigrants, and the Cypriots, are content with this situation and have no wish to become assimilated to any degree at all. On the other hand, the West Indians, while making little effort to accommodate themselves to a different way of life, are demanding equal opportunities and equal treatment generally.[31]

As a result, many West Indians felt that they were demoted in the pecking order behind the needs of Asian immigrants, who had never identified themselves as British, and whose cultural background was vastly different to that of the host community. What evidence is there to support this impression?

A consideration of statistical information on immigration to Britain in the 1950s and 1960s shows the extent to which those coming from the West Indies were declining at the same time as those from the Indian subcontinent were rapidly increasing. Between 1955 and 1960, immigrants from Jamaica and the rest of the Caribbean outnumbered the combined totals from India and Pakistan by more than three to one.[32] The gap between the two was dramatically reduced in the rush to beat the ban on unrestricted immigration from the Commonwealth during the period up to June 1962, when the Commonwealth Immigrants Act put an end to open immigration. Thereafter, as Table 1.2 shows, one sees immigration from India and Pakistan surging ahead of the numbers coming from the Caribbean.

Table 1.2 Immigration from India, Pakistan, and the Caribbean: 1955–67[33]

	India	Pakistan	Jamaica	Rest of Caribbean	Total
1955–60	33,070	17,120	96,180	65,270	219,540
1961–30.6.62	42,000	50,170	62,450	35,640	203,470
1.7.62–1967	95,850	64,340	31,380	27,780	231,830
Total	171,720	131,630	190,010	128,690	654,860

The Commonwealth Immigrants Act also introduced a system of A, B, and C work vouchers for intending immigrants. During the period from 1962 to 1967, 61 per cent of all vouchers were issued to those coming from India and Pakistan, while only 12 per cent of vouchers went to West Indians.[34] The favoured position of Indians and Pakistanis over West Indians was underlined by Rose, who noted, in the issue of 'C' vouchers (which were issued to those who were unskilled and with no specific job awaiting them in Britain), that:

> In this period just over 40,000 C vouchers were issued, of which nearly three-quarters went to Indians and Pakistanis and only 10% to West Indians ... Thus the system was already discriminating against West Indians ... [who] fared even worse with B vouchers. Because there were not enough skilled and professional men and women wishing to emigrate, the West Indies received only 520 vouchers in the five and a half years up to the end of 1967, or less than an average of 100 a year in the whole period, whereas no less than 31,000 went to India and Pakistan.[35]

One sees, additionally, that in the field of education no special provision was made for the children of West Indian families when migration to Britain from the Caribbean was predominant in the period up to 1962. Yet special arrangements were made by local authorities to assist non-English speaking children of Asian immigrants from this time. Nadine Peppard, Secretary of the National Committee for Commonwealth Immigrants recalled that:

> There was little recognition that although the children of West Indian immigrants spoke English, there was still a big linguistic and cultural gap for many of them. None of this was helped by the absence of any reference to important historical figures from their own history. For a long time, the vast majority of schools were ill-equipped to teach other than 'white history'. This was to some extent mitigated for Asian children by the recognised status of Mahatma Gandhi, Pandit Nehru, etc. and by the religious commitment of their extended families and the role played by mosques, gurdwaras, etc.[36]

Patterson, in her 1969 work on immigration and race relations, points out that:

> Some experts believe that the problem of ostensibly English-speaking West Indian children who are in E.S.N. (educationally sub-normal) schools and D-streams, so far largely ignored, may be

a bigger one even than the needs of non-English speaking children, on which the main effort has so far been concentrated.[37]

There was an obvious pressing need to assist non-English speaking children to acquire knowledge of English as speedily as possible, and it was partly to achieve this objective that special classes and the provision of specialist teachers was made in the early 1960s. What is harder to comprehend is the initial inability of some teachers and education authorities to accept the fact that those West Indian children, who Patterson describes as speaking 'Creolese',[38] might be other than ESN or D-stream material. Hatch's research on the school curriculum in 1962 revealed that while the textbooks 'portrayed the African as being more primitive than he is today',[39] India, by contrast, 'is given a fairly prominent place in all history textbooks'.[40]

Health concerns, particularly among Pakistani immigrants in the early 1960s, raised the priority level in education for those coming from the subcontinent. A British Medical Association survey in Birmingham during the period 1960–62 revealed tuberculosis rates among men of 0.67 per thousand for the English, 1.3 for the Caribbean, 4.5 for the Indian, and 94.7 for the Pakistani.[41]

Further provision was made by the government to assist Asian immigrants as part of the Local Government Act of 1966; Clause 11 of Chapter 22, declaring that:

> Subject to the provision of this section, the Secretary of State may pay to local authorities who in his opinion are required to make special provision in the exercise of any of their functions, in consequence of the presence within their areas of substantial numbers of immigrants from the Commonwealth whose language and customs differ from those of the community, grants of such amounts as he may with the consent of the Treasury determine . . .[42]

In the Act's first year of operation (1967/68), figures revealed that the major expenditure of local authorities that had applied for the grant was for education and the corresponding employment of specialist additional staff.

One sees, therefore, that special provision was made at local authority, and subsequently at national government level, that was primarily targeted at assisting immigrants from India and Pakistan in the process of settling in Britain; and that similar measures were never put in place for those coming from the West Indies. This is not to allege any deliberate plan to ignore the needs of the West Indian community in preference to those coming from India and Pakistan after 1960, but merely to suggest that the government began to recognise that many thousands of non-English speaking people with alien cultures and lifestyles were setting up home in Britain and that action was needed to assist them. The link between concerns over health and education made it imperative that measures were put in place to ensure that the nation's health did not suffer as a result of immigration from the subcontinent, and that linguistic difficulties that led to a tendency among those from India and Pakistan to avoid contact with the indigenous population did not allow prejudice to develop still further against a largely unknown potential underclass. As such, efforts to assist Asian immigrants were both logical and necessary.

It appears to be clear that the British government finally woke up to the fact that measures needed to be taken to assist Commonwealth immigrants to integrate at a time when the numbers coming from the Caribbean were no longer of the highest priority. Added to this was the fact that in the period up to 1960, when West Indians had formed the overwhelming bulk of black immigrants to Britain, the intention of successive British governments had been to seek to take measures to deter, and ultimately prevent, black migration. Not surprisingly, many West Indians, who felt that they had borne the brunt of the host community's prejudice and discrimination, did not appreciate the benefits that were seen to have accrued to later arrivals from India and Pakistan. One leading member of the West Indian community observed that:

> In any relationship between Britain, India and Africa – the Africans have always been at the bottom of the social pile, and that same attitude would manifest itself when Asians from the Indian sub-continent came here as well. They became the middle class. You will find that most of the time the British referred to them as hard working, very industrious, very businesslike, small traders and business-people; and we were the scroungers.[43]

One might have assumed that West Indians, with their British-based education system and Christian religion, would, at least in the early years following immigration, have fared better than those arriving from South Asia whose language and religion were different. Apparent commonalities, however, counted for little when it came to living with the British.

Divided by what they had in common: West Indian immigrants and the British

Racial prejudice based upon skin colour was merely one aspect of the overall problem West Indian immigrants encountered in their dealings with the host community in the 1950s and 1960s. A problem of similar proportion was the cultural difference between the two communities that often led to misunderstanding and resentment. Added to this was the tendency throughout the 1950s for well-meaning white people to act as the voice of the West Indian community, rather than encouraging West Indians to express their own views.

In the long-established British tradition of the great and the good seeking to represent the interests of – and making decisions for – those considered to be the least able to speak for themselves, anthropologists and sociologists, representatives from organisations such as the Church of England, the Council for Social Services (CSS), and, in the 1960s, the Commonwealth Immigrants Advisory Council (CIAC), the National Committee for Commonwealth Immigrants (NCCI) and the Community Relations Commission (CRC) all spoke at various times as the predominantly white representative voice of black immigrants. One result of this was that the West Indian Standing Conference (WISC), an organisation set up in 1958 by Caribbean people to represent their interests, was sidelined by the Metropolitan Police on Caribbean issues in favour of dialogue with the NCCI, which was funded by the government and was chaired by the Archbishop of Canterbury. Hall criticised such practices, pointing out that some well-meaning whites actually resented it when black people insisted on exercising their right to speak for themselves:

> A few white people did a lot of good, but some of them got hurt because they didn't allow for the fact that there is a difference between helping me and enabling me. A lot of them wanted to help but not enable. The radical black thinkers and activists of the day wanted to be enabled. It is still the case that when the black individual decides that he or she can represent themselves, some of the very liberal [white] people step aside.[44]

Writing in 1970, Horowitz referred to the attitude of British Conservatives to the decolonisation that was underway in Central and East Africa in the 1950s and 1960s.[45] His observations are worthy of detailed consideration as they have relevance to the debate on black Commonwealth immigration at this time in two key areas. First, although he refers to British Conservatives, there was, in a political sense, cross-party consensus during the period of Conservative administrations that ran from 1951 to 1964 on the subject of black immigration. This was in spite of the condemnation by Labour leader Hugh Gaitskell of the first Commonwealth Immigrants Act: legislation that the subsequent Labour government actually made more stringent in its effect on black immigrants. Second, the issues of decolonisation and multi-racial Britain were intertwined in the mind of the British establishment, whose guiding principles on both questions were that any change to the *status quo* should be evolutionary and spread over a long period. Thus, revolutionary modifications could be avoided in favour of change that would be introduced slowly, and at a time that was considered most propitious to the ruling establishment. On the issue of black immigrants, there were many who advised against legislation to outlaw racial discrimination, arguing instead that educative persuasion over time was better for race relations than the imposition of legal sanctions. As Hall pointed out: 'The liberal agenda was too much of a gradualist approach. In a way it was intended to maintain the *status quo*. We wanted more radical changes.'[46]

The question of race *per se* was invariably placed outside the debate on host community/Caribbean relations in favour of cultural differences, or, as Horowitz describes it in its African framework, 'standard of civilization',[47] as the central issue of political rights, and, one might argue, the issue of equality in Britain. Whenever the race card was played in the British context, references to skin colour were invariably played down and expressions that sought to explain difficulties with West Indian immigrants as stemming from their alien cultures or lifestyles were substituted. As such, racism could, and did, remain as an ingredient that bubbled beneath the surface of mainstream politics and daily life. The effect in everyday terms was that discrimination against West Indian immigrants appeared in many guises, all of which were intended to mask the reality of racial prejudice based directly on skin colour.

Patterson observed that the commonalities that West Indians shared with the British of language, religion, citizenship and an education system that emphasised the British value system, might have been expected to have aided Caribbean assimilation with the British, but that:

> The apparent community is often superficial and masks very real divergencies and sometimes incompatibilities between contemporary British and West Indian social and cultural patterns, as well as some important divergencies between the attitudes and expectations which each group holds in relation to the other.[48]

At this time, the difficulties Patterson outlined were largely confined in London to the few areas in the inner parts of the capital where black communities were developing.[49] But what were the incompatibilities of attitude and expectation to which she refers, and how did they influence relations in social and economic life?

If one looks first at the British, it would, perhaps, be fair to suggest that while West Indians regarded themselves as having a shared nationality, the host community largely saw Britishness in terms of a rank system that was derived from the nation's imperial and colonial past. As a result, black people were considered by many of the indigenous population to be of a lower social standing than the higher-ranking, and therefore 'superior', white British. Such attitudes existed at all levels of British society and were described by Jocelyn Barrow as: 'A feeling of great superiority; feelings that nobody else could come up to your standards even though you trained them to come up to your standards: which largely originates because you had such a powerful Empire.'[50]

Particularly in the 1950s, the concept of marriage, fidelity and family life were considered by most British people to be the pillars that supported an ordered and well-adjusted society. West Indian familial and sexual relationships, on the other hand, were likely to be looked down upon, especially if the female partner was white; or to be criticised for the way in which, at a time when illegitimacy was still considered to be a source of shame in British society, many West Indian couples did not conform to the accepted host community tradition that marriage preceded childbirth.[51] Allied to this was the 'Englishman's home is his castle' mentality in which the front door was the proverbial raised drawbridge behind which the head of the family retreated from and excluded the outside world at the end of the working day.

To many West Indians, home was a place to invite one's friends for a party or general get-together, as well as to reminisce about life 'back home', frequently to musical and alcoholic accompaniment. When one considers that throughout the period under consideration London's Caribbean community predominantly lived in multi-occupancy accommodation, often with grudging white neighbours who had little empathy with West Indian cultures, it is hardly surprising that police were frequent and unwelcome visitors to Caribbean get-togethers, as Hall noted when considering the origins of the deterioration of the West Indian community's relations with the Metropolitan Police:

> It's interesting to ask the question, 'Where did it start to go wrong?' Now my experience, and I have some personal knowledge of this, is that every time we had a party the police used to turn up; not to help us enjoy the party but to threaten us that they were going to smash it up.[52]

Addressing a meeting at the Colonial Office on 19 December 1961, Mr de Souza, speaking on behalf of the West Indies Federation, expressed similar views when he observed that 'the question of noisy parties . . . remained the major cause of friction between West Indians and other local residents'.[53]

Immigrants to Britain from the West Indies, and increasingly from India and Pakistan, found that, even in the mid-1960s, discrimination in employment and housing were little better than in the previous decade.

At a meeting of the Commonwealth Immigrants Committee on 9 February 1965, it was noted that:

> Discussion with the TUC and employers organisations on job opportunities for immigrants would be fruitless at present. It would not be disputed at this level, nor indeed at the level of the local Trades Council, that immigrants should be given equal opportunities at work; but this was not enough to influence attitudes on the workshop floor. Promotion was an especially difficult subject, often leading to disputes and stoppages.[54]

Some trade unions were reluctant to accept black workers as members and, when redundancy threatened, it was not uncommon for unions to take a protectionist stance in favour of white employees, thereby ensuring that their black counterparts were laid off first, in contravention of the traditional 'last in, first out' practice.[55] Jack Jones recalled that during his time with the Transport and General Workers' Union:

> The question of race relations and equal rights wasn't tackled by the trade union movement as strongly as it should have been. I, along with two others, picked it up when I was at the TUC. We established an equality committee. The view then was, 'Oh well, you've got to persuade people' . . . But you've got to have legal rights. There's no other way of dealing with problems like discrimination.[56]

Though the 1950s and early 1960s were periods of general economic wellbeing, West Indians found that as far as certain occupations were concerned, particularly those in the service sector, they were unwelcome. Howard-Drake recalled that in the 1960s:

> We (at the Cabinet Office) went to all sorts of people, big employers like Joe Lyons, where in the early days you couldn't have black people in the front of the shop because the great British public wouldn't buy food that had been handled. They were all right in the back doing the washing up. You couldn't have black girls fitting ladies with underwear. They wouldn't like that. But they could be in the back packing up the underwear. One of the phrases that always stuck in my mind were the banks, who were particularly bad. I said to a director of one of the banks, 'Why haven't you got more coloured faces as assistants?' 'Well', he said, 'The trouble is, all the people we recruit have to be potential managers.' It's one of the most significant remarks I think I ever heard.[57]

It was not until the second Race Relations Act in 1968 that racial discrimination in employment and housing was outlawed. Prior to this time, information on the willingness of employers in both the public and private sectors to take on black workers was difficult to obtain, due largely to a reluctance to maintain information on the racial make-up of the workforce. Rose observed that among employers:

> It was felt that the keeping of such statistics was in itself discrimi-natory and would create racial problems where none or very minor ones existed . . . thus, the usual response to an enquiry was the ritual statement that because the firm did not discriminate it did not keep such records.[58]

A government report of 22 March 1968 acknowledged that there were some members of society who argued that immigration from the West Indies and the subcontinent was more than offset by total emigration and, as a result, concerns over the numbers coming to Britain were unfounded. However, while this may have been true in pure numerical terms, it overlooked the fact that emigration involved people from all over Britain who were overwhelmingly white; while inward migration was largely black, and tended to be concentrated in small pockets of urban areas that had traditionally been associated with social depriva-tion and, in a number of cases, were already showing signs of inter-racial tension.[59]

But what of the attitude of West Indians at the time to the host community: and how real were their expectations of life in Britain in the 1950s and 1960s? Patterson argued that there were three key issues that hampered the ability of West Indians to achieve their objectives in England. These were their initial intention not to remain permanently in Britain, a lack of adaptability, and their exaggerated expectations.[60] One might argue that thoughts of permanent settlement in Britain would have been unlikely for many in the early years following arrival in the United Kingdom. The vast majority of West Indians who came to Britain in the period were young men and women whose priorities, especially those without the financial burden of supporting parents, wives and children back home, would probably have involved experiencing the excitement of life in a different country, getting a job, making money and enjoying themselves: particularly those who came to London, with its international 'big city' reputation. Gladstone Reid, who came to London in 1961 after service in the Guyana police, was typical of many in his initial attitude towards permanent residence in Britain:

> It's years before you make up your mind that this is your home because I think every West Indian when they come here work, and

those that can afford it go home every year and then they come back. It took them a while before they decided they might as well stay here and make this [their] home.[61]

One might also argue that it was perfectly understandable that West Indian immigrants would seek to establish themselves in those parts of the country where they knew that friends or relatives were already living. Their experience of widespread discrimination once they had arrived in England, particularly in the rented sector of the housing market and in certain sections of the economy, would have tended to discourage initiative in looking for work or lodgings in pastures new, away from safe and familiar associations and surroundings.

An undoubted handicap for many West Indians, and crucial to the accusation that they lacked adaptability, was that, although secondary education existed in the West Indies, attendance, though compulsory, was difficult to enforce. Lee suggests that attendance was at best irregular, and for many, nonexistent.[62] As a result illiteracy rates in certain parts of the West Indies were high.[63] The effect of this was that many English workers and employers complained that West Indian co-workers were slow to learn and that this resulted in reduced performance targets. In the industrial sector it was not infrequently the case that English employees, especially those engaged in piece-rate work in which overtime rates were reduced if production targets were not met, were reluctant to work alongside their Caribbean counterparts, fearing a loss in earning potential.

Patterson was unquestionably accurate in her assertion that an expectation on the part of West Indian immigrants that the host community would immediately accept them was, at best, naïve. Webster has identified that the West Indians' all-inclusive view of Britishness was at odds with white society's perception of Britishness, in which inclusive and exclusive aspects were clearly delineated:

> Within the Empire black British subjects were represented as part of 'our people' in a pattern of familial imagery where colonizers and colonized were represented as England's daughters, the colonized as children of Empire and England as their motherland or mother country . . . these constructions of the colonized as 'our people' depended on them being outside Britain – contained and controlled elsewhere.[64]

Essentially, the failure of many West Indian immigrants to achieve economic and social elevation in the early years of large-scale migration to Britain is understandable in view of the failure of white society to allow a climate to develop in which their aspirations might be realised.

In addition, a number of immigrants were less than prepared, in terms of education and skills, to take advantage of opportunities that may have presented themselves. However, when we consider the latter half of the 1960s we see that little had changed for the better. A Political and Economic Planning (PEP) Report in 1967 revealed the continuance of what it described as the widespread 'substantial discrimination in Britain against all coloured immigrants in employment, housing and in the provision of certain services'.[65] While it had been hoped that the passage of time would reduce hostility and discrimination it had regrettably been found that: 'As immigrants become more accustomed to English ways of life, and acquire greater expectations of life in Britain and higher qualifications, so they experience more discrimination.'[66]

After almost two decades of West Indian immigration to Britain, equality, in terms of opportunity and expectation, was an aspiration still hugely unfulfilled: a state of affairs that would require the helping hand of legislation to begin the slow and arduous process of change. Between November 1969 and June 1970, the Home Office commissioned a number of social surveys on public attitudes to the introduction of legislation outlawing discrimination in employment and housing as part of the 1968 Race Relations Act.[67] Some 70 per cent of those surveyed approved of legislation relating to employment; rather less than two-thirds agreed with legislation relating to council housing; while roughly half approved of legislation concerning private housing. Interestingly, approval of the abolition of discrimination in private housing was most widespread amongst those in the lower socio-economic group, while legislation abolishing discrimination in council housing was most popular among non-managerial white-collar workers, but least popular with unskilled manual workers.

The survey also found that, as in the population as a whole, white people in the 'special areas' (selected districts in London and Bradford) were more likely to think that race relations had deteriorated since the introduction of legislation than that they had improved. Black people, on the other hand, were more inclined to think that relations had improved as a result of legislation. One might conclude that, while most people by 1970 were prepared to accept that it was time to bring racial discrimination in employment to an end, it was still quite another matter for the indigenous community to accept that black immigrants now had the right to live next door. It was against this far from welcoming backcloth, that the Metropolitan Police was to exercise its responsibility of policing London's West Indian community. Initially, perhaps, the Met was to take its lead from government and popular discourse, which perceived black immigrants as an unwelcome 'problem'.

Notes

1 Paul, *Whitewashing Britain*, pp.67–69.
2 Ibid. p.81.
3 Ibid. p.81.
4 *Parliamentary Debates (Commons)* (10 December 1948), Vol.459, Cols.789–99.
5 NA HO344/100 This was followed a year later when a Committee was set up under the chairmanship of the Home Secretary, to inquire into the control of immigration of 'coloured' people. See NA HO344/11 Immigration of British subjects into the UK 1950–52.
6 Ibid. Cabinet memorandum by the Secretary of State for the Colonies, 20 May 1950. Prior to being sent home enquiries would be made in the colony concerned to see if relatives might pay the cost of repatriation or make a contribution towards the cost.
7 Ibid.
8 Ibid.
9 Ibid.
10 *Parliamentary Debates (Commons)* (19 July 1948), Vol.459, Col.99.
11 NA HO344/11 'Immigration of British subjects into the United Kingdom', Report by *ad hoc* Committee of Ministers, 1950–52.
12 *Parliamentary Debates (Commons)* (13 June 1951), Vol.488, Cols.2277–8.
13 *Parliamentary Debates (Commons)* (8 November 1951), Vol.493, Cols.452–5.
14 Ibid. Questions on this subject were raised again in the early 1950s. In each case the House was advised of the difficulty of altering Treasury regulations to accommodate the benefits on offer to British firms wishing to invest in Caribbean development. See *Parliamentary Debates (Commons)* (29 April 1953), Vol.514, Cols.2130–1; and (2 July 1953), Vol.517, Cols.559–60.
15 NA CAB124/1191, dated 29 October 1954.
16 N. Deakin, 'Residential Segregation in Britain: a comparative note', *Race*, No.6 (1964–65) p.19. Deakin states that 141,587 local authority houses were built in 1951, while private builders built 21,406. In 1961 local authorities built 92,880 houses, while private builders built 170,366.
17 NA CAB134/1466 Cabinet Meeting 1957.
18 Ibid.
19 NA CAB124/1191. Revised draft on housing, 17 June 1958.
20 NA CAB124/1192 Proposal to restrict right of entry to the UK for overseas British subjects 1955–65 (reproduced with kind permission of Express Newspapers).
21 NA HO376/140. Report dated 22 March 1968.
22 Patterson, *Dark Strangers*, p.230.
23 Ibid. p.232.
24 Interviewed by author, 9 October 2001. See also *The Times*, 'West Indian Settlers II' (9 November 1954), in which reference was made to remarks in provincial papers that Caribbean immigrants spoke passable English and were technically Christians. It continued, 'there is no doubt that at first some of the citizens of Birmingham and Ipswich rather expected to hear the nightly thud of barbaric drums.'

25 This version had clearly travelled the distance from Manchester to Liverpool. Kit-e-Kat was a well-known brand of cat food, which, it was commonly believed by the less enlightened members of the indigenous population, was a staple of the black immigrants' diet.
26 Interviewed by author, 30 January 2002.
27 NA CAB124/1192 a pencil note in an official Cabinet file, in which reference is made to 6,000 immigrants to Britain from the Caribbean for the first six months of 1954, reads 'probably much more than 6,000.'
28 Assistant Secretary at the Cabinet Office from 1963–65, and Under Secretary of State at the Home Office from 1974–78.
29 Interviewed by author, 15 May 2001.
30 NA HO376/140 figures provided for the Ministerial Committee on Immigration and Assimilation 1968.
31 NA HO376/128, and CWI/63412/612/1 Undated, but compiled on or before 26 September 1963.
32 E.J.B. Rose, *Colour and Citizenship: A Report on British Race Relations* (Oxford: 1969), p.83.
33 Ibid.
34 Ibid. p.84. The system of 'C' work vouchers was effectively brought to a close in August 1964.
35 Ibid. pp.85–86.
36 Letter to author, 4 March 2002.
37 S. Patterson, *Immigration and Race relations in Britain*: *1960–1967* (Oxford: 1969), p.268.
38 Ibid.
39 S. Hatch, 'Coloured People in School Textbooks', *Race: The Journal of the Institute of Race Relations*, Vol.4, No.1 (November 1962), p.63.
40 Ibid. p.64.
41 Rose, p.335. Rose also points out that in Bradford in 1961 the incidence of tuberculosis was 23.94 per thousand in Asians, compared with 0.64 per thousand in the whole population, p.334.
42 Patterson, *Immigration*, p.243.
43 Thompson interview.
44 Hall interview.
45 D. Horowitz, 'The British Conservatives and the Racial Issue on Decolonization', *Race*, No.2 (October 1970), pp.169–87.
46 Hall interview.
47 Horowitz, *British*, p.176.
48 Patterson, *Dark Strangers*, pp.219–20.
49 The largest groups were residing in North Kensington, Paddington, Stoke Newington, Lambeth and Hackney. See R.B. Davidson, 'The Distribution of Immigrant Groups in London', *Race*: Vol.5, No.2 (October 1963), p.64.
50 Barrow interview.
51 There were many in the host community who conveniently overlooked the fact that in the days of slavery in British colonies blacks were not permitted to marry and any children they produced were, like themselves, the property of the slave master.
52 Ibid.

53 NA CO1032/331 Immigration into the United Kingdom from the West Indies.
54 NA HO287/1468.
55 Patterson makes the point that in some parts of the country trade unions would not accept West Indians as members. Patterson, *Dark Strangers*, p.117.
56 Interviewed by author, 14 January 2002.
57 Howard-Drake interview.
58 Rose, *Colour*, p.305.
59 PRO HO376/140 Ministerial Committee on Immigration and Assimilation.
60 Patterson, *Dark Strangers*, p.79.
61 Interviewed by author, 11 October 2000.
62 R. Lee, 'The Education of Immigrant Children in England', *Race*, 2 (October 1965), p.134.
63 *Parliamentary Debates (Commons)* (12 July 1950), Vol.477, Cols.1346–8. Rates for illiteracy in the Caribbean given in Parliament in 1950 revealed that in the most recent figures Jamaica's illiteracy rate in the 10+ age group was 24 per cent, while in Trinidad the figure stood at 23 per cent. The highest literacy rate was that of Barbados, where only 7 per cent of the 10+ age group were illiterate.
64 W. Webster, *Imagining Home: Gender, Race and National Identity: 1945–64* (1997) p.26.
65 NA HO307/150. (The first Annual Report of the Race Relations Board) PEP Report dated 17/18 April 1967.
66 Ibid.
67 NA HO376/147 Race Relations Research: public attitudes to immigrants and the Race Relations Act.

Chapter 2

The police and British society in an era of affluence and decolonisation

A dispassionate onlooker of life in London in the immediate post-war years could be forgiven for assuming that Britain was a curious mixture of fantasy and reality. The latter was plain for all to see: the capital's drab, bomb-cratered landscape provided the backdrop for a community for whom the staples of life – food, fuel and clothing – were, and would continue to be for some time, rationed. Despite such hardships, the fantasy that the nation was still a major force on the world stage was alive and well and was to be found in the hearts and minds of many British people; especially politicians of both major parties and members of the elite, who fervently believed that despite the reality of the nation's 'Mother Hubbard' predicament, Britain and its Commonwealth remained one-third of the world's 'big three', along with the United States and the USSR.

As we saw in Chapter 1, Britain's need for additional labour in the immediate post-war years had been the motivating factor that led increasing numbers of West Indians to come to the metropolis in search of regular employment. At the time the host community generally viewed the colourfully clad newcomers with an air of benign detachment; but by the early 1950s many immigrants had come to realise that familiarity with the British merely revealed the worst aspects of their racial prejudices. As a result, the initial indifference of the host community to their new neighbours was gradually replaced by increasing demands from the mid-1950s for government action to control further immigration from the Caribbean.

Much of the 'evidence' that West Indian immigrants were a 'problem' came from local police forces, which were asked by the Home Office to provide information about patterns of immigrant settlement, employment and social interaction. The details they provided tell us more about the British than they do about the immigrant communities. For example, they reveal that, in the absence of any positive information from the government on the way in which West Indian labour was helping to rebuild post-war Britain, traditional supremacist views associated with metropolitan cultural and national hegemony remained firmly in place. Reports compiled by the various police forces during this period suggest that such attitudes were as likely to be found among police officers as the public at large. The failure of successive governments to educate and inform both hosts and immigrants of the implications of black immigration were crucial factors in the creation of an environment in which racial prejudice and discrimination fed fear and mistrust among members of both communities.[1]

The role of the British in policing the lives of the Caribbean community did not begin when they stepped ashore at Tilbury or Liverpool, or alighted from a train at Waterloo station. The overseas arm of the British police service had long helped to sustain a system of colonial government that was tottering on the brink of extinction at the dawn of the 1960s. Policing in the West Indies was, until independence, the task of the Colonial Office, with technical and training expertise provided by the Home Office. Colonial policing had traditionally propped up societies in which small minorities lived privileged lives, in sharp contrast to the majority of the people, who remained economically and politically powerless. As a result, it was likely that a significant number of West Indian immigrants would have held views on the role of the police in society that were directly related to their own experiences in the Caribbean.[2] It had long been a tradition that chief police officers in the United Kingdom were former military men who had served in Commonwealth territories, and serving middle-ranking British policemen were still being selected to occupy senior posts in colonial police forces.[3] New British recruits to the colonial policing service were trained in Home Office police training centres, including many who received instruction at the Metropolitan Police College at Hendon.

The arrival of large numbers of black immigrants from the West Indies in this period raised serious questions about Britain's long-held belief that it was both accommodating and tolerant of immigrant groups. It also coincided with changes that were afoot in public attitudes as, for the first time, young people became economically significant in their own right; establishment values began to be questioned, including the traditional deference that had been shown towards the police; and consumerism and single-issue politics brought a new set of challenges to authority in general, and the police in particular. As a result, the cultural challenge that the police faced in respect of West Indian immigrants, those seen as alien outsiders, coincided with the new challenge of a burgeoning indigenous culture that rejected the moral straightjacket imposed by society on previous generations of young people in favour of self-expression and self-indulgence. How the police service, a body that was largely comprised of former military men who were comfortable with rules and regulations but untrained in concepts of social permissiveness, responded to these challenges will be examined in the chapter's concluding section.

Siren voices, government failings, and what became of the Commonwealth?

At the end of the Second World War the British government viewed the exodus of young white migrants from the United Kingdom to the Commonwealth, particularly to those countries where the populations were predominantly white, or where white minorities held power, as vital to its national interest. There was no desire in Whitehall to see them replaced by black people from the West Indies, who were generally assumed to be culturally, educationally and socially inferior.[4] Paul observed that the Attlee government, as part of its vision of imperial migration, negotiated a series of sponsored deals with various Commonwealth governments after the war.[5] She argues that imperial migration, which continued under successive British governments to the early-1960s: 'Is significant because it illustrates the commitment of successive administrations to the empire/commonwealth as a viable entity worthy of receiving large quantities of one of post-war Britain's scarcest resources – labour.'[6]

However, while governments at Westminster strove to develop the nation's economic and political interests in its former empire, a different picture emerges when one looks at the way in which the concept of the Commonwealth and its people was presented for domestic consumption in the 1950s. In 1958 the Macmillan government was forced to admit that the promotion of the Commonwealth ideal in Britain had been neglected.[7] On 2 November 1958 draft proposals submitted by Charles Hill, Chancellor of the Duchy of Lancaster, revealed that there was little doubt that knowledge and understanding of the Commonwealth in Britain was unsatisfactory. It was suggested that the Commonwealth was largely taken for granted and it was neglected as a school subject.[8] Hill pointed out that in the financial year 1950–51, under the Labour government, expenditure at home by the Central Office of Information on behalf of the Commonwealth Relations Office and the Colonial Office amounted to about £125,000.[9] The corresponding provision in the 1958–59 estimate was a mere £3,000. In his reply to Hill, Macmillan suggested that any efforts to project the Commonwealth in Britain would be unlikely to succeed. He argued that other countries of the Commonwealth:

> Can never mean a great deal to the great mass of the people because they never visit them. This was different for certain parts of the middle-classes, in the days when relatively large numbers of them had jobs in various parts of the Empire.[10]

He believed that the British people had found the transition from Empire to Commonwealth difficult to grasp and saw no simple solution to the problem.

Section III of the Interdepartmental Working Party's report on the Projection of the Commonwealth in the United Kingdom, entitled 'What Needs To Be Done', noted that confusion about the concept of the Empire and the Commonwealth had existed since the First World War and that this had played into the hands of those opposed to 'imperialism' and 'colonialism'. It suggested that, 'most people have reacted by refusing to think about the Commonwealth at all.'[11] This failure to educate the British public of the nature of the Commonwealth's *raison d'être* ensured that many Britons harboured only vague notions of its purpose, and only really knew what it had once been but no longer was. The argument of May and Cohen that the legacy of Empire was crucial to the growth of racism after the First World War, still had validity in the aftermath of the Second World War:

> Racial theories, which by the turn of the century had assumed a material force in their own right, were used to legitimise relation-ships of dominance and disability within the Empire ... the very achievement of military superiority and administrative control over the colonised peoples fed back to the metropolis in the form of stereotypes, mythologies and ideologies which confirmed the sup-posed superiority of the Anglo-Saxon 'race'.[12]

At a time of large-scale black immigration from the West Indies, such ignorance of shared histories, of Caribbean lifestyles and customs, added to traditional British reserve and feelings of decline at the passing of Empire, would have offered the widest possible scope for the develop-ment of racial prejudice and discrimination. Whatever the British were fashioning for themselves as signifiers of their national identity in a period of imperial decline, West Indians had no doubts about their own Britishness; after all, Britain was the 'mother country'. What many of them were soon to discover, as Nadine Peppard noted, was that, 'It did not occur to them that their own idea of the relationship to the mother country did not exactly coincide with hers; that most of the English people with whom they were to come into contact knew little of the Caribbean and cared even less.'[13]

In Parliament the readiness with which a number of politicians argued for restrictions on the entry of black Commonwealth citizens merely fanned the flames on each side of the argument. Their demands for control led them to become what Nicholas Deakin described as, 'siren voices offering a solution where the government could only proclaim with diminishing conviction the indivisibility of British citizenship'. Deakin noted the irony of their actions, in which their arousal of anxieties merely accelerated the migration they sought to control, and exacerbated the social tensions they claimed as justification for their demands.[14] What is particularly significant is that it was local police forces that often provided the information which political and media authorities seized upon to confirm their view that West Indian immigrants were a 'problem', and a danger to social order and cohesion.

In 1953, and again in 1955 and 1957, the Home Office Working Party on 'coloured' people seeking employment in the United Kingdom conducted inquiries into the difficulties they faced in the workplace and into factors that were hindering assimilation with the host community.[15] These inquiries were carried out by local police forces. It would appear clear that, in calling for details of obstacles to assimilation, the Home Office was already well aware that difficulties were being encountered by black immigrants. The police forces all reported in terms that were to become stereotypical paradigmatic references for West Indians living in Britain. The reports alleged that it was frequently found that black immigrants had no desire to associate with the indigenous community; that black men sought the favours of low-class white women 'of the prostitute type'; that they displayed a general lack of social responsibility; that those who had done well spent more time with whites than 'people of their own colour'; and that they were overly sensitive to colour prejudice.[16]

In 1953, Tynemouth Police, reporting on the failure of black absorption into the community, suggested that it resulted from, 'their [black people's] below-par mentality and their underlying suspicion of the white race'.[17] Yet in the same report, local police merely noted that, 'their [black people's] absorption into the community is slow and looked upon with disfavour by the majority of [white] citizens'.[18] In the same year, police in South Shields claimed that, 'the main factor which hinders assimilation is colour, coupled with the lack of education, social intercourse and cultural knowledge of the coloured man'. Yet like police in Tynemouth, it was noted as almost an afterthought that, 'there is a social colour-bar; white inhabitants by a vast majority will not tolerate the coloured people'.[19] Four years later, police reports claimed that while the presence of 'coloured' people was now more or less accepted without comment, 'the degree of assimilation is no greater'. It was suggested that, 'the immigrants themselves have no desire to mix with white people . . . in the main the attitude of the white people seems to range between indifference and tolerance.'[20] It was found that:

> The Nottingham, Wolverhampton and Warwickshire police say that white householders in better class districts resent coloured people buying houses in those districts and when this happens those who can, move out. This tends to support the views expressed by the London police that the present attitude of indifference adopted by white people will last only so long as the coloured people do not encroach on the interests of the rest of the [white] community.[21]

In the face of such blatant racism it seems clear that the failure to assimilate or integrate was at least as likely to be due to the prejudices of the indigenous population.

Such observations were not unnatural, coming as they did from a police service that was overwhelmingly conservative, and whose chief officers had often been men who had served in the colonies. Policing in the colonial context thus had major ramifications for black immigrants. It shaped attitudes and fed expectations among both West Indians and the police, both in the Caribbean and in the United Kingdom: not only with regard to law enforcement, but also in terms of a social structure in which the inequalities and prejudices of West Indian life were perceived to have been replicated in Britain by a police service and a frequently hostile white society.

External influences and internal problems: policing at home and in the West Indies

In the 1950s and 1960s Britons were recruited, as they had been for many years, to police colonial territories. This was in spite of the fact that decolonisation was now accelerating rapidly. Policing in its colonial context had fostered a style of policing that ranged from semi-judicial paternalism to authoritarianism and led directly to much of the confusion and frustration experienced by many West Indians in London when they sought help from the Metropolitan Police with their problems. British recruits to colonial police forces were never recruited to perform routine constabulary work but to manage those who did. New recruits from Britain with no previous policing experience invariably took up appointments at the rank of inspector after completion of their basic training. Indeed, the rank of sergeant had traditionally been the pinnacle to which local police officers in the Caribbean might aspire.[22]

Experienced middle-ranking British policemen who joined a colonial force could expect to take up a senior position of at least superintendent rank.

It was the intention of the Colonial Office that the West Indies would be policed along similar lines to policing in Britain. However, in the absence of overwhelming popular support, colonial policing often relied on the use or threat of force to maintain public order and imperial power; as was the case in St. Lucia in 1937, when the Island Council urged the Governor to request Whitehall to send one of His Majesty's ships and a naval aeroplane to fly over striking agricultural labourers.[23] Colonial governors had wide powers to control publications considered to be seditious, and political activists, such as Marcus Garvey, were imprisoned for alleged inflammatory political speeches.[24] At a meeting on 15 July 1954 Colonial Police Force Commissioners acknowledged the legacy of ill feeling that still existed towards the colonial power. It was noted that there was hostility both to rule from London, and the way in which colonial police were seen as the embodiment of imperialist repression:

> The conference recognised that it was most important for police and public to establish friendly and frequent contacts in the everyday life of the territory, so that the confidence thus engendered in the public would serve to counteract their traditional feeling of resentment towards the police as being the strong arm of the imperialist power.[25]

The British were confident that, in the post-colonial period, policing arrangements in territories they had ceased to administer would continue to function along lines that had been drawn up in Whitehall.

As territories moved towards independence the Colonial Office sought to separate control of the police from local politicians by the creation of Police Service Commissions, which would have a quasi-judicial function and would be made up of people from outside politics.[26] What this meant in practice was placing control of the police in the hands of those who were not democratically elected, but who were favourably disposed to the Westminster point of view. The desire of the British government to influence the way in which policing would function in independent former colonies shows that while Britain may have been moving towards post-colonial times, it was not yet in post-imperial times. Put simply, Whitehall believed that local politicians could not be trusted to operate a police service that was fair and impartial, especially where territories appeared to be dominated by a single political party, viewpoint or ethnic or racial group. Colonial policing, and the transition to independence, can be seen as an example of Britain's desire to retain what could be salvaged from its dominant status over those it once governed. Above all, it emphasised British supremacist attitudes towards those who were neither from the United Kingdom or white-skinned. Such was the situation in the West Indies as the age of British imperial rule drew to a close.

For the first half of the twentieth century Metropolitan Police Commissioners were invariably men with distinguished military backgrounds who had served extensively in the colonies. They had all lived through the age of imperialism and in many cases had played a significant part in its maintenance. Indeed, Sir John Nott-Bower, Commissioner of the Met from 1953 to 1958, had been a member of the Indian police at the time of the Amritsar Massacre in 1919.[27] Worse still was the fact that a number of appointees took office when their best years were behind them; Sir Harold Scott becoming Commissioner in 1945 at the age of 58; while Nott-Bower was 61 when he succeeded Scott. The likelihood that such individuals would have brought sorely needed innovation and modernisation to the Met was largely wishful thinking.[28]

Although the Met addressed the problem of ageing commissioners with the appointment of 47-year-old Joseph Simpson in 1958, an allied problem, and one that was not addressed, was that of a police service led by ageing senior officers. In 1969 the Home Office examined the retirement pattern of police officers in the inspector to chief superintendent ranks.[29] It was found that during the previous ten years, 73% of inspectors who retired on pension did so with between 25 and 30 years service. Only 4% stayed on until reaching age limit (55 years of age) before retiring. The majority of chief superintendents, however, over 55%, retired during the intervening years between reaching 30 years service and age limit. A further 29% remained until age limit was reached before leaving the service. It was believed that many chief superintendents remained as long as possible because they had been promoted late in service and, as a result, wished to, 'enjoy the fruits of their promotion and to average their pay for pensionable service.'[30]

Although the report did not deal with ranks above chief superintendent, it would be logical to conclude that the financial inducements that persuaded chief superintendents to stay as long as possible would have had even greater influence on the minds of those of higher rank, such as the Met's commanders and assistant commissioners. Senior officers, in the twilight of their careers, raised in the age of empire, and who were generally possessed of an extremely conservative outlook, would have been unlikely to tackle new problems of racial discrimination with a progressive mind and firm hand. Indeed, London's first black officer, Norwell Roberts, believed that negative attitudes towards black people were endemic in the Met, when asked if racist junior ranks were a reflection of racist senior officers in the 1960s:

Absolutely: remember when these PCs gave me a hard time there would be no good me turning to the sergeant. He would think the same, as would the inspector. He'd be thinking the same. And so it went, right the way up.[31]

One cannot disregard the fact that home and colonial recruits to the police service in the 1950s were men, many of whom had been raised on the myths of the British Empire, promoted through the medium of popular culture: stories in which black natives kow-towed to their British masters, who, to the eternal gratitude of the simple black folk, had treated them with paternal kindness and had brought them order, religion and civilisation. Such attitudes may have been shaped by the popular culture of the nineteenth century but, as Jeffrey Richards noted, they continued to be displayed in the twentieth century by more modern cultural fashions, notably the cinema.[32] An officer who joined the Met in 1951 after military service in Egypt recalled the popular appeal of such imagery for his generation:

We were brought up in the age of Empire and when at school had had dinned into us that we must be proud of our country, the Monarch and the Empire. The Union Jack was flown in some areas on flag poles erected in the back gardens and yards of most houses quite frequently, as well as on public buildings. Schoolteachers would often point out the red areas on world maps, and the red areas seemed to cover most of the world. We were nationalists to the core, even in deprived areas.[33]

The tough line that was often taken by police in the colonies in order to suppress challenges to its authority was, albeit less severely, mirrored on the streets of London. An officer of the period recalled the way in which uncompromising policing tactics were used by the Met against an immigrant community that was seen as a challenge to its authority:

That was largely about 'come to heel'. Fit in with the way we, the Brits say, then everything will be OK ... It was still very much a colonial approach. These whatever you call them will come to heel. You've got this group of black people who've come over here and they don't want to be policed and so on. Well they'll just jolly well have to learn that they've got to be. So OK lads, you just give them the stick. I mean that in a metaphorical sense. It didn't work, and it hasn't worked.[34]

Some early West Indian immigrants, who were aware of police partiality and oppression in their own countries, may well have been predisposed

45

to see policing in negative and repressive terms once in the United Kingdom. Many were to find themselves confounded by an understandable failure to comprehend the written and unwritten rules of the game by which the British police and society operated. Those in the indigenous community who regularly came into contact with the Met knew that it was unwise to argue with, or respond negatively to, a police officer's demand or request. West Indians who determinedly insisted that the Met uphold their rights or pursue a complaint found that, not infrequently, this resulted in unwanted visits to police stations and magistrates' courts.

In the 1960s colonial attitudes were even to be found in the specialist department at New Scotland Yard (NSY), which was intended to foster good relations with the black community. On 6 March 1964 a report was submitted to the Assistant Commissioner 'A' Department (ACA) by A2 Branch. This department was the forerunner of the Met's A7 (1) Community Relations Branch, and had specific responsibility for establishing and developing liaison with representatives of the West Indian community. The report dealt with a proposal to inaugurate talks by representatives from the Jamaican High Commission to Metropolitan Police officers at the recruit training school at Hendon. The writer suggested that in order to assess the suitability of a black speaker who was to talk on race relations, the best course of action would be to subject him to a free-for-all discussion with training school staff and allow him the opportunity for further talks if he, 'emerged successfully from such a baptism of fire'.[35] As if to remind the speaker that black people should consider themselves as living on the margins of British society, A2 Branch suggested that the most suitable subject for the talk, 'would undoubtedly be "Living in a white community" '. The writer noted that Miss Peppard of the London Council of Social Services (LCSS) had suggested that the Met consider organising personal contact for its officers with members of the West Indian community, as this would be more likely to develop an awareness of, and empathy with, Caribbean cultures than merely attending a lecture. The response of A2 Branch was in keeping with the rest of the report, and merely emphasised its author's belief that black people were an inferior underclass in a white society:

> It would seem beyond argument that enforced daily contact with coloured people would be far more conducive to good understanding than a whole series of lectures. Whether the results would necessarily be what the LCSS so obviously hopes, is another matter; one does not become childlike through working with children.[36]

Such attitudes graphically illustrate both the Met's inability to understand the concept of community relations, and its reluctance to accept that it had anything to learn from 'outsiders'. The implicit illusion to one of the most distasteful features of imperial discourse (that colonial subjects were dependent and excitable 'children', rather than autonomous adults) also suggests the persistence of neo-colonial attitudes within the Met into the mid-1960s.

In the immediate post-war years such views were bolstered by a belief that most people held the police in high regard. However, the positive representation of the London 'Bobby', which had developed over many decades and which epitomised what were believed to be his enduring qualities of good-natured tolerance and political impartiality, came under increasing fire during the course of the 1950s and 1960s. Unfortunately, it created a culture of resistance in the Met that made a more positive attitude towards race relations less, rather than more, likely.

Popular representations of the London police: from deference to realism

Observers of policing in Britain have consistently subscribed to the theory that the police function is firmly grounded on a popular consensus which empowers the police to enforce laws and regulate activities that the vast majority in society believe are necessary for the prevention and detection of crime, and the maintenance of peace and tranquillity. All major political parties endorse this philosophy as a central pillar of their home affairs strategy, and since the 1966 general election it has been a regular feature of political manifestos. The British media have, by and large, traditionally supported this line in its recognition of those values that have maintained the consensus view of national life. Though the failures and indiscretions of individual office-holders make them fair game for press assassination, the media endorse and strive to uphold the system by which the various organs of government operate; as such, the police are in a favoured position. Individual cases or events, miscarriages of justice, and the implementation of unpopular policies may invoke the media's wrath, but the police's role in society is supported and valued.

The high regard in which the Metropolitan Police was traditionally held said much about Britain's traditional insularity and complacency.[37] The idealised depiction of the London 'Bobby' as the world's finest continued even when, as Emsley points out, it became apparent (at least by the 1930s) that in detection and traffic matters there was much to be learned from foreign police forces.[38] This popular representation, a view that was endorsed by the property-owning middle class and those with no first-hand experience of police procedures, was often at odds with the experience of the residents of the less affluent parts of London. However, it remained a staple in cinema representations of the police in Britain until the late 1950s.

The outbreak of war in 1939 prompted a revolutionary shift in British filmmaking. The upper-class hero now had a new rival for the nation's affections: the worker, doing her/his bit in the war effort. Ealing Studios continued this spirit of comradeship and the promotion of the 'ordinary hero' after the war, and, from the Metropolitan Police's perspective, the 1950 film *The Blue Lamp* was a high water mark in terms of public appreciation and esteem. The film encapsulated the aspirations of a generation of filmmakers who wished to capitalise on the 'New Jerusalem' optimism of 1945, and use it as a springboard for a series of Ealing films in which wartime camaraderie would, it was hoped, continue and develop in the hands of a more egalitarian post-war society. Ealing's penchant for films emphasising social cohesion began to focus on new threats to the British way of life once the war was over. Richards observed the way in which the focus changed from that of external threat to one of internal malaise:

> The Ealing view of Britain and the British, of the life of service and duty under discipline, passed in peacetime from the war against the enemy without – Germany – to the war against the enemy within – the criminal.[39]

Central tenets of each film were the principles of order and conformity to society's value system. Be it criminals, the Burgundians of Pimlico, or the errant marital partner, the need to conform was paramount. Thus, Tom Riley's (Dirk Bogarde) violent criminality inevitably leads him to the gallows (*The Blue Lamp*, 1950); the Burgundians finally see the delusion of self-fulfilment and the 'joy' of shared austerity (*Passport to Pimlico*, 1949); and Rose (Googie Withers) ultimately accepts that she is better off with her boring, asexual husband, George, than indulging rediscovered lustful desire for her sexually attractive and violent one-time boyfriend, Tommy (*It Always Rains on Sundays*, 1947). But if, as Richards claims, moviemakers now saw crime as Britain's biggest menace who were its victims and its perpetrators?

In the broadest sense the principal victim of crime in post-war Britain was society itself: a society whose value system was considered to be under threat from a younger generation that had become dysfunctional as a result of wartime upheaval, family breakdown, and the growing influence of alien (principally American) cultures. These commonly held views ultimately led to the identification of a succession of errant scapegoat groups: spivs, cosh-boys, teddy boys, mods and rockers, black and Asian immigrants and black youth; a number of which were to acquire folk-devil status. Crime is invariably the end product of many destabilising causes and British social-problem films of the 1950s used the subject as a backdrop to highlight wider social concerns; in particular, violent and disaffected youth, the erosion of traditional family values, the state of the nation and colour prejudice.

The Blue Lamp was the first feature film made in Britain to portray uniformed police constables in leading roles. The Met had hoped that it would aid recruitment and the *Police Review* spoke for many in the media in its estimation of the impact the film would have on the general public:

> One effect it is bound to have on most people: once you have seen it you look at all policemen with a new respect and affection, and are buoyed up by the illusion that, though very occasionally they may get killed, nothing else can ever conceivably go wrong with them.[40]

In the film, PC Dixon's murderer, Tom Riley, epitomises society's anxiety over the behaviour of young delinquents in post-war Britain: a point picked up on by Andrew Spicer, who argues that one reason why British films focused on delinquent youth at this time was because they:

> Displayed an essentially middle-class commitment to a law-and-order paradigm in which the society and state were beneficent. Hence their use of the delinquent . . . as unstable and vicious, rather than tough and exciting. The society the delinquents disrupted was orderly and paternalistic embodied in kindly policemen, caring probation officers and progressive clergymen.[41]

In *The Blue Lamp* Riley's failure to conform is dealt with in such a way that the social and economic circumstances that would have helped to create him are ignored and remain unresolved. In its attempt to address post-war social problems the film fails to tackle the causes of crime. It is Riley who is solely to blame, and not the society that created him. John Hill has argued that it is the rationale of containment that is characteristic of the need for a positive resolution in such films; for, as he points out, 'if the causes of the problem are located in the individual, then *prima facie*, there is no need for a reconstruction of the social order'.[42] However, the didactic solutions that such films tended to offer – conformity and public-spiritedness – were, even by the time of *The Blue Lamp*, largely out of step with the aspirations of a nation that was fed up with bread and margarine, a collective philosophy of 'make do and mend', and whose members were desperate for a splash of colour and excitement in an otherwise grey existence.

While *The Blue Lamp* had been something of a public-relations coup for the Metropolitan Police, the 1959 film *Sapphire* broke new ground in its depiction of a racist police detective, Inspector Learoyd (Michael Craig). The film's topicality, coming as it did only months after racist disturbances in Notting Hill and in the same year as Kelso Cochrane became the first racist murder victim, ensured that it had an important moral message. It also highlighted West Indian society's obsession with a ranking system that placed those with the lightest skin tones in the most favoured positions. Throughout the film, Learoyd's racism is only mildly rebuked by his senior officer. Whether by accident or design, the film accurately depicted the Met's failure to address racial discrimination. Sir Peter Imbert believed that the force could have done much more to tackle colour prejudice among its officers during this period:

> I don't know if we had the machinery for getting rid of them [racist officers], but I think we were at fault, that we ignored it when we saw it or heard it. We weren't big enough to say, 'That's not acceptable. It's out of order.'[43]

The decline in cinema attendance at the end of the 1950s was matched by a corresponding increase in television audiences. At the same time, the gentleman senior police officer, characterised in British films by Jack Hawkins and Nigel Patrick, was replaced by a new tough-guy cop; epitomised in films such as *Hell is a City* (1960) by Stanley Baker, and by Stratford John in TV's *Z Cars*. The new approach to television's depiction of the police, in which conflict often figured as the antithesis to George Dixon's (*Dixon of Dock Green*) paternalism, was largely a reflection of the new reality of policing at street level, in which individuals and errant groups were increasingly seen to challenge police and state authority.

One might argue that *Z Cars* played a role in the changing face of policing in the 1960s. The Met's Commissioner, Sir Joseph Simpson, speaking in 1964, took a positive line in support of the programme and stated that it showed in a lifelike way the problems the police had to meet: suggesting that, 'I think the public realise from this programme that the police cannot always use kid gloves.'[44] The down-to-earth approach of the cops in *Z Cars* may well have played into the hands of Simpson, coming as the series did at a time when crime in London was spiralling upwards and low recruitment and manpower wastage were major concerns. The programme's popularity may also have inadvertently acted as a softening-up process by which the public became accustomed to an aggressive style of policing that was more confrontational than the residents of Dock Green would have been familiar with. The fact that Simpson felt the time was right to authorise the establishment of the notorious Special Patrol Group (SPG) in 1965, the year after his speech in support of *Z Cars*, would suggest that the no-nonsense approach was to be the order of the day in the Met, as well as on TV.

By the second half of the 1960s both film and television were dealing with yet more controversial policing issues, including that of police corruption: something that would have been unthinkable in the era of *The Blue Lamp*. The hard-nosed film and TV cop was still plying his trade, but in films such as *The Strange Affair* (1967) he now indulged in framing the innocent and committing perjury: though he was still depicted as the one 'rotten apple' in an otherwise healthy barrel. Such representations painted a picture of policing that was far more real than the police service was willing to admit. The infamous Challenor case had raised serious questions about police propriety, and complaints of harassment and victimisation by the West Indian community were too numerous to be brushed aside; though the Met still argued that such complainants were largely unrepresentative, or were overly sensitive to the issue of race.

The 1968 BBC programme *Cause for Concern*, which dealt with the experiences of black people who had been framed by the police, had been acquitted and subsequently received damages for malicious prosecution, prompted the police to invoke legal sanction to prevent the programme being broadcast; claiming that it was, 'unfair, unobjective, grossly distorted, highly defamatory of police officers and libellous'.[45] However, the experiences of a former officer and a current inspector of relations between the Met and the West Indian community when new recruits, would appear to support the view that the programme exposed the reality of policing in London for many West Indian immigrants:

> It was bad when I went to Harrow Road in 1968. Even when you went out [with an experienced officer] learning beats they would show you how to fit them [West Indians] up.[46]
>
> One manifestation [of racist attitudes] was the playing card. I've never talked about this before. We're talking about the early-'70s, and hopefully a lot of these officers will be retired: in fact, they'll all be retired. Officers would play cards: those who lost would have to go out and arrest a suspect. If you produced the Ace of Spades you would have to go out and arrest a black pickpocket; and they would do so. One famous quote from a person I worked with has stuck in my mind all of my career and is to do with the term 'stitching up', which was common at that time. He said 'Look David, don't get me wrong. We don't stitch up just anybody. We only stitch up those who are guilty.' Trying to justify something that is unjustifiable.[47]

The decline of media deference towards the police prompted complaints from the Met that it got a raw deal from the press and other influential groups.[48] In the mid-1960s the Met's Press and Information Branch was seriously understaffed, but as Simpson pointed out to his chief superintendents:

There was no point in providing additional staff unless they were to be trusted and respected by all police officers. Mutual confidence was an essential requirement and Press and Information officers must be provided with the information they required if they were to do their jobs properly.[49]

In the minutes of the discussion that ensued it was noted that, 'discord between the police and the press would never be completely eradicated'.[50] Thus, at a time when the Met was increasingly the subject of critical public scrutiny, a deep sense of mistrust existed at the highest levels of the force towards the media. By refusing to co-operate fully and openly with the Met's own Press and Information Branch, senior police officers effectively tied the hands of the very body that had been created to portray them and the organisation in a positive light with the media and the public.

Controlling and regulating the permisive society

In 1962 the Royal Commission on the Police reported on the state of relations between the police and the public.[51] The Commission's findings emphasised the division within the police service on the question of community relations. Chief police officers, central government departments and police authorities were unanimous in the belief that there was no evidence of serious deterioration in the relationship. On the other hand, the federated ranks of the police (constable to chief inspector) and the Magistrates' Association believed that there had been a significant decline, some holding that, 'the traditional standing of the police was in grave danger'.[52] The Royal Commission concluded that:

> We have noted that, both among those who hold that there has been a general decline in the relationship between the police and the public and among those who hold that there has not, a substantial area of agreement as to the factors which at present imperil that relationship. Thus almost all the evidence draws attention to the changed attitudes, as compared with those of pre-war days, of the public with whom the police have to deal; a decay in respect for properly constituted authority and a tendency to question the justification for measures which formerly would have been accepted without challenge ... and a variety of social changes, particularly the increase in the vehicle-owning population, which have brought the constable into contact with sections of the community with whom previously he had little or no dealings.[53]

Put simply, the Royal Commission found that there had been a noticeable deterioration in public attitudes and deference to the police since the war; and, at the same time, the police's workload had increased thanks to an upsurge in crime and the need to regulate the increased use of private motor transport. New legislation had added to police duties and increasing numbers of people were coming into contact with the police for breaches of the law. It should not be overlooked that, with the massive increase in its workload, the Met had only 271 more officers in 1966 than it had in 1938.[54] As a result, the force did not have enough officers to adequately cater for all of its commitments. The shortage of officers led the Met to concentrate on what it was most comfortable with: the enforcement of the criminal law and maintenance of the peace, and ensured that little was done to develop community relations. What efforts were made in this area were largely of the token variety, in which the public was encouraged to assist the police to achieve the police's own objectives (fighting crime, maintaining the peace and regulating traffic), with little attention given to the wishes of the community, and no say of any kind for their elected representatives.

From the 1950s one sees that a range of measures were introduced to regulate public rights and social behaviour at a time when British society appeared to become more affluent and liberal. Tim Newburn has argued that this was a period in which the power imbalance between the middle and the working classes was reduced, with the inevitable consequence that, 'the heightened volume and visibility of "alternative" ways of behaving and styles of living ... progressively undermined long established beliefs in the existence of, and necessity for, a single and uniform morality'.[55] This, he claims, led those with most to lose from such changes, 'to forms of protest dedicated to the idea of reversing threatened changes and upholding traditional norms and values'.[56] Thus one sees the introduction of a whole raft of legislative activity from the 1950s that was intended to regulate public behaviour; including *inter alia* betting and gaming; prostitution and sexual offences; obscene publications (and the 'Lady Chatterley' trial)[57]; liquor licensing; restrictions on the rights of Commonwealth citizens to enter the United Kingdom; the rejection of attempts to liberalise the law on homosexuality (the Wolfenden Committee Report, 1957); and the retention of capital punishment for murder (Homicide Act, 1957). The reality was that, from the mid-1950s, the British establishment, faced with increasing affluent consumerism, developing youth sub-culture, receptiveness to 'alien' American cultures and increasing numbers of black colonial immigrants, was ill-prepared to respond positively to its new challenges.

In the 1950s and early 1960s many police officers joined the Met after completion of military service. They were often men who were comfortable with rules, regulations and hierarchical command structures. In consequence they tended to find liberalising social developments, such as 'youth culture' and the 'permissive society', at odds with the police's prevailing conservative outlook. Jocelyn Barrow, a leading campaigner for racial equality in this period, claimed that the 1960s was an era in which people born in the post-war period were seeking a type of freedom that British society was not used to providing. She argues that none of the agencies – police, social workers, teachers, etc. – were being given the skills that were necessary to deal with changing attitudes:

> At a time when society was shifting its moral values and codes the people who were supposed to ensure that those moral values and codes could be respected didn't know what to do, and, as far as the police were concerned it could be that the training the police got did not provide them with the skills needed to police a multi-ethnic society. They had all the prejudices that everyone else has . . . I think they used a great deal of aggression and stridency and physical force because they were frightened. But they did that with their own society.[58]

The lack of preparedness was particularly evident with regard to West Indian immigrants. Neither Whitehall nor the Met had initially envisaged a role for the police in areas of immigrant settlement other than the time-honoured ones of law enforcement and regulation. Government policy throughout the 1950s was to restrict and deter further black migration. It is likely, therefore, that building relationships with West Indian immigrants would have been low on the Met's list of priorities, as the Institute of Race Relations noted:

> Confining of the police to a purely regulatory role may well have had something to do with the deterioration of relationships, which began to be noticeable in the early-1960s and which found expression in the increasing number of protests raised by organisations like CARD (Campaign Against Racial Discrimination) and the West Indian Standing Conference.[59]

In the absence of a progressive outlook towards a changing society the Met had only its old 'fall in line or else' approach when dealing with a community from which it was increasingly set apart: a philosophy that the public was less and less prepared to go along with. The Met's problems were compounded by an excess of ageing senior officers, men who had been raised in the age of empire and whose expressed views on colonial immigrants were generally in keeping with those of a prejudiced and discriminatory population. The huge rise in crime, and the Met's ever-increasing commitments, meant that the force, which was massively under strength, could do little other than to focus its resources on its traditional enforcement role, something that alienated the public still further. The junior ranks, many of whom were recruited from the armed forces, were poorly led and largely untrained and unprepared to adapt to the liberalising impact of the social changes that were underway in the 1960s. They, like the public at large, were ignorant of, and lacked empathy with, Caribbean cultures and lifestyles: failings that successive government from 1945 had done little to correct.

Notes

1 Colonial students attending courses in the United Kingdom were however offered induction courses on life in Britain by the British Council in the early post-war period, the cost being met by the students.
2 See L.A. Chase, 'West Indians and the Police: Some Observations'; in *New Community*, Vol.3, No.3 (Summer 1974), p.205, who argues that 'West Indians have always resented white, and indeed all, policemen because of the function of the police in slave society.'
3 Joseph Simpson's appointment as Commissioner of Police of the Metropolis in 1958 was the first such appointment of an officer who had come through the ranks from Constable to Commissioner since the Met was established in 1829.
4 See B. Schwarz, 'Conquerors of Truth, Reflections on Postcolonial Theory', in B. Schwarz (ed.) *The Expansion of England* (2001), p.181.
5 Paul, *Whitewashing*, p.25.
6 Ibid. p.26.
7 See L.J. Butler, *Britain and Empire* (2002), p.xii, who argues that 'until the Second World War, and arguably beyond it, the British Empire was to a great extent taken for granted by successive British governments, regarded as a "natural" feature of Britain's complex of overseas relationships.'
8 NA CAB124/1515 Report on the projection of the Commonwealth in the United Kingdom.
9 Ibid. Of which £40,000 had been spent on films, £30,000 on lectures and £25,000 for the Colonial Touring Exhibition.
10 Ibid. In 1958 the decision was taken to re-name Empire Day as Commonwealth Day.
11 Ibid.
12 R. May and R. Cohen, 'The Interaction Between Race and Colonialism: A Case Study of the Liverpool Race Riots of 1919', *Race and Class*, No.2 (October 1974), p.112.
13 N. Peppard, 'Into the Third Decade', *New Community*, Vol.1, No.2 (January 1972), p.93.
14 N. Deakin, 'The Politics of the Commonwealth Immigrants Bill' *The Political Quarterly*, 39, 1 (January–March 1968), p.45. See also *Parliamentary Debates (Commons)* (7 February 1961), Vol.634, Col.1929.
15 NA HO344/106 Chief Constables' replies to questionnaires on numbers and conduct of coloured people in their area, 1953. Follow-up surveys were

conducted by police in 1955 and 1957, see NA HO344/117 Information from Chief Constables 1955–1956.

16 Ibid.

17 NA HO344/106.

18 Ibid.

19 Ibid.

20 Ibid.

21 Ibid.

22 See, for example, *Police Review* (1 January 1960), p.3, in which applications were invited for police posts in Kenya, Hong Kong, Nyasaland, Uganda and Northern Rhodesia. Gladstone Reid, a former Guyanese police officer, recalled that prior to independence, all senior police officers in Guyana were white. Interviewed by author, 11 October 2000.

23 NA CO318/427/11 Trinidad and Barbados riots 1937: West Indian repercussions.

24 NA CO318/399/3 Movements of Marcus Garvey.

25 NA CO1037/2 Colonial Office working party on the position of police forces in the later stages of constitutional development 1953–1954. See also PRO HO376/135, which refers to an address by the Jamaican High Commissioner to senior police officers in England and Wales in March 1967. He pointed out that, as far as policing in the Caribbean was concerned, 'there was still some considerable aftermath of the impression created by previous [colonial] organisations . . . West Indian immigrants had a great uncomprehending faith in the power of government. The police were associated with government in their minds and whenever they met racial overtones this convinced them that the government was opposed to them.'

26 NA HO287/250 Operational control of colonial police forces: policy on policing in the colonies 1956.

27 An exception to the tradition was Sir Harold Scott, who was Commissioner from 1945 to 1953. He had been a career civil servant with a Home Office and Prison Service background.

28 For a critical assessment of Scott and Nott-Bower see D. Ascoli, *The Queen's Peace* (1979), pp.269–71.

29 NA HO377/72 Report No.8/69 An assessment of the promotion prospects for the period 1969–78 with special reference to the effect of the graduate entry scheme and the special course.

30 Ibid. Police pensions were calculated on an aggregate of the final three years of an officer's service. It followed that officers promoted late in service would wish to remain in their higher rank for at least three years in order to accrue maximum pension rights, in addition to their increased salary. Officers reached retirement age at 55, but annual extensions could be applied for up to the age of 60. In the 1950s and 1960s an officer became eligible to receive a full pension upon completion of 25 years service.

31 Interviewed by author, 2 April 2002.

32 J. Richards, 'Imperial Heroes for a Post-Imperial Age: Films and the End of Empire', in S. Ward (ed.) *British Culture and the End of Empire* (Manchester: 2001), p.129.

33 Ex PC P. Scruby, letter to author, 18 December 2000.

34 Ex chief superintendent S. Higgins, interviewed by author 21 November 2000.

35 NA MEPO2/9854 Police relations with the West Indian community.
36 Ibid.
37 See C. Emsley, 'The English Bobby: An Indulgent Tradition' in R. Porter (ed.), *Myths of the English*, (Cambridge: 1992), pp.114–35, for a fuller description of changes in the popular perception of police since 1829.
38 Ibid. p.125.
39 J. Richards, 'Basil Dearden at Ealing', in A. Burton, P. O'Sullivan and T. Wells (eds.) *Liberal Directions: Basil Dearden and the Postwar British Film Culture* (1997), p.130.
40 'The Constable and the Law', *Police Review*, Vol.41, No.2977 (27 January 1950), p.57. A dissenting voice in the general euphoric praise the film received was provided by the *Daily Herald* (20 January 1950), which argued that the film ignored the plight of the poorly paid, overworked and poorly housed London bobby and that better pay and pensions 'would do all the recruiting required.'
41 A. Spicer, 'The Emergence of the British Tough Guy', in S. Chibnall and R. Murphy (eds.) *British Crime Cinema* (2001), p.82.
42 J. Hill, *Sex, Class and Realism* (1986), p.56.
43 Sir Peter Imbert, interviewed by author, 20 February 2002.
44 *Sun*, 24 November 1954.
45 L. Chase, 'West Indians and the Police', *New Community*, Vol.3, No.3 (Summer 1984), p.207.
46 Mr. C. Edwards in conversation with author on 15 January 2003. To 'fit someone up' is a term used by police and criminals to refer to the practice by which an innocent party has incriminating evidence planted on him/her, or a (police) witness in a criminal trial commits perjury in order to obtain that person's conviction.
47 Inspector D. Lewis, interviewed by author, 18 December 2003.
48 NA MEPO2/10435 At the Commissioner's Conference with chief superintendents on 11 January 1966 it was generally agreed that 'The Police Council, Home Office, MPs, church magazines, Courts of Criminal Appeal, magistrates and the press appeared to be against the police.'
49 Ibid.
50 Ibid.
51 NA HO287/85 Report of the Royal Commission on the Police, Chapter VII, p.331.
52 Ibid.
53 Ibid. p.334.
54 NA MEPO4/213 In 1938 the Met had 18,511 male officers. On 31 December 1966 the corresponding figure was 18,782.
55 T. Newburn, *Permission and Regulation: Law and Morals in post-war Britain* (1992), p.159.
56 Ibid. A good example of which was the rise of Mary Whitehouse and her National Viewers and Listeners Association (NVALA).
57 For a critique of proposals to ban the sale of horror comics see Marghanita Laski, 'Horror Comics', *New Statesman and Nation* (30 April 1954), p.612.
58 Dame Jocelyn Barrow, interviewed by author 9 November 2001.
59 R. Rose and associates, *Colour and Citizenship: A Report on British Race Relations*, (1969), p.335.

Chapter 3

Only on our terms: the Met's unhappy dialogue with representative organisations

The small welfare department that had been maintained in the Colonial Office in the 1940s to deal with problems of colonial immigrants was closed down in 1951, and, as Patterson observed:

> Until 1965 . . . for over a decade of large-scale Commonwealth immigration, there was no British Government department or agency directly or solely responsible for immigrant welfare or integration . . . Basically . . . the whole matter of integration, was left to, and regarded as, the responsibility of local authorities, the voluntary associations, and possibly the High Commissions.[1]

The voluntary associations largely filled the void that was left by government inertia in the 1950s, and took the lead in dealing with the complex task of integrating black immigrants into a grudging white society. Not only were there a whole host of welfare issues to tackle for West Indian migrants, many of whom were fundamentally unprepared in material and cultural terms for life in Britain; but there was the infinitely more difficult task of persuading a reluctant indigenous populous that benefits were to be had from membership of a racially, and culturally, diverse society.

Consultative arrangements between the various agencies representing the interests of West Indians living in London and the Metropolitan Police gradually evolved in the 1950s and 1960s. Such dialogue enabled the Met to obtain a clearer picture of the belief – widely held among black immigrants – that it was a racially prejudiced organisation. The discussions were, however, largely ineffective in changing police attitudes to what a significant number of senior Metropolitan officers regarded as the essence of the problem: the immigrants themselves.

The chapter begins with a summary of the principal organisations dealing with racial integration and West Indian representation in the 1950s and 1960s, a number of which were established in the aftermath of racial disturbances in London and Nottingham in 1958. Welfare services were set up by Commonwealth governments, which, after the demise of the West Indies Federation in 1961, became the responsibility of the various high commissions. The remainder could roughly be grouped into four types: those voluntary associations that were run by immigrants for immigrants, including the West Indian Standing Conference and the West Indian League; those bodies whose membership was comprised of immigrants and members of the indigenous population, including the British Caribbean Association (BCA),[2] the Campaign Against Racial Discrimination (CARD) and Voluntary Liaison Committees (VLCs) – the last of which operated from 1965 with support and guidance from the National Committee for Commonwealth Immigrants (NCCI); and bodies set up with government backing to look at race and immigration, such as the Commonwealth Immigrants Advisory Council (CIAC), the NCCI, and its statutory successor, the Community Relations Commission (CRC). Finally, there were organisations actively involved in tackling problems associated with racial discrimination and immigration – though not exclusively, and only as part of a more varied caseload – such as the National Council for Civil Liberties (NCCL), the Citizens' Advice Bureaux (CAB) and the British Council of Churches. The Race Relations Board (RRB), through its Local Conciliation Committees, had limited powers to receive, consider and endeavour to secure settlement of alleged cases of discrimination, but court proceedings required the approval of the Attorney General. The Board's remit was extended by the Race Relations Act 1968.

For many of these organisations, concerns about policing in London tended to focus on the problem of relationships between police and immigrants, and a perceived unwillingness by the Met to treat black people, either as victims or offenders, fairly. This was a different problem to the widespread social and economic effects of racial prejudice existing in the key areas of housing, employment, education, health and social interaction; though, as will be seen, many West Indians felt that it was in these areas – where the British police had traditionally performed only a limited role – that police inaction, or unwillingness to act, caused widespread resentment. Social and economic problems that were associated with racial discrimination would eventually be addressed, albeit in a somewhat restricted way, by government legislation. The question of discrimination by the police was, however, specifically excluded from such legislation, as it was from the remit of the Race Relations Board.[3]

There is considerable evidence to support the belief that police relations with the black communities took a turn for the worse in the late 1950s, and continued to deteriorate throughout the 1960s. One might well ask why, when there were so many representative organisations and pressure groups working to eradicate discrimination against black migrants – some of which were in receipt of funding from local authorities and the NCCI – this should occur. How might the failure of those who, with the best of motives, sought to improve communication with the Met on the thorny problem of immigrant/police relations be explained? As will be seen, the diversity of the representation, and lack of a united voice, enabled the Met to pick and choose who it spoke to, and, perhaps more importantly, to whom it would listen. Allied to this was the Met's refusal to regard liaison as being anything other than a self-defence mechanism by which it appeared to be actively working to address the concerns of the West Indian community, but failing to back up positive words with good deeds.

In considering these issues it will also be necessary to deal with several related matters. How did the Metropolitan Police Commissioner and his senior colleagues view the various representative organisations; and what changes to force policy, if any, were implemented at grassroots level? What does the consultative process with the Met tell us of the representative bodies; and were some more effective than others in their efforts to effect change in the deeply rooted conservative nature of the police service? The evidence would suggest that the Met was reluctant to involve itself in what it saw as the preferential treatment of the black community, particularly from the mid-1960s when legislation to outlaw racial discrimination first appeared; and that it was selective in determining whose views on the policing of London's black communities were relevant and worthy of consideration, favouring officially sponsored, white-led organisations rather than immigrant voices.

The work of the Special Branch (SB) was particularly influential in the Met's approach to representative bodies, and the individual members of community liaison panels and workshops who were actively seeking to improve race relations at the time. Special Branch files from the period indicate that police were as interested in the political allegiances of those taking part as they were in the causes they espoused. What was the perceived threat that such people posed to national security; how influential were Special Branch intelligence reports on Metropolitan Police race relations policies; and does this tell us anything of the politics of policing and its impact on the political objectives of immigrants at the time? Legislation was introduced in the 1965 and 1968 Race Relations Acts to eradicate racial discrimination in key areas.[4] Senior Met officers believed that such legislation would create particular difficulties for the police. What were their concerns, and what lessons can be drawn from their negative approach to the Race Relations Act 1965, which introduced a specific criminal sanction for incitement to racial hatred?[5]

Throughout this time, the Metropolitan Police remained a *de facto* self-regulating body, and the exclusion of policing from the remit of the Race Relations Board meant that black complainants, aggrieved by police acts or omissions, had no alternative but to seek redress through a complaints procedure that, as statistics showed, treated them less favourably than white complainants. In 1968, the Home Office, in its evidence to the Select Committee on Race Relations and Immigration, gave blanket support to the police and asserted that the cause of friction lay at the door of the black communities. What inferences can we draw from these remarks, and to what extent were they merely a reflection of the degree of influence that the Met exercised over the Home Office Police Department at the time?

For much of this period the Metropolitan Police was labouring under the misapprehension that relations between itself and the black communities were improving, when, in truth, its association with immigrant representatives and other concerned bodies was characterised by condescension, mistrust and suspicion. The Met simply did not grasp the information it received from representative organisations on the state of relations between police and black people, of their concerns regarding the Met's failure to harmonise enforcement of the law with an awareness and appreciation of black public opinion. In his annual report for 1967, Sir John Waldron, the Metropolitan Police Commissioner, spoke of police empathy for the problems associated with immigrants and, in Macmillanesque tones, suggested that – as far as policing was concerned – black people had never had it so good:

> Police understanding of immigrants' problems is deep, police liaison with immigrant groups and contact with individuals is healthy and even an example to some other official organisations – and yet, the more militant groups rant about police victimisation and brutality, and the mass media take up the cry, stating that never have relations been more strained. This is nonsense: police action or inaction will always give cause for complaint – but never had the immigrant groups less cause for complaint than now.[6]

Was Waldron right to make such claims, and were militant activists and the press seeking to destabilise good relations between immigrants and the police: if so, with what aim in mind? Or was it rather the case that the Met involved itself in discussions with immigrant representative organisations principally for its own purposes, and that, for this reason, it failed to recognise the objectives and aspirations of a broad range of bodies that were seeking to make the police more accountable, as well as more culturally and racially aware?

A surfeit of representation?

Associations representing the interests of West Indians in early 1950s Britain existed at both local and national level. Such groups, made up largely of expatriates, were concerned with the welfare of their country-men and women, who were mainly to be found in England's industrial towns and cities. The pattern of migration to Britain from the Caribbean tended to be based upon continuing association with those from one's island or colony. As a result, identifiable communities were re-estab-lished in English towns and cities: such as the Jamaicans in Brixton, Barbadians in Reading and Anguillans in Slough. A number of distinct island associations were formed, primarily to cater for the welfare, spiritual, social and economic needs of members, and also to maintain links with home. Patterson observed that, by the late 1960s, there were at least 30 different Caribbean organisations in London alone.[7] The vast majority of those coming to Britain in the early period were men, whose common aim was economic self-improvement. Many of them planned to stay for a limited period of time and benefit from the higher wages on offer in Britain, before returning home or moving on to bigger and better things. Only a minority arrived in Britain with the intention to settle permanently.

The West Indian Standing Conference (WISC) had been set up in the aftermath of the Notting Hill disturbances as a co-ordinating body for the various organisations representing the interests of West Indians living in London.[8] It sought to address topics that were of particular concern to West Indians and to raise such issues with central and local government, the police and other relevant agencies. In its support role, the WISC received backing from the Migrant Services Division of the West Indies Federation, until the latter was dissolved in 1961.[9] Part of the problem that the WISC faced was the fact that a significant number of the associations representing Caribbean interests in London were local in character, seeking to pursue the welfare interests of their own group members rather than to advance pan-West Indian causes. It should be borne in mind that while English people at this time generally assumed that West Indian immigrants were a homogeneous social group, this was far from being the case. People from one island or territory often felt that they had more in common with those in the 'mother country' than with immigrants from other parts of the British Caribbean. Nadine Peppard, Secretary of the NCCI, and later the CRC, recalled that:

The early West Indian immigrants ... had been brought up to think of themselves as completely British: for those who had experienced the education system, the curriculum was exactly the same as ours. As the true nature of the situation developed, they often said that they knew more about Agincourt and the kings and queens of England than they did about the next island.[10]

The Immigrants Advisory Committee of the London Council of Social Services was established in 1958. Membership of the Committee included High Commission officials, government representatives and others who were actively involved in immigrant affairs. The Committee gave information and assistance to all bodies interested in the welfare and integration of immigrants from overseas.[11] The National Council of Social Services provided co-ordinating meetings for VLCs. It fulfilled no proactive welfare role for immigrants; neither did it endeavour to educate the host community. However, as the major national social service organisation, it was consulted and was one of the three organisations whose representatives formed the short-lived predecessor of the NCCI,[12] the National Advisory Committee for Commonwealth Immigrants (NACCI).

In 1962 the Commonwealth Immigrants Act was passed; legislation that for the first time restricted the rights of Commonwealth citizens to come to Britain. In the same year, the Home Secretary, R.A. Butler, set up the Commonwealth Immigrants Advisory Council. Its purpose was to:

Advise him on any matters he might refer to it ... affecting the welfare of Commonwealth immigrants in this country, and *inter alia* ... to examine the relationship between action by local officials of Government departments and local authorities on the one hand, and the efforts of voluntary bodies on the other, in furthering the welfare of immigrants.[13]

The first National Committee for Commonwealth Immigrants was established by the CIAC.[14] This consisted of a small committee, which supervised the tasks of its liaison officer, which were:

To bring to the notice of local authorities and voluntary bodies the experiments and methods of work of other bodies and any other relevant information and ... suggest new experiments and methods of work in areas where numbers of immigrants had settled.[15]

In September 1965 the CIAC was replaced by a new, and enlarged, National Committee for Commonwealth Immigrants under its chairman, the Archbishop of Canterbury. It had an advisory officer and an annual budget of £6,000.[16] Its terms of reference were:

> To promote and coordinate on a national basis efforts directed towards the integration of Commonwealth immigrants into the community. In particular the Committee was required to:
>
> (a) Promote and co-ordinate the activities of voluntary liaison committees and advise them on their work
> (b) Where necessary, assist in the recruitment and training of suitable men or women to serve these communities as full-time officials
> (c) Provide a central information service
> (d) Organise conferences, arrange training courses and stimulate research
> (e) Advise on those questions which are referred to them by Government or which they consider should be brought to the attention of Government.[17]

By 1968, the government had developed a two-pronged strategy to tackle racial discrimination. It believed that legislation had a part to play in preventing discrimination on racial grounds and in influencing attitudes. It also believed that legislation needed the support of voluntary and administrative action and effective social policies.[18]

The work of the NCCI was put on a statutory basis by the Race Relations Act 1968, when it was renamed and replaced by the Community Relations Commission. Though the Commission continued to deal with issues that had been the province of the NCCI, the CRC's role was intended to reflect a move in emphasis away from the difficulties associated with immigration, and towards the problems that were likely to be encountered by black people who had been born, or had grown up, in Britain. The work of the ever-increasing number of voluntary liaison committees (VLCs), many of which contained representatives from the West Indian and Asian communities, was seen as crucial to the success of the government's race relations policy. Some VLCs had been in existence for a number of years but, by the mid-1960s, they had been revamped and brought into line with the new ones that were being established in all of the principal areas of immigrant settlement in London and around the country. They relied largely on local authority funding and support and were primarily intended to develop positive community relations, rather than merely focusing on 'the welfare of coloured people.'[19]

The Campaign Against Racial Discrimination was established in 1964 as a multi-racial pressure group, the objective of which was to seek the elimination of all forms of racial discrimination in Great Britain. It was particularly active in challenging government legislation on immigration, and made recommendations to amend the 1965 Race Relations Act, which were subsequently incorporated into the Race Relations Act of 1968. The Race Adjustment Action Society (RAAS) was an organisation that appeared in early 1965, under its leader Michael de Freitas, the self-styled 'Michael X'. It advocated unity among black people living in Britain to 'redress the balance of insecurity, fear and disunity in which we live'.[20] One outcome of RAAS was the creation of 'Defence', a body that provided legal assistance to black people in trouble with the police. The difficulty for activist organisations such as RAAS, and indeed for all associations claiming to speak for West Indians living in Britain at the time, was the lack of a collective voice, which was largely the result of their isolation from each other in their island or territorial homes. As Nadine Peppard recalled:

> The difference between the people was not just political. They were simply complete strangers to each other. Not only was Jamaica geographically some distance from most of the others ... many could not even understand the accents of the others. It is not surprising that this absence of a corporate Caribbean identity carried over when they came to Britain. While they were generally not aggressively antagonistic to each other, there was some degree of prejudice and they did not easily come together in co-operation. Nor were the vast majority interested in setting up or joining a black movement.[21]

The lack of a unified approach and shared objectives, particularly when it came to dealing with the police, played into the hands of the Met: an organisation that, at the time, saw little need to change its own approach to the community it served.

Different wavelengths: representative voices, the Metropolitan Police and its Special Branch

The Metropolitan Police Commissioner, Sir Joseph Simpson, was concerned that West Indians constituted over half the black population of what he described as 'London's troubled areas', and, on 2 July 1959, he visited Mr Garnett Gordon, Commissioner of the West Indies Federation (WIF), with the intention of establishing a working relationship. He seemed to have been less motivated by a desire to enhance the cause of racial and cultural harmony than by personal and corporate self-interest, for, as he stated:

My aim was to establish a channel of liaison between this office and his office so that there would be no excuses for any allegations that police had refused to co-operate with responsible representatives of the coloured people in the various districts.[22]

Simpson was heartened that Gordon and members of his senior staff appeared to show, in his words, 'common-sense', in their apparent acceptance of his less than favourable assessment of West Indian society, a viewpoint that was to have profound effects for West Indians who applied to join the Met during Simpson's stewardship of the organisation. According to Simpson:

All three of them acknowledged the sort of weaknesses and defects which we experience in coloured people and above all, deplored the circulation of rumours and the making of allegations which are unsupported by reasonable, if any, evidence ... He [Gordon] appreciates too; the coloured person may resent good advice, even reasonably given, due to an inferiority complex or to criminal or unpleasant traits in the character of the person spoken to.[23]

Simpson's solution to the problem of liaison with the West Indian communities was the appointment of Chief Superintendent Best of 'A' Department to act as the official police liaison officer. Best was to receive details of complaints from the WIF and take steps to 'smooth out difficulties or misunderstandings in the various sub-divisions.'[24] On 5 October 1960, Best received a letter from Mr Johnson, the Secretary for Migrant Services at the WIF. Johnson expressed concern at the current state of relations in the Notting Hill area:

From reports received from leaders of West Indian Organisations in the area of North Kensington (Notting Hill), over the past three months, I have gathered the impression that there is some latent tension between West Indians and white residents in the area, together with a growing atmosphere of unhappy relations with the police.[25]

One week later, on 13 October, Johnson again wrote to Best. On this occasion he gave details of an alleged assault by police on a West Indian male, and added:

I have two reports from West Indian leaders of organisations in Greater London that there is a growing feeling among West Indians that the police appear to act unfairly with them, and there appears to be an unfavourable growing atmosphere of unhappy relations between West Indians and the police.[26]

In replying to Johnson's letter, Assistant Commissioner Webb stated with apparent surprise that 'local senior officers are unaware of unhappy relations between the coloured population and the police.'[27]

On 16 May 1963, Simpson attended a meeting at the Home Office with the Jamaican High Commissioner, Mr Lindo. It was noted in the minutes of the meeting that Lindo:

> Made a long statement about his anxiety – as a result of representa-
> tions made by responsible members of his own people – concerning
> what he thought were deteriorating relations between coloureds and
> what he called the junior ranks of the police service [sergeants and
> constables] . . . it was clear that the chief thing in his mind was the
> tendency for his people to be questioned by police or moved on
> when they concentrate on street corners, as is their wont, and he
> feared that a hot summer might create a brittle situation.[28]

Simpson was surprised to hear that the relations had deteriorated, as his impression, based upon police reports of incidents involving black and white groups, was that 'the situation had improved considerably since 1960.'[29] His observation – perhaps purposefully – somewhat missed the point. The issue concerning the Jamaican High Commissioner was that of relations between black people and the police, and not relations with white society at large.

In spite of warnings from leaders of London's West Indian communi-ties of deteriorating relations between immigrants and police, the liaison arrangement that had been put in place during the life of the West Indies Federation ended abruptly when the Federation was dissolved in 1961. Had the Met worked to re-establish links, this time with the various high commissions in the immediate post-WIF period, it would undoubtedly have been better informed as to the state of relations between West Indian immigrants and its officers.

Following the May 1963 meeting with Lindo, Simpson decided that he would re-establish liaison. However, he insisted that it should take place only with the Jamaican High Commission. Though they were clearly the largest group of West Indians living in London at the time, his decision meant that other West Indian representatives in the capital had no formally agreed direct access to senior Metropolitan Police management. The decision was likely to cause ill feeling within the West Indian community, not only because Jamaicans appeared to have a better chance of having grievances against the police brought to the attention of the Commissioner and his colleagues, but also because many of the others had blamed Jamaica's decision to leave the West Indies Federation for the organisation's collapse.

The Metropolitan Police approach to representative associations at this time was characterised by a defensive reluctance to accept criticism from without, frustration that West Indian immigrants did not always behave in the same way as white British people, and an unwillingness to acknowledge that a change of attitude was needed if black communities were to have confidence in the police. An illustration of this is given by chief superintendent Norman's address to the West Indian Students' Union on 11 March 1966.[30] At the time, Norman had special responsibility for West Indian affairs at New Scotland Yard, a post in which he would have been expected to develop what Waldron had described as 'a deep understanding of immigrants' problems'.

Norman informed his audience that the Met had no special attitude towards immigrants. He said that West Indians were a problem because 'of their penchant for complaining that police had been too officious towards them, or that police were not doing their job properly'.[31] He added that West Indians had a fondness for litigation and that they resented advice given by the police. He went on to tell them what the police in England considered to be an acceptable standard of behaviour, and, at the same time, how he expected them to behave:

I said that the traditional attitude in England was for members of the public to accept advice or orders from policemen, if not with good grace at least without argument. This to my mind was a good thing, as someone has to be the boss on the streets and give the orders. Police naturally resented having every order questioned, and I said that it would make for better relations if immigrants were prepared to accept advice or orders more readily.[32]

Such remarks can hardly have been calculated to convince those attending the meeting that the Met empathised with, or understood, the concerns of the black community. Norman's remarks, given his position as the Met's link with the West Indian community, would tend to suggest that the attitude of senior police officers at the time was based upon a belief that conflict between police and West Indian immigrants stemmed directly from negative black attitudes to police authority. The Met's solution to the problem, as expounded by Norman, was to emphasise that there had to be a boss, and that someone was the police. As soon as the West Indian community understood that they should accept the word of police without argument, the better it would be.

At question time the topic of black policemen arose. The general view of the students was that no black person, whatever his qualifications, would be accepted for appointment. Norman, in his liaison role with the West Indian communities and with his direct access to the Met's highest-ranking officers, must have known that it was Metropolitan

Police policy at the time not to recruit black men to the service. His reply to the students was therefore disingenuous:

> I ducked this one by saying that up to the present suitable candidates had not offered themselves. There was some disagreement with this but as none of those taking part in the discussion was able to quote a case the matter was dropped.[33]

While the Met's approach to liaison with the immigrant communities left much to be desired, dialogue did take place, and a number of Met officers played a positive and active part in the work of local VLCs. By July 1969, there were 38 police liaison officers serving on committees in London, of which 17 had voting rights.[34] A meeting was held at New Scotland Yard on 7 November 1966, at which the Commissioner met with Maurice Foley MP, and police delegates from divisions with large numbers of immigrant residents.[35] Two of the four police officers at the meeting were members of local committees.[36] The police delegate from Camden felt that representation on such committees was favourable because: 'It gave police an opportunity to be "kept in the picture" so far as community affairs were concerned . . . but . . . he found an element on these committees which resented the presence of a police officer.'[37]

Relations between police and other members of VLCs were not always harmonious. A good example of the difficulties described by the officer from Camden was that provided by the Kensington and Chelsea Inter-Racial Council (KCIRC), which had its inaugural meeting on 2 August 1966. This group had been established with the backing of the NCCI and the borough council and the local police superintendent, David Helm, had been invited to become a member. The group's stated objective was to work with the council to develop cordial race relations in the borough. It is interesting to note that policing was not considered to be an issue deserving special attention at the first steering committee meeting.[38] Immediately following the meeting, Superintendent Helm reported to his senior officers his concern over the *bona fides* of certain West Indian members of the group, particularly a Mr Frank Bailey, and suggested that rather than delegating the liaison role to a junior ranking officer, he wished to attend personally to 'keep an eye on proceedings'. He reported that, 'the chairman and the secretary [who were white] are both very responsible people who will do their utmost to keep this Inter-Racial Council on the right lines'.[39] Helm submitted a copy of his report for the information of Special Branch.

Over the succeeding 12 months the structure of the group changed: the West Indian, Bailey, had now become chairman, and a number of other members had been drawn from the West Indian community. When the KCIRC appointed a liaison officer, Mr James Cummings, a 52-year-old

Trinidadian, Helm carried out a Special Branch check on him and noted that 'He is well known to the Council of Civil Liberties and was a member of the Communist Party ... Mr Cummings strikes me as a very aggressive type, with obvious experience of public speaking.'[40]

By February 1968, the KCIRC had decided to establish a number of sub-committees to look at various issues of concern to the local community. Policing was now top of the list. The KCIRC met again on 10 March 1968. By this time Superintendent Paterson had replaced Helm as the police representative. At the meeting Bailey pointed out that Helm, during his period as a member of the committee, had been reporting on him to Special Branch, and that Helm had described him as 'a dangerous agitator'.[41] A report on the meeting was submitted to the ACA, who noted that:

> Regrettably, this sort of work is largely among the completely irresponsible members of the coloured community ... this incident does underline the importance of establishing some central depart-mental direction in this field, and ... A7 Branch is being set up primarily for this purpose.[42]

The example of the KCIRC shows how the Met was happy to work with a committee, the white chairman and secretary of which it believed would always conduct its affairs in a manner that was acceptable to police. However, when the committee came under the chairmanship of a West Indian whose views were more independent and less acquiescent than had previously been the case, the Met, rather than striving to work with the new committee in order to address issues of concern regarding policing, chose to take exception to individuals and points of view that it saw as a direct challenge to its privileged position. The problem, the Met believed, was people such as Bailey, the 'black agitator' chairman, and his supporters who didn't play by its rules. Gurdial Bhamra, one of London's earliest Sikh police officers, recalled his experiences of the type of community representative that was most welcomed by senior Met officers:

> Police always produce people from the community, someone who is willing to say 'your police are wonderful. It's what's wrong with the Asian community or the black community. They're not doing this, they're not doing that right.' I can remember some time ago when I was an inspector at Hackney. A conference was organised on two issues; one was racial crime, blacks and Asians as victims, and the other one was domestic violence. On the issue of racial crime, they brought a teacher, or head-teacher out to speak, an Asian bloke. He spent nearly an hour talking about racial crime and as far as he was

concerned there was no racial crime. There were no racial assaults. As far as he was concerned, those people who were assaulted must have done something wrong . . . As far as the police were concerned, those who were listening, they were so happy because he was saying that the police were wonderful.[43]

In its dealings with voluntary associations representing the welfare of black people, the Met was primarily interested in ensuring that the structure of the organisations were such that those holding positions of influence were favourably disposed to its viewpoint. What such individuals had to offer as a force for change and improvement was of less consequence. As a result, criticism could be kept to a minimum. This viewpoint was well illustrated by Tony Smythe of the NCCL in an address to the Police Federation in June 1971, in which he pointed out the shortcomings in the police's eternal quest to ensure that it was always represented in a positive light:

> It is necessary to make a distinction between criticism of the police and constructive observations . . . I would urge you to get criticism in perspective. Criticism from outside the force may be proportional to the lack of self-criticism within. Whenever one does raise with the police the question of criticism, one always has slung back the question of morale – 'You can't say that sort of thing.' This is a very dangerous state of mind to get into. You [the Police Federation] should value criticism and you should not be misled by sentimental support. There are real areas of concern . . . There is a fear of scrutiny from outside.[44]

When the Met had to deal with those in positions of authority who were less inclined to view its policies with approval, it assumed a defensive posture and sought to discover if unwelcome skeletons from the past might be unearthed. Background checks would be carried out on those taking part in liaison meetings to ascertain whether or not their political leanings were likely to cause problems. In this regard, the Met worked hand-in-glove with its Special Branch (SB).

The Metropolitan Police Special Branch was established in 1883, with the original objective of combating Irish 'Fenian' terrorism. Special Branch officers are drawn from serving officers in the Metropolitan Police. The work of the Branch in this period, and its recruitment policy, was summarised and set out in the *Metropolitan Police Instruction Book*:

> The duties of this Branch include enquiries concerning the security of the State, and naturalisation of aliens, special duty at ports and airports, and the protection of foreign Royalty and Heads of State,

certain Cabinet Ministers and other important persons. Appointments to the Branch are made from male and female Uniform or CID Constables who are well educated: a good knowledge of a foreign language or shorthand is desirable ... applicants who are recommended for the duty are required to pass a special examination before being appointed on probation. They must be prepared to perform duty at any place to which they may be assigned.[45]

The most obvious aspect of the Branch's work that would have been relevant to West Indian immigrants was that of state security. That being the case, Special Branch officers would have taken an interest in the political activities of West Indians and many others whose views were, or may have been considered to be, outside the parameters of acceptable political activity. Intelligence obtained by SB pertaining to those who were leading figures in the immigrant communities, as well as those who were actively campaigning for improved race relations, was disseminated to the Commissioner and his senior colleagues, who would have undoubtedly considered and acted upon the information supplied. Some examples may help to show the persuasive influence of SB on Metropolitan Police policy toward the West Indian community.

Special Branch reports claimed that, prior to the disturbances in Notting Hill in 1958, there were no political associations of West Indians in that area. However, as a direct result of racial tensions, two welfare organisations allegedly became politically active. These were the Coloured People's Progressive Association (CPPA), and the National Association for the Advancement of Colored People (NAACP).[46] It might be argued that the very process of seeking better social and economic conditions and an end to racial prejudice were inherently political acts, and this poses the question, what activities did Special Branch deem to be threatening to state security? It claimed that control of both organisations had been seized by extreme left-wing elements and that an alliance had been established between the Coloured People's Progressive Association and a Trotskyist group that became known as the Socialist Labour League.[47] SB made special mention of a leading figure in the NAACP, Claudia Jones, who was described as: 'A well-known West Indian communist, who came to this country in 1955 rather than await deportation proceedings against her because of communist activities in the United States of America.'[48] The report went on to assert that Jones was editor of the *West Indian Gazette*, the circulation of which had increased from 500 to 7,000 copies each month, and that all members of the editorial board were communists.

On 9 September 1959, ACA Webb attended the office of the WIF for a meeting with Gordon, who, during the discussion, asked whether it might be possible for police to be represented at the committee meetings of coloured peoples associations. In answer to what, on the surface, appears to have been a positive proposal to improve police/immigrant relations, and one which was in keeping with Gordon's constructive attitude on the subject, Webb pointed out that 'there was definite policy against police officers talking to or appearing with Committees of persons where there was the slightest indication of political favour'.[49] Gordon's reply that 'politics should not normally enter into the Coloured Peoples Associations' shows that the ACA's negative response took him by surprise.

Gordon would have been unaware of the information compiled by Special Branch on prominent West Indian individuals and organisations, details of which would have been made known to Webb before their meeting. It appears safe to assume that, as a policy decision had been taken that the Met would not talk to, or appear with, black associations for fear of showing 'political favour', the subject of relations between the two had been discussed at the highest level at Scotland Yard. If the decision had been taken for political reasons, as seems to have been the case, there can be little doubt that Special Branch reports on the background of association members – a significant number of whom were described as communists or as communist sympathisers – would have been a crucial determining factor in negating, or seriously limiting, the chances of persuading the Met to enter into dialogue with any constructive purpose.

In September 1963, the London Council of Social Services organised a three-day seminar entitled 'Integration or assimilation?'[50] The conference, which was chaired by Alderman J.E. MacColl from Paddington, was attended by a cross-section of people drawn from university, trade union, local authority and other representative backgrounds. The work of some London VLCs was discussed, as well as problems associated with housing, education, employment and migration. On 10 February 1964, the ACA asked for a check of Special Branch records on speakers and delegates who had attended the conference. Many of the delegates were described as communists, or as having communist sympathies – including the High Commissioner of Trinidad and Tobago. Others were described as having, or having had, connection with the Campaign for Nuclear Disarmament (CND) and, in one case, as having 'supported the National Council for Civil Liberties'.[51]

Such observations expose the fallacy of the argument of many senior police officers that the police service steered a course of political neutrality; for, as Reiner points out: 'The police are inherently and inescapably political: "The civil police is a social organisation created and sustained by political processes to enforce dominant conceptions of public order" ' (Skolnick, 1972, p.41).[52] The police service and its Special Branch may well have claimed neutrality in party political terms, as it always served the government of the day, but politics has always been a consistent and vital ingredient of police policy decisions. The British parliamentary system, structured as it is in such a way that the administration and methodology of government remains unaltered whichever of the main parties is in power, relies upon its police service to maintain the *status quo*. In consequence, the police, in its role as the enforcer of establishment attitudes to crime, political protest and public order, was, and continues to be, the physical embodiment of government ideology at street level. At a time when the need to counter communism was still central to the thought processes of those at Westminster, it logically followed that the police Special Branch would view those seeking to challenge the established order of things – including West Indian representatives and others who campaigned for a more egalitarian society – as subversives. A former Special Branch officer, Sir Peter Imbert, confirmed this view: 'It was probably a nonsensical conclusion that they were communists but in those days, of course, the great Russian bear was looking over everyone's shoulders and anyone who was perceived to be a troublemaker was labelled a communist.'[53]

Legislation and the representative process: the RRB, the NCCI and the Met

Early government plans to introduce legislation to tackle problems of racial discrimination were ill conceived and extremely limited in their scope. A senior civil servant of the day recalled the reaction to the government's proposal to provide a criminal sanction against racial discrimination.

> I remember clearly ... the Home Office under pressure with an incoming Labour Government to introduce legislation. They drafted a Bill that would have made discrimination a criminal offence ... we were independent enough to say that this is absolute nonsense. You cannot make discrimination a criminal offence, a civil offence yes. I think it went to Committee as a criminal offence ... I can't remember the details but I think it only had about three clauses in it. But it got torn to pieces in Committee.[54]

For its part, the Met viewed the introduction of legislation to tackle discrimination with much trepidation. Simpson called for a secret response to the proposed legislation from his area commanders following their discussion of the matter on 1 December 1964. Waldron made no attempt to hide his disquiet:

If this becomes law, minority interests will deliberately provoke incidents and police are going to be placed in an impossible position if they are obliged to institute proceedings against licensees and others with respectable reputations on the word of the [black] complainant and his witness, some of whom may be lying.[55]

While police at the time were labouring under the mistaken assumption that they would be required to enforce anti-discrimination legislation, some of their observations shed light on more general attitudes to the black community.[56] The Commander of Number One Area suggested that social discrimination, of the unspoken sort, which had long been accepted and understood by British people, had operated to the advantage of society before the influx of black people, and added:

The ordinary white citizen generally accepts his place in society and makes no attempt to gatecrash places where he would not only feel out of place but is clearly unwelcome. Coloured people do not have the ability to do this and for the most part they are hypersensitive over colour . . . It must be concluded that coloured people are more conscious of their rights than their obligations and any kind of legislation on the lines suggested will result in an avalanche of complaints . . .[57]

The Commander of Number Four Area pointed out that the proposed legislation would create 'a specially favoured class and spotlight the very difference which all our efforts are directed to remove'.[58] The planned criminal sanction for discrimination was dropped at the committee stage of the Bill's progress, but this did not deter Waldron from making further adverse comment on potential beneficiaries of the Bill:

One is left with the impression that the Government, badgered by their intellectual left wing to introduce this legislation, will be happy to see it played down, for they realise only too well that working Labour is as intolerant of colour as any other class. It will be left to the Director of Public Prosecutions to make the difficult 'political' decision that only cases in which 'black' people are concerned will be appropriate for proceedings; if it is the Liverpool Irish, Cypriots or Maltese who are involved, I am sure that we will hear little more . . . If as one would hope this situation is accepted more as a declaration of intent to which all sensible people should listen rather than as an ideological piece of legislation indifferent to the feelings of the average Englishman, we should not have too many head-aches. On the other hand, it will give the National Council of Civil Liberties and other trouble makers ample opportunity to stir up racial animosities in order to upset police and authority generally.[59]

Relations between the Met and representative bodies were undoubtedly affected by the personal relationships of the individuals involved. This was certainly the case regarding the Met's dealings with the WISC, an organisation the Met sought to marginalize largely as a result of personal difficulties with WISC's executive. On 4 April 1967 WISC's executive attended a meeting at New Scotland Yard to which they had been invited by the head of A2 (2) Branch, chief superintendent Merricks.[60] The WISC representatives expressed concern at the way in which complaints against the police were dealt with, and its chairman suggested that, in order to improve local relations, his organisation would provide the Met with details of responsible members who could work with police to improve relations. In return, he asked if he could be supplied with details of police liaison officers. Merricks advised him that he would provide such information later, and noted that:

> This meeting, though serving a useful purpose, underlined once again the basic difficulties of dealing with West Indians. Namely that although many, if not most, of their grievances can be shown to be misconceived, they remain stubbornly if not cynically convinced that this force practices discrimination.[61]

The WISC proposal appears to have been a simple and straightforward effort aimed at improving relations with the Met, and yet Merricks sought confirmation from the NCCI before agreeing to the WISC proposal. This suggests that certain representative organisations were more highly regarded by the Met's senior officers than others. The government-funded NCCI, and later the CRC, appear to have been viewed more favourably than organisations that did not have government backing; but this poses the question: how representative were the NCCI and CRC; and how would other bodies have viewed such preferential treatment?

A number of immigrants believed that the NCCI, the RRB and the later CRC were created to stifle the legitimate concerns of immigrants. Hall has argued that the preference shown by the Met to officially sponsored representative organisations, such as the NCCI and CRC, was made worse by the failure of such bodies to engage in dialogue with the West Indian community and its representatives:

> The problem that we had was that sometimes these good white people, having agreed what they would want us to achieve with our people, wouldn't even tell us. If we don't know the agenda, then often you have difficulties.[62]

There were many who believed that the RRB was something of a paper tiger. Those who complained to it about the police were merely informed that the Race Relations Act of 1968 'did not extend to complaints against police while they are working in their operational role . . .'[63] Complainants were left to pursue their grievance through the unsatisfactory police complaints procedure. Dorothy Kuya recalled her experiences as the general secretary of a VLC, and argued that VLCs that wished to assist complainants might find that they were ordered to desist:

> The few who did take up things were in trouble with the Commission [CRC]. We were always getting phone calls from the Commission . . . to lay off a lot of things; police things and drug things . . . The CRC and NCCI were organisations that were set up to control. They weren't set up to look at the problems and deal with the problems and what they've done is continually appointed people who go along with that.[64]

An added difficulty was the fact that in the period between the creation of the NCCI and the RRB and the passing of the Race Relations Act in 1968, government officials began to question the position and status of both the NCCI and RRB. Perceived problems in the structure of the NCCI where highlighted in an internal report:

> There are signs . . . that it is becoming self-perpetuating. The main Committee and its Finance & General Purposes Sub-Committee are becoming embroiled in staff matters and questions of routine administration, and some of the panels now seem to be meeting more for the sake of meeting than to deal with important problems . . . Further, we shall shortly be moving into a situation in which the concept of a Committee specially created to deal with Commonwealth immigrants will be out of date as the emphasis shifts to the problem of second generation British born coloured people rather than to the problems of the newly arrived immigrant.[65]

In his Annual Report for 1968, the Commissioner of the Met (Waldron), reported the setting up of the force's Community Relations Branch, A7 (1), and went on to explain the rationale of the new unit:

> The social consequences of a rapid influx of coloured citizens from overseas throughout the Metropolitan Police District . . . are still comparatively new and provide matters of concern. This is a field in which police are among the first to become involved, since it is when difficulties and misunderstandings due to incompatibility and different habits and ways of life become major social problems that police come into the picture.[66]

The Met now had local liaison officers and a central department charged with the task of discovering the nature of black peoples' difficulties and misunderstandings where social problems might arise. The stumbling block to progress was that, while the Met could now expect to be better informed of potential problems, it still saw the solution in terms of necessary changes that would have to be made by the black community in order to fit in with accepted white attitudes to policing, rather than the need to question its own approach to people from the Caribbean and the problems they encountered.

An example of this is to be found in the Met's response to questions posed by the Select Committee on Race Relations and Immigration. On 12 December 1968, the Committee considered evidence supplied by the Home Office. Part III of the White Paper *Immigration from the Commonwealth*[67] had set out the government's view on the benefits and the dangers of large-scale Commonwealth immigration to Britain:

> The United Kingdom is already a multi-cultural society and Commonwealth immigrants make a most valuable contribution to our economy . . . At the same time it must be recognised that the presence in this country of nearly one million immigrants from the Commonwealth with different social and cultural backgrounds raises a number of problems and creates various social tensions in those areas where they have concentrated.[68]

The Select Committee considered the role of the police and sought answers from the Home Office to four questions:

1. Could the police do more to keep in touch with the immigrant community? Explain circumstances where police discrimination has been alleged? Help bring parents in touch with schools etc.? Help Youth Clubs? Talks to immigrants in schools?
2. Are the Home Office satisfied with training given to the police regarding race relations?
3. Should police advise young immigrants when a breach of the Race Relations Act is alleged?
4. Would more policemen be welcome?

The response from the Home Office Police Department was clear. If problems existed between immigrant communities and the police, the fault was not to be found at the door of the police service.

The Home Office claimed that the police would always like to do more, but they also had a large number of responsibilities that needed to be considered before any one aspect of policing could be prioritised. It had to be borne in mind that the primary task of the police was the preservation of the peace by preventing and detecting crime. There was a limit to what the police could achieve alone. The police should be able to rely on the co-operation of leaders of immigrant communities and associations. Allegations of discrimination by black people against the police were largely the result of their over-sensitivity and were not supported by evidence. In any event, it was claimed, young people and the Irish 'have more to put up with from police activity in the pursuit of criminal offenders and the maintenance of order than coloured persons'.[69]

Many of the difficulties in police/immigrant relations were, it was alleged, the result of a failure of the latter to adjust to a lifestyle that was in keeping with British ideas of reserve and decorum. As a result, police were accused of discrimination when they were called upon, often by neighbours, to deal with noisy 'shabeens' where alcohol was being sold illegally. It may well have been the case that an immigrant received roughshod treatment from police in his own country and this may have affected his attitude to the British police. The reply ended with the suggestion that there was a disposition among some immigrant associations or individuals to make indiscriminate allegations against the police. Such allegations were not conducive to good police/immigrant relations.[70]

On the specific subject of complaints, the report identified that while there appeared to be proportionately more complaints made by black complainants than whites, the number of complaints that were substantiated was less. The somewhat odd conclusion drawn from these figures was that when police investigated such allegations against themselves, and invariably found them to be unsubstantiated, it naturally followed that police had not discriminated against black complainants and that the initial (black) complaint had been either malicious or unfounded. A more impartial observer might be forgiven for drawing a different conclusion: one in which, in percentage terms, more black people complained against the met because they had legitimate grievances, and that their complaints of police discrimination were considered to be unfounded largely because the accused (the police) sat in judgement of themselves.

The representative process: the barriers to effective communication with the Met

Consultation with the Metropolitan Police on issues of race and diversity and the problems facing black immigrants was a largely unrewarding process in the 1950s and 1960s. No liaison arrangements between the Met and organisations representing the interests of London's West Indian communities appear to have existed until after the killing of Kelso Cochrane in May 1959; despite the fact that racist disturbances in Notting

Hill in the late summer of 1958 had provoked a wave of public disquiet. In the decade that followed, the Met showed a greater willingness to discuss the concerns of West Indian people at senior level, with high commissioners, and at local level with a variety of representative bodies. While it welcomed dialogue with those it deemed appropriate, it did so largely on its own terms; namely, so that it could be better informed of the potential threat to public order, criminal activity and the political conduct of those who were believed to hold extremist political views.

London's West Indians faced many problems in their daily lives prior to 1965, when limited legislative measures were introduced to combat racial discrimination. Of these, the most important concerns, and ones that would not be legally outlawed until the Race Relations Act 1968, were those relating to the widespread prejudice in employment and housing. These key issues, along with discrimination in public places, prompted immigrants and their supporters in the host community to resolve to bring about change. Many believed that, as in the Caribbean, the local police could and would resolve domestic, housing and employment-related disputes. They naturally assumed that the Met would do the same. However, the Met was ever conscious of the distinction between the criminal law, which it dealt with, and the civil law, which it didn't, and sought to avoid. Waldron had acknowledged the difficulties this caused in a report to Simpson on 4 January 1965:

> I can well understand that many coloured people when they bring their troubles to a police station desk or to an officer in the street think that they are being treated in an offhand manner or with lack of interest or sympathy if they are merely referred to a magistrate or a Citizen's Advice Bureau. Police in the colonies are not liked but they are feared and respected and when they give an on-the-spot decision in a civil dispute, provided the officer is of some rank or experience, it is generally accepted and obeyed. This is, of course, in direct contrast to the instruction we give our constables but it might be worth considering in a predominantly coloured area whether or not we should take a more definite line in these civil disputes.[71]

Establishing effective liaison with the Met was an extremely challeng-ing process, made more difficult by the fact that the Commissioner and his colleagues had their own view on the purpose of such dialogue. When Simpson set up a consultative arrangement with the WIF he did so to forestall criticism of the Met in the aftermath of an allegedly racist murder, rather than to review police strategies, or with any desire to encourage racial awareness amongst his officers. When the WIF was disbanded in 1961, the Commissioner failed to encourage or pursue liaison with other bodies. It was only when pressed by the Jamaican

High Commissioner to establish a working relationship two years later that the process of dialogue with immigrant representatives was reintroduced. The result was that, during the intervening period, the Met developed a wholly unrealistic assessment of its relationship with West Indian immigrants and assumed that relations were much better than they actually were.

The Metropolitan Police was unquestionably selective in deciding which organisations it would do business with regarding immigrant welfare and community relations. Success or failure often depended on the personal chemistry between police and delegates (as was the case with the WISC); whether or not those in charge of a particular organisation were favourably disposed to the Met's viewpoint; and the political background and views of the various representatives. If any of the criteria was found to be unsatisfactory to police, the likelihood was that little or no credence would be given to the views expressed. One organisation that the Met appeared to favour was the government backed NCCI (later the CRC). Despite the Met's support, the General Secretary of both the NCCI and CRC, Nadine Peppard, felt that the Met's attitude to consultation left much to be desired:

> To my knowledge, the Met was not open to establishing any sort of consultation arrangements with lay bodies, except with the West Indian High Commissions, which I suspect was largely a matter of lip-service or, after 1962, tracking down people who were in the UK illegally. I worked closely with the High Commission officers and we discussed current problems on a continuing basis, but they very rarely even mentioned the police. In general, the police were regarded as racially prejudiced and unhelpful, though in certain areas, like Notting Hill, things were much more highly charged.[72]

The Met's selectiveness was divisive and led not only to feelings of exclusion, but to resentment at the apparent favouritism shown to organisations such as the NCCI, some critics going as far as to suggest that it (the NCCI) was merely a government creation to stifle black protest.[73]

Special Branch reports on organisations and individuals that were seeking to improve life for black people in Britain at the time tended to suggest that many of them were communists or communist sympathisers. When one considers that Waldron could describe an organisation such as the National Council for Civil Liberties as 'trouble makers' it appears reasonable to conclude that those assumed by the Met to be active communists would have had little chance of persuading it of their good intentions. The result was that individuals and organisations which were so described were kept at arm's length by the Met; or, in those situations where the Met sat on committees with such persons, they were treated with suspicion and subjected to a continuing cycle of monitoring and reports that merely helped to perpetuate antagonism and mistrust.

Despite the establishment of a Community Relations Branch at New Scotland Yard, and liaison at local level, the Met failed to recognise its own shortcomings in its dealings with the West Indian community. While, in its own words, it would have liked to have done more, it suggested that the real problem was that West Indians tended to be over-sensitive when stopped by police, that they misunderstood the nature of life in Britain, and that they may well have developed negative attitudes towards police in this country as a result of damaging experiences with police in their homelands. They also had a tendency, the Met claimed, to make allegations against the police that were invariably found to be baseless. In short, the problem and its solutions, as far as the Met was concerned, lay with the West Indian community itself. Louis Chase, a public relations officer at the WISC during this period, had no illusions about what he saw as the Met's motivation for establishing liaison: '[The West Indian] Conference suspects that "liaison" was a subtle and successful way of the police infiltrating black organisations to find out what is going on, who is who, and to recruit black spies and informers.'[74] It was hardly surprising; therefore, that the Met's response to the problems voiced by what it saw as the left-wing, troublesome representatives of the West Indian immigrant community, was the proverbial deaf ear.

Notes

1 S. Patterson, *Immigration and Race Relations in Britain: 1960–1967*, (1969), p.114.
2 The BCA, for example, included a cross-party group of MPs among its membership.
3 Established by the Race Relations Act 1965.
4 Racial discrimination was made unlawful in prescribed public places, viz: hotels, restaurants, cafes, public houses, places of public entertainment or recreation, etc. by Section 1 of the Act of 1965. The 1968 Act made it unlawful to discriminate in the areas of housing, employment, the provision of goods, facilities and services and broadened the definition of 'places of public resort' in the 1965 Act.
5 Section 6, Race Relations Act 1965.
6 NA MEPO4/215 – Report of the Commissioner of Police for the Metropolis: 1967.
7 Patterson, *Immigration,* p.315.
8 A Birmingham Branch of WISC was later also established.
9 Patterson, *Immigration*, p.316. The Migrant Services Division had itself taken over the support role that had been created by the Jamaican-backed British Caribbean Welfare Service, which had been set up in 1955.

10 N. Peppard, letter to author, 20 February 2001.

11 Patterson, *Immigration* (1969), p.293.

12 The other bodies were the Institute of Race Relations and the Commonwealth Immigrants Advisory Committee.

13 NA HO376/159 Select Committee on Race Relations and Immigration: Home Office evidence 1969. The Council produced four reports, two on housing, and one each on integration and immigrant school-leavers.

14 Ibid. (Command 2266).

15 Ibid.

16 NA HO376/65 Consideration of the future structure of the Race Relations Board and National Committee for Commonwealth Immigrants 1967. By April 1967 the annual budget for the NCCI had been raised to £150,000.

17 Ibid.

18 NA HO376/159.

19 Patterson, *Immigration*, p.295.

20 Ibid. pp.323–4.

21 N. Peppard, letter to author, 8 May 2001.

22 NA MEPO2/9854.

23 Ibid.

24 Ibid.

25 Ibid.

26 Ibid.

27 Ibid. The letter was dated 26 October 1960.

28 Ibid. The Royal Commission on the Police discussed the subject of deteriorating relations between the police and public in 1962. The findings are contained in Chapter VIII, 'The Police and the Public'.

29 Ibid.

30 NA MEPO2/9854.

31 Ibid.

32 Ibid.

33 Ibid.

34 NA HO287/1455 Working Party on police training in race relations: minutes 1970.

35 Patterson, *Immigration*, p.117. In March 1965, Foley was placed in charge of a small task force established to co-ordinate government action with local authorities and voluntary bodies on immigrant affairs.

36 NA MEPO 2/9854 These were the Ealing International Friendship Council, and the Camden Committee for Community Relations.

37 Ibid.

38 The meeting took place on 4 January 1966. The areas identified for special attention were; race relations and discrimination; housing; public relations and education; employment; social services.

39 NA MEPO2/10638 Police representation on proposed Kensington and Chelsea Inter-Racial Council 1966–69.

40 Ibid.

41 Ibid.

42 Ibid.

43 Ex Inspector G. Bhamra, interviewed by author, 20 November 2001.

44 T. Smythe, 'The Police in Society', in P. Southgate, *Research and Planning Unit Paper 29*, Home Office (1984), pp.26–7.

45 MP *Instruction Book*, Ch. 2, paragraph 64, *IB* amendment dated 15 November 1975.

46 NA HO325/9 Racial disturbances in Notting Hill, activities of extreme organisations: deputation of MPs to see the Secretary of State 1951–61.

47 Ibid.

48 Ibid.

49 NA MEPO 2/9854.

50 It is interesting to note that police reports of the seminar referred to its title as 'Immigration to assimilation?'.

51 Ibid.

52 R. Reiner, *The Politics of the Police* (Lewes: 1985), p.2.

53 Interviewed by author, 20 February 2002.

54 Howard-Drake interview, 15 May 2001.

55 NA MEPO 2/10489 Race Relations Act 1965. Commissioner's and Solicitor's observations on the proposed Bill, amendment to Police General Orders 1965.

56 A criminal sanction was introduced as part of the 1965 Race Relations Act. Section 6 made incitement to racial hatred a criminal offence and was the only section directly affecting the police.

57 Ibid.

58 Ibid.

59 Ibid.

60 NA MEPO 2/9854 Police liaison with the West Indian community in London.

61 Ibid. Those present from the WISC were Mr Maxwell (Chairman), Mr Dyke (Vice Chairman), Mr Crawford (Hon. Secretary) and Mr Hunte (Public Relations). Assisting Merricks were Mr Rae (A1 Branch) and chief inspector Lee (A2).

62 Hall interview.

63 NA CK 2/572 Singh v Police: case outside scope of Act 1969.

64 D. Kuya, interviewed by author, 3 May 2001. This view was, however, strongly refuted by Nadine Peppard (former Secretary of both the CRC and NCCI) in her letter to the author of 29 July 2001, in which she claimed that VLCs were autonomous bodies.

65 NA HO376/65 Report on the future of the RRB and NCCI (27 April 1967).

66 NA MEPO 4/216, p.10.

67 Cmnd 2739, August 1965.

68 NA HO 376/159.

69 Ibid.

70 The writer of the report is believed to be Mr. Richard A. James, who was later to be appointed Receiver of the Metropolitan Police.

71 NA MEPO 2/9854.

72 N. Peppard, letter to author, 3 April 2001.

73 See D. Howe, 'On the Race Issue, All Have Made Asses of Themselves', *New Statesman* (30 April 2001), p.35.

74 L. Chase, 'West Indians and the Police', *New Community*, Vol.3, No.3, Summer 1994, p.208.

Chapter 4

The Home Secretary's over-mighty subject: the Metropolitan Police

The structure of the police service in England and Wales in the 1950s bore many of the hallmarks of its nineteenth-century ancestry. A multitude of autonomous and independent police forces existed that, outside of the metropolitan area, were based upon borough, city and county boundaries. In urban areas a watch committee, consisting of local councillors was the police authority, while in county areas police committees were made up of local councillors and justices of the peace.[1] Each was part-financed by a government grant that could be withheld, wholly or in part, if one of Her Majesty's Inspectors of Constabulary (HMICs) submitted an adverse annual report on the force's performance.[2] The Police Authority for the Metropolitan Police was the Home Secretary. Uniquely, therefore, the Met was free from the control of local politicians and justices of the peace,[3] but was the only force in the country for which the Home Secretary bore direct responsibility and in respect of which a government minister could be called to account by Parliament.[4]

The government recognised that the time for reorganisation of the police had arrived when, on 16 December 1959, the Prime Minister, Harold Macmillan, advised the House of Commons that there was to be a Royal Commission on the Police.[5] Its terms of reference were:

To review the constitutional position of the police throughout Great Britain, the arrangements for their control and administration and, in particular, to consider:

1. the constitution and functions of local police authorities;

2. the status and accountability of members of police forces, including chief officers of police;
3. the relationship of the police with the public and the means of ensuring that complaints by the public against the police are effectively dealt with; and
4. the broad principles which should govern the remuneration of the constable ... having regard of the need to attract and retain an adequate number of recruits with the proper qualifications.[6]

The independence of the police and their relationship *vis-à-vis* those who paid their wages had never previously been satisfactorily resolved. In considering the crucial question of police accountability and the control and direction of policing in this country, the Royal Commission found that:

> The present legal status of the police, in denying that they are either Crown servants or the servants of a police authority, accords them a position of exceptional independence. It follows that they are subject to little legal control in carrying out their duties. Like everyone else they are subordinate to the law; but the effect of this is rather to restrain them from unlawful activities, than to order the manner in which they carry out those that are lawful. The problem of controlling the police can, therefore, be re-stated as the problem of controlling chief constables.[7]

In this chapter we will consider the background to the setting up of the Royal Commission, together with its recommendations on the control and accountability of chief police officers, as contained in the 1964 Police Act; as well as examining the more active role adopted by the Home Office in the 1960s, when, for example, it sought to influence the direction of the Metropolitan Police over specific issues, such as Unit Beat Policing and the recruitment of black police officers. Home Secretary Roy Jenkins (1965–67) championed the case for the introduction of Unit Beat Policing after he had seen it in operation on a visit to Chicago. There were advantages and disadvantages in transferring a method of policing that had proved successful in a large city in the USA to the streets of London. As we will see, the scheme worked best in suburban districts of the capital where there were well-established communities. It was far less successful in inner-city locations of high immigrant settlement. Jenkins was also one of the prime movers in the drive to recruit black policemen. His successor as Home Secretary, James Callaghan (1967–70), was more cautious than his predecessor, and, in reviewing Home Office policing policy over the second half of the 1960s, it will be suggested that the drive for reform of the police service, that had so characterised the Jenkins era, became noticeably slower under Callaghan.

The Royal Commission on the Police: the demand for greater political accountability and the anomalous position of the Met

The constitutional position of the police came under increasing scrutiny in Parliament in the second half of the 1950s. Growing concern was expressed that the government had no legal sanction over police forces outside London; neither was it able to initiate disciplinary inquiries into the activities of provincial police forces. The government's initial response, as expressed by the Home Secretary, R.A. Butler, suggested that there were no imminent plans to remedy these defects:

> It is an essential feature of the police system of this country that disciplinary control is vested not in the central government but in the local disciplinary authorities ... I am perfectly content to interpret the duties of Home Secretary as they have been handed down to me, to keep the Queen's peace by a division of responsibility.[8]

On 9 April 1959, Frank Allaun MP asked Butler if he would introduce legislation to enable him to take full responsibility for police matters outside the Metropolitan area that involved national policy. Butler declined to do so, and added that, 'An essential feature of our police service is that it is organised and controlled on a local basis.'[9] This meant that, while MPs could ask questions of the Home Secretary on policing in London, they were effectively forbidden from raising parliamentary questions about policing anywhere else in the country. Butler continued to argue against the need for an inquiry, when asked in the Commons if he would consider setting up a Royal Commission on the Police, only seven months before Macmillan announced that such a Royal Commission was to be appointed.[10] This begs the question: why did the government change its mind on the issue?

There had been a number of high-profile confrontations between chief constables and police authorities during the 1950s. These included alleged corruption by the chief constable of Brighton, and the suspension of the chief constable of Nottingham for his refusal to disclose information to his police authority: the police authority's action subsequently being overruled and the chief constable's reinstatement ordered by the Home Secretary.[11] By the end of the 1950s, problems of police accountability and direction were more apparent than ever before; not only to those local representatives whose task it was to maintain a police service, but, more significantly, to those in Parliament who could – if they possessed the will to do so – bring about change.

Hand-in-hand with concerns over the lack of political accountability for the activities of the police was the question of the way in which complaints against the police were investigated. The problem was highlighted on 18 June 1959, when Butler was questioned in the Commons about the arrest of two 'respectable citizens' who were allegedly beaten and kicked by police officers; as a result of which both needed hospital treatment. Butler's reply merely emphasised the degree to which he, as both Home Secretary and Police Authority for the Met, was content to leave to the police decisions on what action should, or should not, be taken against its own members: 'I referred this complaint to the Commissioner, who has investigated it very fully and finds no grounds for disciplinary action or for the institution of criminal proceedings. I accept this conclusion.'[12] The subject of Metropolitan Police accountability for the treatment of those in police custody was again raised in the Commons on 20 July 1959, when the case of Guenter Podola was discussed. Podola had been arrested for the killing of a police officer. He was beaten to such an extent during the course of his arrest that he was detained in hospital with serious injuries. Butler refused to inform the House how his injuries had been sustained, claiming that the matter was *sub judice*, despite the fact that the alleged assault by police on Podola had nothing to do with the allegation of murder he faced. In its later evidence to the Royal Commission, the National Council for Civil Liberties criticised the way in which the system of complaints was handled by both the Met's Commissioner and the Home Secretary:

> In the Metropolitan area a complaint to the Home Secretary results in a brief statement that maintenance of public order is the responsibility of the Commissioner of Police, to whom a copy of the letter of complaint has been sent. No further word is received from the Commissioner or from anyone else.[13]

The Royal Commission, under its Chairman, Sir Henry Willink, presented its findings in 1962. It noted that at the beginning of the 1960s the Home Office exercised some degree of supervision over the police service in three ways. Through the Police Council for Great Britain it acted as a negotiating body and advised Secretaries of State on all matters connected with police pay and conditions of service.[14] Under the guidance of the Home Office, regular conferences took place with the chief constables of England and Wales; and a Common Police Services Committee, comprising representatives of police authorities and the Home Office enabled the government to be appraised of the views of all the component parts of the police service on operational matters.[15]

The Royal Commission sought to introduce:

(i)   A system of control over the police, and a basic organisation which, while enabling them to perform their duties impartially, will achieve the maximum efficiency and the best use of manpower.
(ii) Adequate means within this system of bringing police to account, and so of keeping a constitutionally proper check upon mistakes and errors of judgement.
(iii) Arrangements for ensuring that complaints against the police by the public are effectively dealt with.[16]

When considering the position of the Metropolitan Police, the Royal Commission identified that the relationship of the Commissioner and the Home Secretary was vastly different to that existing between a provincial police authority and its chief constable. Their assessment of the arrangement painted a picture of close supervision, in which the Home Secretary approved orders and regulations for the government of the Metropolitan Police, exercised direct control over the executive work and administrative policy of the Met and concluded by saying:

> Moreover, for the discharge of his responsibilities the Home Secretary is answerable to Parliament in a way that no police authority is accountable to its local authority.[17]

Indeed, the Royal Commission considered certain aspects of Metropolitan Police procedure as an example of good practice.[18] This somewhat rosy depiction of organisational supervision and efficiency was, however, at odds with reality.

In October 1964, a confidential Home Office report was prepared entitled, 'The Secretary of State's role in relation to the Metropolitan Police'.[19] The report suggested that the Home Secretary's relationship with the Met was far from clear, but added that, 'there are obvious advantages in leaving it vague'.[20] It went on to say that, while most people assumed that the relationship worked efficiently, the nature of the relationship was such that supervision of the Metropolitan Police – by far the biggest police force in the country – was much less stringent than existed in every other police force. Other forces were subjected to two levels of supervision, the police authority and HMIC, while the Met was subject only to one. Outside London, the situation was such that many people had a direct interest in the operation and management of the local force, and would have had a vested interest in ensuring it was efficiently run.[21] The report continued:

The Metropolitan Police are under much less effective control than provincial forces, and this is hardly surprising in view of the administrative arrangements. There is neither the machinery available to supply us [the Home Office] with information, nor the staff to evaluate it and act upon it.[22]

The report alleged that there was no established systematic procedure in the relationship between the Commissioner's office and the Home Office. Although there was regular dialogue between the two when specific complaints against the Met were brought to the attention of MPs, the relationship was, from a Home Office perspective, unsatisfactory. The Home Office, it was claimed, merely relayed information to others that the Met chose to divulge, and consequently was unable to address or identify problems in Metropolitan Police policies and procedures. The report concluded:

Thus it is rare for the Home Office to follow up a case with the Commissioner in such a way that defects brought to light have been or are being remedied. On the contrary, it has probably been tacitly assumed that the Commissioner would put his own house in order ... our role ought to be beyond that of passively waiting for things to be referred to us, particularly after they have gone wrong, and then dealing with them piecemeal with an eye almost exclusively on the political aspects and barely at all on the implications of the matter on the efficiency and well being of the force.[23]

It appears obvious that the Home Office's role in the policing of London at this time was essentially that of trusting the Met's Commissioner to run his force in an efficient manner, while attempting to square political circles in the aftermath of mistakes or alleged wrongful acts by the Met and its officers. Clearly, it would be difficult to argue that the Home Office exercised adequate control and supervision of the Met.

In Circular 170/1964, the Home Office advised police authorities of the procedural changes that were to be introduced as a result of the Police Act 1964. One provision of the Act was that police authorities would be entitled *inter alia* to information on the deployment and allocation of the force, the state of crime generally (or in particular parts of the area), and the circumstances of an incident that gave rise to complaint. The Act enlarged the role of the Home Secretary and gave him sanction over the actions of police authorities in certain circumstances;[24] all of which appeared to make the position of the Home Secretary and the Commissioner of the Met appear ever more bizarre:

Certainly it would be hard to defend a situation in which he [the Secretary of State] knows less about the force nominally under his control, comprising about a quarter of the police in the country, and throwing up the most acute problems of recruitment, crime, traffic, etc. than he does about other forces. To sum up, if the Secretary of State's role were merely that of police authority he should know more, and do more, than he does.[25]

On 30 January 1967, Mr Waddell of the Home Office wrote to Sir Philip Allen regarding relations with the Metropolitan Police.[26] His letter focused principally on shortcomings within the Met rather than with the level of Home Office supervision. Waddell believed that the problems of liaison between the Home Office and the Met lay in three key areas. It was common, he argued, for major decisions to be taken at Scotland Yard without prior Home Office consultation. As a result, the Home Office found that it was frequently invited to rubber-stamp decisions already agreed by the Commissioner and his senior colleagues. Worse still, the Home Office did not know enough of what went on to enable it to operate as quickly and effectively as it should. The Yard's internal machinery was cumbersome – sometimes ill co-ordinated – and perhaps worst of all, the outlook of those at Scotland Yard, 'tended to be excessively conservative and hostile to new ideas'.[27]

The Commissioner (Simpson) had been asked, in his evidence to the Royal Commission on 21 March 1961, if the Met was less efficient than smaller forces. His reply appeared to confirm Waddell's observation that senior ranks at the Yard were set in their ways and reluctant to embrace creativity: 'I think there is some slight tendency on the way up to stifle ideas. We run what we think is a very efficient team to a great extent by precedent. Ideas do not come too easily to some people.'[28] Middle-ranking police officers dealt with much of the Yard's day-to-day correspondence with the Home Office. It was found that they were largely unsuited to this type of work, but that they were resentful of the possibility that their posts might be 'civilianised'. Sir Robert Mark recalled the way in which the Met functioned at the highest level, and the hostility that existed between police and the Met's civilian staff when he joined the force as an Assistant Commissioner in 1966:

The whole organisation was uncoordinated to a remarkable degree. There was only a nominal pretence of democratic management. The Commissioner exercised unchallenged authority ... until 1968 the division between police and civil staff was tangible. An observer might have been forgiven for thinking that they were more concerned to oppose or frustrate each other than to maintain a common objective.[29]

The feasibility of civilianisation at the Yard was an issue that management consultants hired by the Home Office had been asked to consider. The problem was that the Met's civilian arm lacked a career structure, paid low wages and generally attracted staff of limited ability. The force's problems appeared to stem from its sheer size and the scale of the job it had to do; the vague supervisory status of the Home Secretary; and the poor quality of middle management in the Met at a time of major social change and reform. The Home Office itself was not immune from criticism. Waddell admitted that it often appeared to be slow and inclined to focus excessively on points of detail. Perhaps most important of all, and something that would always be the Commissioner's trump card when dealing with Home Office officials, it had, 'an imperfect grasp of operational requirements'.[30]

When contrasted with the relationship between chief constables and police authorities, that which existed between the Home Secretary and the Metropolitan Police Commissioner appears to have had little to commend it. Rather than a body of locally elected representatives having a vested interest in providing a policing service to meet the needs of its own community, the Met's police authority was an individual politician whose own constituency might be outside London, and who was directly responsible for a number of other contentious political issues, not least of which were the prison service and immigration. The limited nature of the Home Secretary's powers over the Commissioner's policing policies, coupled with his officials' imperfect grasp of operational requirements, ensured that the Commissioner was his very much his own boss in the day-to-day running of the Metropolitan Police.

In giving evidence to the Royal Commission, Simpson had been asked, 'Does the Home Secretary ever take the initiative in these matters and say – I would like you to issue the following order?' His reply encapsulated the nature and extent of the convention that had for many years covered not only the relationship between the Metropolitan Police Commissioner and the Home Secretary, but also that of every chief constable and police authority in the country:

> No, Sir. He might on occasions write and say some complaint had been made, and our procedure according to *General Orders* was so-and-so, would I re-consider it and consider perhaps a suggestion that has been put up by somebody from outside, say a Member of Parliament, and in that case of course I would look at it and write and say whether I thought there should be such an amendment. But normally the initiative is left to the Commissioner.[31]

An example of this was provided by Dick Taverne, who recalled a meeting he had attended at the Home Office when a minister of state, with the then Home Secretary, Roy Jenkins, and Simpson, which graphically illustrated the Home Secretary's peripheral role in the Commissioner's policing strategies:

> There was this incident at which I was present when there was discussion with Joe Simpson, and Roy Jenkins said, 'Why are so many of your police officers, who've got lots of things to do, spending time in "cottages" trying to track down homosexuals?' Simpson said, 'With great respect, Home Secretary, that is an operational question and you cannot dictate to us what we'll do. But I think there is some reason behind your complaint and I will investigate.'[32]

Such a statement by the Commissioner of the Metropolitan Police to the Home Secretary clearly reveals the degree of independence to which Simpson believed he was entitled. It also highlights the difficulties the Home Office faced in its efforts to inculcate new ideas and practices in an organisation (the Met), the leadership of which was renowned for its conservatism and unwillingness to change. However, Simpson argued that his position was, in some respects, far more difficult than that which provincial chief constables faced.

He claimed that, unlike his provincial counterparts, Section 5 of the Metropolitan Police Act 1839 governed his actions; the effect of which was to subject his orders to the approval of the Home Secretary. While this may have been the case in law, the observations of Waddell and others that the Home Secretary and the Home Office Police Department lacked knowledge of operational matters to such a degree that they invariably went along with decisions emanating from New Scotland Yard, clearly demolishes much of Simpson's argument. Simpson also claimed that funding arrangements for the Met were detrimental to the force's efficiency, and here there is evidence to support his statement. Prior to becoming Commissioner, Simpson had served as chief constable in other police forces and was aware of the way in which local police authorities operated. He told the Royal Commission that:

> By and large my experience is that the local authority is somewhat more generous in certain ways that central authority. For instance the Home Office may say that certain things are too expensive. I turn round and say, 'such and such forces have them.' They say, 'They are locally run; if that authority is prepared to spend that amount of money we do not think that is an issue we could cross swords on and we must allow it.'[33]

A further impediment to efficiency was the London Allowance paid to Metropolitan Police officers, which amounted to a mere £20 per year.

Such a small sum did nothing to persuade prospective applicants to choose the overworked and under-strength Met, rather than a provincial force, where the pressure of work might be less intense; and, perhaps more importantly, the quality of life and house prices would invariably be more in tune with an applicant's aspirations and salary. The Home Office was aware that the Treasury was in favour of increased pay differentials to assist the Met, but recognised the two-pronged opposition to the Met's demands for an increase in the London Allowance:

> Any considerable increase in the London Allowance would be strongly opposed by the Police Federation, who feel strongly that conditions of service should be uniform over the whole country . . . the Royal Commission in their interim report came down firmly in favour of a standard wage on the ground that the weight of responsibility carried by the policeman was the same all over the country.[34]

One of the Royal Commission's principal objectives had been to introduce procedures to ensure that complaints against the police would be dealt with effectively.[35] Simpson defended the system by which the police themselves inquired into allegations made against them. His argument was that there were a number of ascending levels of seniority in the Met at which a dissatisfied complainant's grievance would be independently reviewed, and that:

> If it is suggested for the very, very few people there are that they cannot be appeased by that, they cannot believe that somebody who wears a blue uniform is in a position to deal with that complaint properly, I do not see much opportunity of ever satisfying them.[36]

Efforts were made at the report stage of the Police Bill to address the deficiency in the police complaints procedure. MPs expressed concern that the proposed bill contained no machinery for reassuring the public that complaints were properly dealt with by police officers. When the matter was before the Commons, Sydney Silverman MP enlightened the House as to the nature of public dissatisfaction with the police complaints procedure:

> There was a feeling that justice was not being done, and that it was not being done because the police were not accountable to anyone, if any member of the public made a complaint, because they judged the complaint themselves, because they judged it in secret, because they judged it without the complainant being represented . . . without the complainant knowing what was being said for him or

against him in the secret inquiry formed of the people against whom he was making his complaint.[37]

Silverman also suggested that the fact that the Police Federation was opposed to the proposed amendments to the Bill was all the more reason for the amendments to be incorporated.

The Home Secretary, Henry Brooke, then dealt with the proposed amendments. He explained that the Met's policy of recording every complaint and referring all allegations of crime to the Director of Public Prosecutions (DPP) would be adopted nationally. However, the Police Act failed to address the primary cause for concern among those who had expressed doubts about the investigation of police complaints: namely, that the police continued to investigate all allegations against themselves. A number of those seeking to introduce an independent element into the complaints procedure argued that Police Disciplinary Boards might display bias in favour of their own officers. The problem, in reality, lay not at this final stage of the process, but at an earlier stage – with the difficulties faced by the officer(s) deputed to investigate the complaint.

Allegations that might be described as 'criminal' frequently related to accusations of assault by police officers on complainants. It was not uncommon for such accusations to be countered by claims that the complainant's injuries were the result of his/her own violence towards police while being arrested. Indeed, it was frequently the case that, arising out of allegations of assault by police officers, complainants had themselves been charged with (and commonly convicted of) assaulting police. In such circumstances it often transpired that the only witnesses to the incident were other police officers – particularly if the alleged incident occurred in a police station. The investigating officer's findings, when presented to the DPP, would therefore leave the latter little alternative but to recommend no action against the accused officer(s). In non-criminal matters,[38] the same evidential problems would apply but no referral to the DPP was made. Not surprisingly, only in those allegations in which the evidence was unquestionable, 'bang-to-rights' in policing parlance, was there any likelihood that the allegation would be presented to a formal disciplinary hearing. The result was that, in both criminal and non-criminal allegations against police officers, the public was left largely frustrated and dissatisfied with the outcome of complaint investigations.

Simpson was much respected by the Met's rank-and-file and his attitude to disciplinary matters suggests one reason why he was held in such high esteem. Addressing the Commanders' Conference on 12 June 1962, he informed delegates that he had decided to overrule the decision of a Discipline Board to reduce a sergeant to the rank of constable for neglect of duty and altering an official record. While he believed that the decision of the Board had been correct, he argued in support of his decision that, 'his [the sergeant's] length of service was such that if he had been reduced he would probably never have recovered his rank'.[39] In the minutes of a later meeting with commanders, Simpson stated that his philosophy in disciplinary cases was that he, 'adopted the practice of the Court of Criminal Appeal and, even if he felt that a punishment had been light, he did not increase it'.[40]

The Home Office and the police: changing policies for changing times

During the 1960s government ministers and the Home Office began to take more proactive measures to encourage a more enlightened approach among senior police officers to all aspects of policing, including the question of race relations, and – for the first time – the recruitment of black policemen. This was undoubtedly due in no small part to the election of a Labour government in 1964, a government whose more progressive members (at least in the early days) favoured the adoption of 'a much easier attitude to immigration'.[41] Dick Taverne had no doubt of the then Prime Minister's commitment to the concept of multi-racial Britain: 'Harold Wilson was very good on these issues. I think Harold Wilson was absolutely determined to do everything possible to end racism. I think it's one of the very few things he believed in.'[42] Such aspirations had been less apparent in government circles under the previous Conservative administration.

Though the Conservatives had introduced the Police Act reforms, there are indications that, as late as 1963, the Home Office was extremely reluctant to be associated with any suggestion that black police officers should be recruited into the police service. At the launch of the National Police Recruitment Campaign on 23 January 1962, the Home Secretary, R.A. Butler, when asked by journalists about the possibility of black recruitment, was widely reported as saying that, 'So far it has been found neither necessary nor expedient to appoint coloured policemen, but that there was no bar to it and I certainly would not exclude it.'[43] The Home Office considered Butler's remarks with great care and was anxious to avoid any suggestion that his statement implied that the government actively supported the recruitment of black policemen. Its position on the matter was set out in a Memorandum of 9 April 1963, which stated:

> The statutory responsibility for appointing constables rests with chief constables in counties, watch committees in boroughs and the Commissioner in the Metropolitan Police force. The Secretary of

State has no authority to intervene . . . we have been careful to avoid expressing any opinion on the merits of having coloured police-men.[44]

This statement prompted a rethink of Whitehall's position. The Home Office recognised that there existed an underlying objection to the appointment of black or Asian policemen: namely, the probable reluctance of sections of the community to accept them; not to mention other police officers, with whom they would have to work.[45] That being the case, it was disingenuous to suggest that it saw no difficulty in their appointment and was prepared to leave such matters in the hands of chief police officers to determine. The Home Office position was illustrated in an internal memorandum of 17 April 1963. The writer, Mr Glanville, recognised that, whatever the argument for black policemen, relations between the police and public were, 'sufficiently difficult and delicate to have been specially considered by the Royal Commission', and that:

It is very doubtful whether it is really in the interests of the coloured community to press that coloured people should be admitted to the police: the public might well – however irrationally – resent being 'moved on' or prevented from parking by a coloured policeman, to say nothing of more serious matters.[46]

One might argue that here is a working example of the 'vague relationship' between the Secretary of State, the Home Office and those charged with the appointment of police constables. The Home Office can be seen to disassociate itself from any connection with the Home Secretary's remarks on black recruitment, and to further suggest that, whatever the Home Secretary believed to be the case, he was in no position to say who should be appointed as a constable: such decisions being the responsibility of chief constables and the Commissioner. Despite the desire of some at the Home Office for a more hands-on role in policing, the usefulness of the 'vague relationship' lay in the fact that it enabled the Secretary of State and the Home Office to maintain their positions of influence and guidance over the police service while, at the same time, allowing them to avoid accountability for every police force other than the Met; and to pass the buck to chief police officers on contentious issues, such as responsibility for operational matters, black recruitment and police complaints. The Home Office observation also suggests that, as the subject of police relations with the community was already a matter of concern, the advantages and disadvantages of black recruitment were an added complication it could well do without.

What is strikingly clear is how similar were the views of chief constables, the Commissioner, the Police Federation and Home Office officials on the issue of black recruitment. There was a common consensus that, while not rejecting the possibility, the time was not yet right for experiments to be made. Their attitude was summarised by Taverne:

> We've got to be very careful about this (black recruitment) because the cause of race relations isn't going to be helped if the blacks or Asians we recruit are inferior in quality and it's very difficult because there's a lot of suspicion on the part of the ethnic minority community . . . That was the general attitude. The sense that you really have to push hard was not something that most chief constables embraced.[47]

This was fine as long as the Secretary of State was of a similar mind, as was the case with Butler; or was ineffective, as was the Labour government's first Home Secretary in 1964, Frank Soskice. But the position was radically altered when Roy Jenkins was appointed to replace Soskice as Home Secretary in December 1965.

Jenkins was determined to reorganise and modernise the police service and was responsible for the introduction of Unit Beat Policing (UBP) in England and Wales. He argued passionately in support of racial equality, and urged chief police officers to be more receptive to the idea of black recruitment. On 18 May 1966, Jenkins informed the Commons that he had carried out a review of police areas throughout the country. He stated that he had considered the recommendations of the Royal Commission on the Police regarding amalgamations, but that the continuing increase in crime, and its changing pattern, justified a more far-reaching reorganisation than was contemplated by the Commission.[48]

He explained that no rigid formula had been adhered to in determining the size of the new police forces; the sole criterion had been that they should be of a size most likely to achieve full efficiency in the prevention and detection of crime and the control of traffic. There was much opposition to the proposals, as Taverne recalled:

> It was both chief constables and local authorities. It was very much the local government officials, the treasurers of the police authorities, who all said that democracy would come to an end if their own particular force was merged with the police force next door. In fact, it meant that their jobs would come to an end.[49]

Taverne believed that it was principally to avoid lengthy and potentially obstructive discussions on police amalgamations that Jenkins and Home Office Ministers decided that such decisions would be taken quickly and arbitrarily:

We had a session one afternoon and we simply looked at the map and said, 'Let's put that one in with that one.' We had the Chief Inspector of Constabulary there and said, 'Do you think you could defend that [decision] in court?' He said, 'Well, I suppose so.' 'OK, we're going to do that. Now what about this one? Hey, wait a minute; we've got Buckinghamshire stranded on its own. Can it go in with Reading?' And that's how it went: very decisive, arbitrary in some ways, but effective: the only way to do these things.[50]

Two other areas of concern for Jenkins and the Home Office were the low educational standard of the majority of police recruits, and the extreme conservatism of senior police officers. Charles Morrison raised the subject of police academic standards in a Commons question to the Home Secretary, when he asked how many graduates there were in the police forces of England and Wales.[51] The House was informed that there were only 69 graduates in total.[52] There were 19 graduates in the Met, 2 in Manchester, 1 each in Liverpool and Cardiff, and none in Birmingham. In light of these figures, Jenkins asked Taverne, then Minister of State at the Home Office, to submit a report on what could be done to recruit graduates to the service. His report recommended a career structure for suitably qualified applicants, which offered the chance of further training at the Police Staff College and a fast-track pathway to promotion. The Police Federation did not welcome the proposal:

They've [graduate recruits] got to go through the mill because you can't have people who are being discriminated in favour of. The fact that they've got a good degree doesn't mean that they're going to be any good as a copper.[53]

Despite the Federation's objections, the Graduate Entry Scheme was adopted and introduced nationally from 1967.

On 10 October 1966, Jenkins spoke to members of the Institute of Race Relations. He urged public bodies, the police in particular, to review their recruitment policies towards school-leavers from immigrant families. He acknowledged that the position in Britain was more difficult than existed in the United States, largely because of the language difficulties faced by a number of recently arrived migrants to Britain. He cited the work carried out by Police Commissioner Leary in New York, and praised the vigorous way in which he had encouraged Puerto Ricans to join the New York City Police Department. Comparing Britain and the United States, he went on:

Perhaps our progress is bound to be slower than New York's, with its enormous experience of absorbing new immigrant communities.

> But I will not rest content until I see far faster progress being made
> in our public services. And I see far more coloured policemen,
> firemen, ambulance men – yes, and coloured magistrates – than we
> have today.[54]

The major problem facing the police at the time was shortage of
manpower, the Met in particular being several thousand officers below its
establishment strength. Jenkins had been impressed by methods of
policing he had seen on a visit to the United States, and, in 1966, he
initiated Home Office trials of Unit Beat Policing, a concept that was based
on policing strategies used in Chicago. The pilot site for the scheme was to
be – somewhat oddly, given its American 'big city' model – at the town of
Accrington in Lancashire. UBP offered a number of attractive possibilities.
The traditional beat system was to be replaced by resident beat officers
who would live at, or near, their place of duty; and whose hours of work,
and manner in which their duties would be performed, would be based
upon local needs and conditions. Mobile constables in 'Panda' cars would
support them, each covering the same area as two of the foot patrols. Some
traditional beat patrols were to be retained for city and town centres. The
mobile patrols and traditional beat officers would deal with the bulk of
routine non-emergency calls while resident beat officers would be
encouraged to build relations with local people and play an active part in
the life of the community. All this would be backed up by high-speed
immediate response vehicles to deal with emergency calls, and a team of
CID officers, who would offer advice to patrolling officers on crime
matters.[55] The success of UBP depended upon the introduction of a reliable
personal radio system that would enable each patrolling officer to contact
colleagues and their base station. Each officer was to submit intelligence
reports to a collator sergeant, whose job it was to analyse information
received and disseminate it to local police and surrounding divisions.

The Police Federation welcomed the scheme and believed that it
offered its members greater mobility and job satisfaction. Jenkins and the
Home Office hoped that improved police mobility would lead to greater
efficiency and a reduction in crime. Greater public satisfaction would be
achieved, it was thought, by improved communication; especially with
resident beat officers. However, the real bonus from the Home Office
perspective was that the scheme appeared to offer all these advantages
without having first to solve the police service's acute manpower
shortages. Divisional Circular No. 10/1966 issued by the Lancashire
Constabulary on 27 May 1966 set out the *raison d'être* of UBP on the eve
of its introduction in Accrington:

> According to a recent survey it has been agreed that this force would
> require an addition of about 1,000 men to adequately police the

County by traditional means. As there is very little likelihood of recruiting this additional number of men it becomes increasingly necessary to utilise the available manpower to the best possible advantage.[56]

Resident beat officers were encouraged to cultivate, 'at least one informant in every street, not necessarily a paid informant, but someone who knows the inhabitants and is inquisitive enough to find out what is going on'. Advice on who might qualify as such a police confidant included, 'the woman who is always peeping behind the curtains, the window cleaner, and the retired man who keeps his eyes open'.[57] The essence of the resident beat officer's contact with the community was to discover what the local criminals were up to. What becomes apparent, when considering the type of individual the police were encouraged to cultivate links with, is that the benefits of such a dialogue had little purpose other than to assist the police with their own inquiries. This appears to have been the sole purpose of the liaison guidelines and any benefits accruing to the local community would have been a supplementary bonus.

The Met agreed to trial the scheme on each of its four districts in August 1966. It quickly became apparent that Accrington had little in common with London's policing needs. It was acknowledged that caseloads were very much higher on London divisions than in Accrington and that, particularly in the inner London areas chosen for the experiment, there were fluid and largely anonymous societies in which different problems existed, not only from day to day, but for different parts of each day.[58] The Met eventually decided to trial UBP on only two divisions, those at Bromley and Harlesden, though it was adopted later by the force and was found to be particularly suited to the more residential outer London divisions.

Jenkins hoped that UBP would improve job satisfaction for police and would provide a better service for the community. Many policemen, especially those who became resident beat officers, felt that they derived great satisfaction from it. One such officer described his experience of UBP:

The home beats were paramount. They were not moved for demo's [demonstrations] or anything else. Everything else was positioned to back up the home beat. You worked your own hours in uniform or plain clothes. You had complete discretion. You had to spread the word, fly the flag, collect intelligence, lecture the schools and keep order. The law was back and white. The bit of grey of varying hues in between was your working area. You made the decisions.[59]

Other officers were less enthusiastic. Simpson argued that it was one thing to provide Panda cars to enable policemen to get from A to B; the difficult job would be to get them out of the cars to walk the beat. To a great extent Simpson's argument was well founded. Manpower shortages, and an ever-increasing workload, meant that Panda car drivers were invariably kept busy going from one call to another; and, over a period of time, they spent less and less time out of their vehicles, patrolling in the manner envisaged by the architects of UBP.

A major drawback with UBP was that it was less suited to life in the inner city than it was to the suburbs. While many resident beat officers lived as part of the community in the more settled residential outer divisions, the same could not be said for the poorer areas of inner London – especially those in which there were large communities of black immigrants – and of which a sizeable minority of people lived lives that were essentially transient. Developing dialogue with local people, an essential element of UBP that resident beat officers were required to perform was therefore much more difficult than in established suburban communities.

Statistics provided at the Third National Law Enforcement Symposium, held in St. Louis in 1970, revealed the enormous disparity in percentage manning levels between the Met and United States police forces operating UBP.[60] Chicago, which had been the model for the introduction of UBP to Britain, had an estimated population of 3.5 million and a police force of 15,000 officers. New York's population of 8 million had some 29,800 officers, while London, with a population of 8.5 million, had only 20,000 police officers.[61] For London to match the ratio of police officers to the population existing in Chicago, the Met would have needed an additional 16,000 officers.

The intention of UBP was to enable under-strength police forces to provide an improved service, based upon a two-pronged strategy: foot and mobile patrols communicating with each other and working together; and an enhanced ability to collect and disseminate intelligence on criminals in the community. There does not appear to have been any steer from senior officers to develop positive community relations, or to take specific measures to build bridges with immigrant communities. The police service still saw its role in stark black-and-white terms – to catch villains and to keep the peace.

A new Home Secretary, the power of the Police Federation, and let's not rock the boat

James Callaghan, a career politician who, as Chancellor of the Exchequer, was still smarting from his apparent humiliation over the devaluation of the pound, replaced Jenkins as Home Secretary in November 1967. The reforming vitality of Jenkins was replaced by Callaghan's more pragmatic approach and an empathy with the police that had been built up over a number of years. Callaghan's official biographer, Kenneth Morgan, observed that:

> A more familiar area of Home Office work for Callaghan was the handling of the police. Here he had the strong advantage – one which aroused much suspicion in the ranks of the libertarian left – of personal connections with the force, through his work as parliamentary consultant for the Police Federation 1955–64. He had a good working relationship with the Federation's officials, with several chief constables, and with his appointee as the Commissioner of the Metropolitan Police, Sir John Waldron.[62]

Morgan makes the point that Callaghan was later criticised by the police for his support of civil liberties and goes on to say that, 'This should be kept in mind when Callaghan is claimed to be a particularly reactionary Home Secretary, far less libertarian than Roy Jenkins, his predecessor.'[63] Others held different views. Dick Taverne recalled that, in his role as Home Secretary, Callaghan was neither reformist nor libertarian: 'Socially he's a conservative. He was a puritan. He wasn't so much interested in the causes of crime as making bloody sure we caught the criminals. He had that sort of approach to things – big stick – rather than anything else.'[64]

Taverne attempted to persuade Callaghan to take up the cause of prison reform, as this was an area that Jenkins, despite his successes, had not dealt with. At the same time, he suggested to Callaghan that he should offer the police a revision of the right to silence in criminal trials – something which the police had long campaigned for – as long as they would agree to the introduction of an independent element in the investigation of police complaints; a subject which many informed observers believed was long overdue. Though Callaghan later instituted prison reforms that had been pushed through by Roy Jenkins in the Criminal Justice Act of 1967, he failed to introduce an external element in police complaints procedures.

In his autobiography, Callaghan stated that in his first 12 months as Home Secretary, 'I was piloting through Bills on subjects as diverse as gambling, race relations, the criminal law and immigration'.[65] Taverne again paints a different picture of Callaghan's reforming role, this time regarding the bill on gambling:

> He [Callaghan] tried to stop the very important gambling reforms which Roy [Jenkins] had launched, and which I was in charge of. He

was going to make a disastrous decision because, had he stopped the reform, gambling would have gone underground, and once you've got the mafia in – which you'd have got – the whole of our criminal fraternity would have been operating at a different level.[66]

Nadine Peppard, the General Secretary of the NCCI, and later the CRC, believed that there was a vast difference between the approach of Callaghan and Jenkins to their duties as Home Secretary:

There is no question that it was when Roy Jenkins was in office that so much anti-discrimination legislation was enacted (the drive, the commitment and legal expertise of Anthony Lester being of great help). And, certainly, when Jim Callaghan took up the reins, it was abundantly clear that there would be not only a slow-down and change of tone, but something of a reversal, as manifested by the Commonwealth Immigrants Act 1968, restricting the numbers of Kenyan Asians allowed to enter, and the omission of prior discussion with the NCCI about it, which would inevitably undermine its work.[67]

Of particular significance during Callaghan's period as Home Secretary, and, hence, Police Authority for the Met, was his (and the Home Office's) *volte-face* on the Home Affairs Committee's proposal to introduce a specific police disciplinary offence of racial discrimination: the main opposition to the proposal coming from the Police Federation. At this time, well over half of Britain's black population were residing in the Metropolitan Police District (see Figure 4.1) and one might logically assume that the proposal would have had particular implications for police officers in London.

A draft of Callaghan's intended address to the Commons on the issue was unambiguous in its tone and apparent intention:

The House may be interested to know that, after consulting the Police Advisory Board, I have, by regulation, amended the police discipline code to provide that it shall be an offence for any police officer to discriminate against anyone on grounds of colour, race, or ethnic or national origins. I am in no doubt that under the existing code, chief officers of police would have taken disciplinary action against any officer guilty of such discrimination but I thought it right (and the Police Advisory Board, on which all police associations are represented, agreed with me) that specific provision should be made for this type of offence.[69]

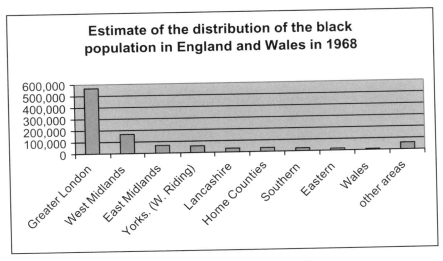

Figure 4.1 Demographic information on immigration[68]

Callaghan clearly misinterpreted, or misheard, the response of members of the Police Advisory Board (PAB) to the proposal. On 22 May 1968, the PAB met to consider, among other matters, the government's intention to outlaw racially discriminatory acts by police officers. Delegates were informed that it was the government's belief that it was, 'important to demonstrate in every possible way that discriminatory action was out of accord with the will of the community ... Its value was in its contribution towards emphasising to citizens of all races that discrimination has no place in the national life.'[70]

The proposal was unacceptable to the representatives of the local authorities and police organisations. They argued that there was no problem of racial discrimination by the police, and that existing regulations covered abuses of authority; the proposal would be a slur on the police and would be resented by them; publicity to the change would lead to an increase in immigrant complaints; police would (if the amendment was introduced) avoid unnecessary involvement with 'coloured persons'; and, if the proposal were pressed, it would lead to resentment by police of 'coloured people'.[71] Over the following months police opposition to the proposal remained solid, while Callaghan and the Home Office, alarmed at the level of opposition to the amendment, tried to extricate themselves with the minimum of adverse publicity from what they saw as a no-win situation. It would be useful at this point to consider the grounds upon which PAB members rejected the proposal; in particular, their claim that there was no problem of racial discrimination by police.

Table 4.1 Complaints against the Metropolitan Police in selected categories[72]

Nature of complaint	Unsubstantiated	Substantiated	% Substantiated
Attitude to Public	747	32	4.1%
Other alleged Offence[73]	909	12	1.3%

As far as the Met was concerned, the question of racial discrimination had by this time become a burning issue among all shades of West Indian opinion in London. In a memorandum to Maurice Foley MP, the Jamaican High Commissioner, Mr Lindo, described the way in which many in the West Indian community viewed the police:

There is growing cause for concern about the incidence of complaints by Commonwealth citizens in the United Kingdom against methods sometimes used by the police in dealing with them. There are allegations of brutality, provocative behaviour eventually leading to arrest on such charges as obstructing the police, assault, and behaviour likely to cause breaches of the peace, 'planting' or 'framing' and arrests without immediately stipulating the offence involved.[74]

One sees how slim were a complainant's chances of having a complaint upheld when figures for recorded complaints against Met officers for 1968 are examined (Table 4.1).

For those whose complaint against a Met officer was for racial discrimination, the chances of success were even worse. In 1969, of 41 complaints alleging racial discrimination by Met officers, not one was substantiated.[75]

On 6 August 1968, Callaghan was informed by the Home Office Police Department that an impasse had been reached on the proposed amendment. A compromise solution had been sought, but without success, and the exit strategy now appeared to be the preferred option; rather than a lengthy battle with the Police Federation:

The choice as we [Home Office Police Department] see it, lies between pressing on with the original proposal and making a clean withdrawal ... It is clear that if you were to proceed with it, the emotional attitude of the Federation leadership would stimulate a good deal of resentment, which might rub off on coloured people, within the rank and file of the service ... If the withdrawal were to be made in September, it would be likely to have been forgotten by the time Parliament returns.[76]

The fly in the ointment as far as Callaghan and the Home Office were concerned was the fact that both the Joint Parliamentary Under Secretaries of State, Elystan Morgan and David Ennals, believed that the PAB's objections were groundless. They argued that:

Although it was appreciated that any clash between the Government and the Police Federation should be avoided whenever possible, to retreat from this issue would in itself be likely to create an imbalance in the relative position of the two sides concerned, that might take a long time to redress. It would also mean conceding to the police a case which in this connection they do not have.[77]

In October 1968, Callaghan presented a document entitled 'Race Relations – The Police' to the Cabinet. He described how it set out the weight of opposition to the proposed discipline code amendment, and added that:

The absence of any rational basis of objection does not make it easier to decide whether to accede to it or to over-ride it ... there is some risk that this feeling might emerge not only as resentment against the Government but also as resentment against the coloured community.[78]

He concluded by stating that to go ahead with the proposal would do more harm than good. His claim that there was no support for the amendment flew directly in the face of the demands of a number of MPs and race relations organisations that were seeking to take the investigation of racial discrimination allegations against police out of the hands of chief police officers.

On 21 November 1968, a letter was sent from the Home Office to the Met's Commissioner, Sir John Waldron, asking him to arrange a meeting with Frank Cousins, then Chairman of the Community Relations Commission (CRC), in order to explain the 'efforts being made by police to establish good relations between the police and the coloured communities'.[79] Referring to the proposed discipline code amendment, the writer added: 'you should not disclose the information which I gave you in confidence that the Home Secretary is ready to abandon this proposal'.[80] On 15 May 1969, Callaghan met with Messrs Gale and Pamplin of the Police Federation. It was agreed that the proposed discipline code amendment would not be introduced, and it was noted in the minutes of the meeting that:

In seeing them [Gale and Pamplin] out, the Home Secretary secured agreement to mutual silence on the question of a special provision on race relations in the Discipline Code. This applies not only to the [forthcoming Federation] Conference but to the indefinite future.[81]

What this issue highlights is the way in which the Police Federation and its supporters, by misrepresentation of the facts and veiled threats as to the evils which may befall the black community if it didn't get its way, was able to defeat a government proposal that, had it been incorporated into the discipline regulations, would have been widely welcomed by members of the black community and those who sought reassurance that both government and police took the issue of racial discrimination seriously. As Nadine Peppard rightly pointed out, during Callaghan's stewardship of the Home Office the cause of race relations in Britain took a backward step.

Tinkering at the edges: bringing the Met under control

During the 1950s, demand for greater political accountability of police forces by Parliament, coupled with concern over the police's inability to attract and retain sufficient officers to satisfactorily perform all of its functions, led to the setting up of the Royal Commission on the Police. Many of the Commission's findings had little impact on the Met – the most undermanned force in the country. The Secretary of State's supervision of the Met was seen to be so inadequate that senior officials in his own department drew attention to the fact that the Commissioner regularly took policy decisions without prior Home Office approval. Such supervision as there was appears to have been driven by political expediency – usually after things had gone wrong and with at least one eye on any possible political implications for the Home Secretary – rather than with any primary concern for the efficiency of the Metropolitan Police. The Home Secretary and Home Office were also culpable, because of their failure to keep informed of operational policing demands. It was hardly surprising that, faced with officials who were unacquainted with the intricacies of policing, the Commissioner should himself decide what was the best course of action to take, and seek approval later. The fact that Simpson felt able to tell the Home Secretary not to meddle in operational matters stemmed from a convention that had been established for many years: a convention that was written into the Police Act 1964:

The effect of the Act is that the chief constable will not be subject to orders or directions from either his police authority or the Secretary of State, but he will be accountable to them for certain of his functions.[82]

Having officials at the Home Office who knew little about policing, and middle-ranking police officers who were largely unskilled at writing detailed reports, did little to help communication between the Home Office and New Scotland Yard. The remedy lay in recruiting well-educated civilian staff, but low rates of pay and the lack of a properly organised career structure hampered the Met's ability to recruit and retain non-police staff of the highest calibre. The Met was chronically short of policemen and was subject to Home Office financial restraint in a way that chief constables in areas with more favourably disposed police authorities were not. This meant that, at times of economic belt-tightening, the Met invariably fared worse than other forces: as was the case in 1967, when the Home Office put a ceiling on police recruitment for the year.

Conservative governments between 1951 and 1964 had shown no inclination to campaign for the recruitment of black policemen, and the Home Office followed this line. One clearly sees that, prior to the election of a Labour government that year, officials were anxious to disassociate themselves from any suggestion that they were in favour of such a policy. Roy Jenkins' time as Home Secretary was characterised by support for cultural diversity and his recommendation that public bodies, the police in particular, should look to recruit black and Asian people to their ranks. The problem was that, while he could encourage chief constables to accept black recruits, he was in no position to tell them which individuals to accept. Consequently, the Commissioner and his colleagues were able to continue their 'maybe tomorrow' approach, largely as before. The process was not helped when Callaghan replaced Jenkins at the Home Office. His natural inclination placed him shoulder-to-shoulder with the Police Federation and traditionalist chief police officers, and during his stewardship reform of the police was largely placed on hold. This is not to say that he was ineffective. He encouraged steps to root out corruption in the Met and took a firm line on law-and-order issues. But his appointment of Waldron to succeed Simpson showed a lack of initiative and foresight at a time when the Met was in need of dynamic new leadership.

Policing in 1970 had, in many ways, changed considerably from the way it had looked 20 years earlier. The number of police forces had been dramatically reduced, and every force was now subject to a greater degree of political accountability than had previously been the case. The 1964 Police Act introduced a national standard for dealing with complaints against the police and established certain rights for complainants; including the right to attend discipline hearings and to be informed of the outcome of a discipline investigation. The Wilson government had taken a positive line on equality of opportunity and in the second half of the decade the first black police officers began to appear on the streets.

But a consideration of the broader questions reveals that many of the earlier contentious issues remained unresolved. The police still investigated complaints against themselves. The right of chief police officers to determine the way in which they would utilise their resources to deal with operational matters was now enshrined in legislative tablets of stone. The Home Secretary remained as police authority for the Metropolitan Police and the London boroughs, despite the considerable contribution of the capital's ratepayers to the Met's budget, continued to have no say in the policing of London. Lord Scarman, in his report on the 1981 disturbances in Brixton, expressed the view that policing expediency in London had the clear potential to be detrimental to the wishes of local people:

> The opportunity to ignore local opinion (but not national) exists for the Metropolitan Police; and he would be a bold man (bolder than I) who would affirm that the existence of an opportunity does not breed the temptation to make use of it, especially when it is convenient or saves trouble.[83]

Lack of political control enabled the Met to pay lip service to the Home Secretary's call for more black police officers at a time when a number of contemporaries argued that such a move would have been of great benefit to police relations with the black community. This, coupled with the government's climb down over the proposal to introduce a specific discipline offence of racial discrimination in the face of opposition from the Police Federation, merely emphasised both the weakness of the Home Office Police Department and the unwillingness of the police service to see beyond its own prejudices on the question of race.

The Royal Commission on the Police may well have concluded that the time had come to control chief constables.[84] The fact remained, however, that, in spite of the Royal Commission's aspirations, the Metropolitan Police Commissioner could still, and did, tell the Home Secretary to mind his own business.

Notes

1 The Police Authority for the City of London Police was the Common Council of the City of London.
2 The grant amounted to one-half of the cost of the annual policing budget.
3 The Metropolitan Police Commissioner and the four Assistant Commissioners were all *ex officio* justices of the peace.
4 At the time the Royal Commission on the Police was established in 1959 there were no less than 125 police forces in England and Wales and a further 33 in Scotland, one of which had only 18 police officers.

5 *Parliamentary Debates (Commons)* (16 December 1959), Vol.615, Cols.1452–5. The Chairman of the Commission was Sir Henry Willink.
6 Ibid.
7 NA HO287/85 Report of the Royal Commission on the Police, p.34.
8 *Parliamentary Debates (Commons)* (2 May 1957), Vol.569, Cols.337–8.
9 *Parliamentary Debates (Commons)* (9 April 1959), Vol.603, Cols.369–70.
10 *Parliamentary Debates (Commons)* (7 May 1959), Vol.605, Cols.67–8.
11 S. Spencer, *Called to Account: the Case for Police Accountability in England and Wales* (1985), p.23; and C. Emsley, *The English Police*, pp.171–2.
12 NA HO325/9.
13 NA HO287/85 Evidence given by the NCCL to the Royal Commission on the Police on 24 January 1961.
14 This consisted of representatives of all police ranks, local authority associations and the Home Department. See *Report of the Royal Commission on the Police* (1962), p.20.
15 Ibid.
16 Ibid. p.7.
17 NA HO272/2 *Royal Commission Report*, p.70.
18 This concerned the fact that the Met had for some years been operating a system of recording complaints. See *Royal Commission Report*, p.26.
19 NA HO287/25 Metropolitan Police: relationship with Home Secretary, formation of a committee to ensure closer relationship: history of the Metropolitan Police from 1829 to date (1961–69).
20 Ibid.
21 Ibid. The report suggests that these would have included HMIC and staff officer, the chairman of the police authority and its clerk, the several members of the police authority, the Under-Secretary in charge of the Police Department at the Home Office, and Home Office Ministers.
22 Ibid.
23 Ibid.
24 For example, if a chief constable deemed that information in his possession was too sensitive for him to disclose when asked for details by the police authority he could appeal to the Home Secretary, who was empowered to determine the issue. The Home Secretary was also to be supplied with an annual report by each chief constable.
25 NA HO 287/25.
26 Ibid.
27 Ibid.
28 NA HO 272/53.
29 R. Mark, *In the Office of Constable* (Glasgow: 1978), p.82.
30 NA HO 287/25.
31 NA HO 272/53 (21 March 1961), p.5.
32 D. Taverne, interviewed by author, 9 February 2001. The term 'cottage' is used to describe venues such as public lavatories, where men congregate for the purpose of importuning for sexual purposes.
33 NA HO272/53 Commissioner of Police of the Metropolis, evidence to the Royal Commission on the Police.
34 NA HO 287/274.

35 NA HO287/274.
36 NA HO 272/53.
37 *Parliamentary Debates (Commons)* (12 March 1964), Vol.691, Cols.812–39.
38 Such as rudeness and over-officiousness.
39 NA MEPO 2/10431 Commissioner's Conferences 1962.
40 NA MEPO 2/10435 Commissioner's Conferences 1966.
41 Taverne interview.
42 Ibid.
43 NA HO 287/1453 Home Office view on whether it should urge police forces to recruit from ethnic minorities 1965–69.
44 Ibid.
45 Ibid.
46 Ibid.
47 Taverne interview.
48 *Parliamentary Debates (Commons)* (18 May 1966), Vol.728, Cols.1341–48.
49 Taverne interview.
50 Ibid.
51 *Parliamentary Debates (Commons)* (4 February 1966), Vol.723, Col.300.
52 This figure includes 21 who had obtained external degrees during their police service.
53 Taverne interview.
54 NA CK 2/16 Race Relations Board – Chairman's correspondence with the Home Secretary.
55 Other facilities included dog-handler patrols, and, in a number of forces, mounted patrols.
56 NA MEPO 2/10596 Mobile unit policing (Accrington Scheme): implementation of the scheme in the Metropolitan Police District 1966.
57 Ibid.
58 Ibid. The observations of Detective Superintendent Newman.
59 Ex PC D. King, letter to author, 5 March 2001.
60 NA HO 377/88 The symposium ran from 28 March to 14 April 1970. Report of the Home Office Police Scientific Development Branch.
61 Ibid.
62 K.O. Morgan, *Callaghan A Life*, (Oxford: 1997), p.300.
63 Ibid. p.301.
64 Taverne interview.
65 J. Callaghan, *Time and Chance*, (1987), p.232.
66 Taverne interview.
67 N. Peppard, letter to author, 15 March 2001.
68 NA HO376/140. Report dated 22 March 1968. Ministerial Committee on Immigration and Assimilation.
69 NA HO 376/81 Security implications 1968, undated draft, but written on or before 9 April 1968.
70 NA HO 287/1466 (PAB (68) 2) Proposed amendment to the Police Discipline Code 1968–69.
71 Ibid.
72 NA MEPO2/10790 (1968).

73 This category covered all allegations that would have been included in High Commissioner Lindo's list, but would have excluded allegations of traffic offences committed by Met officers.

74 NA HO 376/135 Police Relations with Immigrants 1965–67, the memorandum was dated 18 February 1966.

75 Ibid.

76 Ibid.

77 Ibid.

78 Ibid.

79 Ibid. The CRC was one of the organisations that had supported the proposal to incorporate an offence of racial discrimination in the police discipline code.

80 Ibid.

81 Ibid.

82 Home Office Circular 170/1964, Section 5(21).

83 Lord Scarman, *Report on the Disturbances in Brixton 10 to 13 April 1981*, Cmnd 8247, para.5.67.

84 PRO HO287/85 *Royal Commission Report*, p.2.

Chapter 5

Recruitment problems, racial awareness training and becoming a real policeman

The process of becoming a police constable is a long and arduous one. The ability to courteously exercise authority over others while displaying an air of calm tranquillity, often in the face of the most testing of circumstances, are qualities that few people naturally possess. Two factors have long been considered crucial in determining whom the police service, on behalf of society, will entrust with the performance of such onerous responsibilities. These are the selection of only the most able applicants, and the provision of the best possible training to enable them to do the job. In this chapter the recruiting and training procedures of the Metropolitan Police in the 1950s and 1960s will be scrutinised, and the Metropolitan Police's policy on the appointment of black police officers, which was considered from the Home Office standpoint in the previous chapter, will be examined in greater detail. As will be seen, it was in the area of racial awareness training for police officers that one of the Met's most crucial and consistent failings was to be found, primarily because the subject was never seen, other than at times of public disquiet or external criticism, as sufficiently important to be a priority.

For the Metropolitan Police, an immediate problem faced at the end of the Second World War, and one that would plague the force for decades to come, was that of under-manning. There were fewer officers to police the capital's streets in the post-war period than in 1939. In 1938, London had 18,511 police officers and the Metropolitan Police was 6 per cent under strength. By 1958, the year of the disturbances at Notting Hill, the number of officers had fallen to 16,661 and the force was more than 14 per cent under its establishment figure. John Gerrard, a former Assistant Commissioner of the Met, believed that in failing to meet is establishment figure, the Met was largely to blame for its own deficiencies:

I think the force made one or two mistakes in recruiting immediately after the war. There were lots of people coming back from the armed forces who wanted to join the police. They were looking for a job and there weren't too many jobs about at that time . . . so they set a very high standard physically, and, I suppose you could say, educationally. They wanted second-class civil service examination or equivalent to get in. With the result that they turned a lot of people down that a few years later they'd have given their eye-teeth to have . . . so they had a golden opportunity to get all the people they wanted . . . unfortunately, because they set these high standards, it rebounded on them.[1]

The problem of under-manning continued, with periodic peaks and troughs, throughout the post-war period and by the mid-1960s there was a shortfall in male officers of over 27 per cent.

The Metropolitan Police was a young force. In 1958 over 10,000 of London's 12,000 constables had joined since the war and the average age of recruits was 23. Sixty-seven per cent of the officers were single men; and, of those, 60 per cent had joined the Met on release from the Armed Forces. In his annual report for that year the Commissioner of Police highlighted the limited experience of his middle-ranking officers, those who would have been in charge of day-to-day policing at street level: 'Sergeants and inspectors . . . are now largely post-war entrants and, as such, they are only beginning to find their feet as leaders and supervisory officers.'[2]

Prior to 1 January 1949, the date upon which the British Nationality Act 1948 became law, an applicant for the police service in England and Wales was required to be a natural-born British subject who was the child of 'parents who are, or were at the time of death, natural born British subjects of pure European descent'.[3] Such a requirement ensured that black Commonwealth citizens were automatically excluded by virtue of their failure to satisfy the nationality qualification. The 1948 Act altered the qualification rule and Home Office Circular 20/1949 introduced new nationality guidelines that were adopted by the Metropolitan Police. Under the new rules a candidate seeking to join the police could be a natural-born or naturalised British subject. This applied to those who had been born in the United Kingdom and Colonies or a Commonwealth country. By the Act, a person who was a British subject before 1 January 1949 (and was not an Eire citizen) remained a British subject. Those born after 1 January 1949 acquired British nationality as a result of the possession of their citizen status either of the United Kingdom and Colonies or of a Commonwealth country. There was now, in theory at least, no longer any impediment on the grounds of nationality to the appointment of a West Indian or other Commonwealth citizen to the police service in England and Wales.

At the Central Conference of Chief Constables, held on 15 November 1962, delegates were informed that the Metropolitan Police policy on nationality qualifications was simply that a candidate must be of British nationality (natural-born or naturalised) to be eligible for appointment: British antecedents were not required. It was pointed out that the rule embraced a large field and, coupled with the Commissioner's discretion in the selection of suitable men, worked satisfactorily. However, while black applicants were eligible under a 'British nationality' rule, the Commissioner did not consider that under present circumstances they were acceptable for appointment in the metropolis.[4]

This was not the first, nor was it to be the last occasion upon which Sir Joseph Simpson expressed his opposition to the appointment of black police officers to the Met. An earlier example occurred at a meeting that Simpson attended on 2 June 1959 at the Home Office to discuss the police response to the murder of Kelso Cochrane (May 1959). Leaders of the West Indian community in Notting Hill, who were keen to foster good relations in the area, had recommended that suitable people of all races should be recruited as special constables to assist the regular police, as they believed it would be helpful in reducing racial difficulties in the area. In response, Simpson remarked that he was opposed to the recruitment of special constables in the Notting Hill area and added that he did not feel it desirable to recruit 'coloured' policemen.[5]

Revised rules on nationality qualifications for the police were again introduced by the Home Office in its Circular 147/1963, which came into effect on 4 July that year. The Home Office was concerned that police forces in England and Wales were failing to adhere to uniform practices in the interpretation of the nationality qualifications. Some of the appointing authorities still required that candidates must be British subjects and of British-born parents while others adopted a less restrictive approach to the guidelines. Whether or not the nationality rules were being widely interpreted, the debate on black recruitment was still an exclusively academic one. No black policeman had been appointed by any of the police forces and some of the chief constables openly expressed their reservations about their appointment; claiming that the time was not yet right for such posts to be offered to black men.

On 16 January 1964, Simpson met with members of the London Council of Social Services (LCSS) to consider relations between the Met and immigrants. He outlined initiatives that were currently in place or under consideration by the Met, including proposals for talks to be given to his officers on the capital's West Indian community. He pointed out that Metropolitan officers met with their colonial counterparts who were attending courses at the Hendon training school but, as Nadine Peppard of the LCSS noted, this was merely a student fellowship.[6] The Commissioner was asked about the recruitment of black policemen and the suggestion was made that there were surely suitable people who ought to be recruited before the issue became the focus of critical attention. Simpson agreed in principle that black officers should eventually be recruited, but added that:

> There have been one or two applicants who have approached the general standard for the force. In each case the man had been asked by the Assistant Commissioner, as President of the Board, whether he had thought out how the public would react to him if he had to deal with them as offending motorists, etc. and whether he was ready to deal with such positions if he found himself in them. In each case the applicant said he had not considered the matter so deeply and, after doing so, withdrew his application.[7]

When one considers the Commissioner's opposition to the recruitment of black policemen at this time and analyses his words carefully, it seems clear that the president of the selection board, confronted by a black applicant, would have urged the candidate to consider most carefully the drawbacks of a police career in his particular case rather than the benefits. It is inconceivable that anyone applying to become a policeman would not have anticipated that he would, at some stage in his career, be required to deal with offending motorists. The probability is that the potential for racial conflict, stemming from an altercation between a black policeman and a white member of the public, would have been made all too apparent to the applicant; as was the case with Norwell Roberts, the first black officer to be appointed by the Met, to such an extent that in the majority of cases the applicant was deterred from proceeding with his application. As Roberts recalled: 'I thought they would definitely fail me on the interview board because they asked questions like, "what would you do if a drunken man calls you a black bastard?" '[8]

Simpson argued that the most propitious route for black recruitment to the Met was through the Cadet Service. Black youths would need to prove their suitability for the police service by a three-year trial as cadets, before the Met would contemplate whether or not to accept the individual concerned. According to Simpson:

> The most likely source of recruitment was through the Cadet Service, where young coloured boys of suitable education could be assimilated and during the full three-year course, it would become obvious whether they were temperamentally suited to become police officers.[9]

Such an observation clearly suggests that, as far as the Metropolitan Police Commissioner was concerned, a black applicant for the police cadets was not merely to be judged on the basis of his own suitability for appointment, but was also to be the benchmark for the suitability of other black applicants. While Simpson respected the contribution of the West Indian community as schoolmasters and nurses, his stereotypical view of black bus conductors – of whom he claimed that a large number had had their licences revoked – showed how strong was his conviction that black people were temperamentally unsuited to the pressures of day-to-day policing:

> They [bus conductors] put up with a great deal . . . They [black bus conductors] had an unfortunate tendency to take off their equipment in moments of excitement and use it to crown offending passengers . . . This is just the time and situation when a policeman cannot afford to get excited and it would not do for us to have policemen who gave way to their emotions in this fashion.[10]

Given such sentiments, it is perhaps no surprise that Roberts, on whose behalf the Home Office had lobbied the Met to appoint him, remained London's only black police constable when Simpson died while still holding office in 1967.

The Met's position on black recruitment was set out in an internal memo to the Commissioner from the Assistant Commissioner 'D' Department on 10 December 1963.[11]

> The truth is, of course, that we are not yet prepared to recruit any coloured men, although the time may not be so far distant when we shall be unable to turn down well-qualified men who have been born and educated in this country . . . In a predominantly white population, coloured police officers would be at a serious disadvantage and it would be unreasonable to expect them to perform the specialised duties of a policeman effectively . . . It is our belief in Recruiting Branch that the West Indians and other coloured people are well aware that we do not recruit coloured men but that an occasional one is encouraged to apply by various societies as a kind of sighting shot.[12]

Such a view was not uncommon among senior police officers. On 14 April 1965, a meeting was held at the Home Office attended by civil servants and a representative body of chief constables to discuss the recruitment of black policemen. For the Home Office, it was pointed out that, following a question in Parliament, the Home Secretary had informed the House that Police Regulations did not discriminate in any way between applicants of differing race, colour or creed and that the Secretary of State had no reason to believe that chief officers, who were responsible for the appointment of policemen to their forces, considered applicants on any grounds other than merit.[13] The subject was of interest to politicians and public alike and the Home Secretary's answer to Parliament begged the question: why, if discrimination was not a factor, had no black regular policemen yet been appointed? The information available suggested that there had been few applicants from the black community to join the police. Those who had applied had all been rejected for failing to meet the required standard for new recruits. The Home Secretary was keen to know if his answer to Parliament was in fact correct and if he could be satisfied that if suitably qualified black men applied to join the police they would in fact be appointed.

The response from the assembled group of chief police officers revealed that, while there was general unanimity that the recruitment of black policemen was desirable in the long term, serious reservations existed about the desirability of their recruitment at the present, or in the immediate future. Such fears were largely based upon their shared belief that black men would be unable to cope with the rigours of policing. For example, four of the chief officers were concerned that black policemen would have problems in their area as there were Irish people who lived alongside the black community and the Irish would tend to make life difficult for black officers by picking on them. Ann Dummett, in her work on racism in England during the period, commented upon such paternalistic racism in the employment field and observed that:

> If he [a black applicant for a job] is told, 'No black bastards wanted', at least he knows where he stands. Some employers will explain to an applicant . . . that it would really be unfair to him to be given a job, because he might find white people nasty to him in the course of his work. This is to kill with kindness, and it is not surprising if the applicant, who wants to make his own decision and take his own risks just as long as he is given the chance to work, is more bitter about this kind of fatherly refusal than about being told he's a black bastard.[14]

All of the chief officers had received applications from black men, each of whom had been rejected. What is particularly striking about their comments is the complete absence of any apparent enthusiasm on their part at the prospect of recruiting black policemen. Mr Capper (Birmingham) said that if he had a suitable applicant he would appoint him, though not without doubts. Mr Ambler (Bradford) said that it was too early to appoint black policemen in Bradford, 'especially Pakistanis . . . a race riot might well ensue'. The Chief Constable of Leicester, Robert Mark, with an observation that surely went to the heart of the matter, suggested that more qualified black men did not apply, believing that they would not be welcome.[15]

The chief officers followed the Commissioner's line in agreeing that the best time to recruit black men to the police force was when the children of immigrants became eligible to join the cadet corps; as it was generally agreed that the second generation would have been assimilated into the British way of life. However, in general discussion some anxiety was expressed that the appointment of black boys to the cadet corps 'might sometimes mean rejecting suitable white applicants'.[16] Such an observation again emphasises the lack of commitment at the highest level of the police service to the creation of a multi-ethnic police force. While the Home Secretary may have believed in the accuracy of his statement to the Commons that police regulations did not discriminate in any way between applicants of differing race, colour or creed, those charged with the task of implementing the regulations at force level were clearly motivated by a desire to interpret them in a way that was far from equal when it came to black applicants.

The Met's manpower shortage and the National Police Recruiting Campaign: 1962–69

The Metropolitan Police took part in the National Police Recruitment Campaign organised for all police forces by the Home Office, which began in 1962. The Met was seriously concerned that the deficiency between its actual strength and its establishment was reaching alarming proportions. Between 1962 and 1964 the deficiency ranged between 12 and 14 per cent. But in 1965, the gap rose dramatically to 27 per cent. By 31 December 1966, the Metropolitan Police was 6,224 men short of its establishment figure of 25,006 male officers.[17] The Met's public relations officer reported that despite the cost of the advertising, it was essential that it continue, as without it the force was unlikely to achieve even its reduced target figures. He believed that, as a result of recent publicity given to public order issues and the difficulty of police work, there was a reluctance to join the police.

Great emphasis was placed on recruitment from the cadet corps into the police service. The system was a proven success: the dropout rate of ex-cadets being considerably less than for those joining the police directly. The obvious disadvantage of the scheme was that there were an increasing number of policemen who, as ex-cadets, had little experience of life outside the police. The Met led the way in the development of the cadet scheme in the 1950s. Speaking to the Association of Chief Police Officers (ACPO) in May 1960, the Home Secretary, R.A. Butler, observed that:

> One way of attracting good recruits who are likely to stay in the service is through the cadet system . . . an increasing proportion of

constables are being appointed from ex-cadets. The increase is quite steep; the proportion of newly-appointed constables who were cadets has increased from 1 in 20 to about 1 in 4 over the last five years and there is every indication that the wastage of ex-cadets is much less than the wastage of other constables ... The Commissioner of Police of the Metropolis is planning a substantial expansion of the Metropolitan Police Cadet Service, with a much-improved system of instruction and training.[18]

As the issue of black recruitment developed, both the police and Home Office concurred that the cadet scheme would provide the most likely source of recruitment. A minute in the Home Office file 'General policy on the appointment of coloured policemen', dated 22 February 1966, records that:

> The main obstacle to the recruitment of coloured men to the police or police cadets is that those who do apply are unsuitable and that those who probably would be suitable prefer careers which in their view will give them a higher status in the community.[19]

A meeting had taken place the previous month at the Home Office, which was attended by officials from the Ministry of Labour's central Youth Employment Executive to consider the recruitment of black police officers and cadets. A senior official of the Executive stated that, to the best of his knowledge, there had been no applications from the black community to join the Metropolitan Police Cadets. It was recognised that the Met did not accept recent immigrants, whether black or white, and that the Met would want black applicants to be born in Britain or to have been educated there since primary school. It was further alleged that West Indians were hostile to the police in their homeland and this spirit of resentment was likely to be absorbed by the children of immigrants born in England.[20] Such a stereotypical observation of West Indian culture among senior staff at the Home Office and Ministry of Labour merely highlighted the difficulties black applicants for the Met would have had to surmount.

At a meeting with chief superintendents on 11 January 1966, Simpson described the efforts that were being made to attract more recruits to the Met. He informed his audience that the problem of recruitment was exacerbated by the Met's high wastage levels. He added that the educational standards for recruits were as low as possible.[21] The number of cadets for that year was to be increased to 500, one-third of the annual intake of new recruits.[22] In an effort to tackle police manpower shortages, the government introduced a number of amendments to the qualification requirements for entry to the police service. The Police (Amendment)

(No. 4) Regulations 1967 gave chief officers of police power to recruit applicants who were unable to meet the previous height requirements.[23] Authority was also given to recruit applicants who did not possess the required academic qualifications.[24] In further attempts to address its shortfall in strength, the Met decided that it would accept recruits who wore glasses or contact lenses. The recruitment age for those who wished to apply from the armed forces was raised to 40.

While advertisements were now being used to attract a broad range of people who would previously have been excluded from the police, none of the recruiting literature made reference to applicants from the black community, despite the fact that both the absence of black policemen and police relations with immigrant communities had been the subject of adverse comment in Parliament, and the Home Secretary had assured the House that police regulations did not discriminate on grounds of colour, race or creed. In 1969 the Home Office conducted a survey of police recruiting and concluded that:

> Our own report suggests that we are attracting too few of the better educated men and there certainly seems a case to be made for a modification along these lines in order to alter the balance of the quality of recruits.[25]

When considering the previous occupational background of recruits it was noted that the police service attracted men from most walks of life, with the exception of factory workers. A majority of men accepted by the police came from the professional, clerical, armed forces and administrative groups and the cadet corps; the very occupations in which members of the black community were least likely to be represented at the time. The general academic standard of recruits was basic. The survey found that 55 per cent of those accepted did not have a GCE 'O' level qualification, and less than one in 20 had obtained a pass at Advanced level.[26]

The Metropolitan Police was found to have a high overall applicant rejection rate, despite the fact that an exceptionally small number failed the education tests. Those who withdrew their application, failed to meet the physical requirements or were classified as 'others' were all considerably more numerous proportionately than in other forces.[27] The 'others' category is interesting for, as a 'catch-all' classification, it encompassed all grounds for which an applicant might be rejected other than specific grounds for refusal (such as failing to pass the entrance exam, defective eyesight, etc.) and would, for example, have included applicants who were considered to be emotionally, temperamentally or in any other way unsuited to police work; such as the black applicants whose presumed knowledge of the English way of life was thought to be inadequate. By December 1969 there were in the whole of the country only 19 black police officers out of an estimated black population of one million.[28]

While the police had reservations about black applicants, the black community's negative experience of the police service proved to be an additional impediment to black recruitment. Nadine Peppard of the LCSS pointed out that part of the failure to attract black recruits was that:

> The coloured community – or rather communities – lack confidence in the police. The situation is not improved by rumours of police ill treatment of coloured people ... most coloured people believe they can do better for themselves in other occupations ...[29]

This view was endorsed in a minute from the Home Office Police Department to Merlyn Rees MP concerning the recruitment of black policemen in August 1969:

> In the evidence to the Committee on Race Relations and Immigration, you undertook to consult the Community Relations Commission about the recruitment of coloured men and women to the police service ... We have followed this up with the Secretary and Deputy Secretary of the Commission and there has been general agreement about the nature of the difficulties with which this particular problem is beset, one of the most important of which lies in removing the suspicion with which police are regarded by the coloured community in certain parts of the country.[30]

Staying out – black policemen and the Metropolitan Police

There are, of course, a number of explanations for the Met's lack of success in recruiting no more than a handful of black officers by the end of the 1960s. The problem was not exclusive to the Met, but was to be found in all police forces at this time. One reason for the scarcity of black recruits was the shared view of senior police officers and the Home Office that black recruitment must not be seen to have failed. Neither was prepared to take a chance that the first black recruits might not stay the course. At the meeting of chief constables and representatives from the Home Office in April 1965, Mr Parker (Home Office), in summarising the salient issued discussed, said:

> There was no quick or easy solution. The recruitment of coloured youths of high standard into the cadets would be worth pursuing ... The first few coloured policemen would have a very difficult

123

time, and the worst thing of all would be to appoint a coloured man who was not really up to standard or not fully assimilated to this country.[31]

Similar views were expressed almost two years later when a meeting was held involving officials from the Home Office and the Central Youth Employment Executive. It was stated that:

> The consideration which had led to the conclusion that the most promising method of making progress would be to encourage suitable coloured youths, preferably those born and educated in this country, to join the police cadets. The question was how this could be done in such a way as to ensure that those who applied were in fact suitable. If many of those encouraged to apply were unsuitable and rejected, this would only make matters worse ... The first coloured cadets would have to be of a higher standard than that required by the Metropolitan Police for white youths.[32]

A consideration of these observations might reasonably lead one to conclude that racism was a feature of police recruitment procedures in the 1960s. If black candidates had to be of a higher standard than their white counterparts in order to have the same chance of being selected, it follows that those responsible for recruiting were not applying the same standards equally to all applicants. As a result, black applicants were discriminated against in favour of white applicants. Norwell Roberts challenged the widely held police view in the 1960s that society was not yet ready to accept black policemen; arguing instead that the real problem was the reluctance of the Commissioner and chief officers to appoint black policemen:

> If senior police officers or those in authority said that they weren't ready to recruit coloured police officers in the '60s because the public weren't ready for them that's another load of baloney. I had absolutely no trouble with members of the public. In fact, at Covent Garden with the market porters, who you would imagine would have given me so much stick they would have driven me out, I had no problem whatsoever. That is absolute crap. The reason why they didn't is because the police force doesn't like change: 1829 to 1967, no black policemen. I suppose it would have been the same when they had people with glasses in, or homosexuals. What are they going to say? 'How are we going to work with a poof? We can't work with these poofs.' They resent change. I had no trouble with members of the public. My only troubles were inside the job.[33]

Roberts' point was well made. In an internal memorandum to Simpson on 17 December 1965, his eventual successor, Assistant Commissioner Waldron, stated, 'I shall always be reluctant to see police officers on uniform patrol wearing spectacles, and I hope that we shall not be compelled to descend to this.'[34]

Along with the Met's tendency to recruit from lower middle and working class backgrounds that were, prior to 1967, exclusively white (with particular preference being given to those from the cadet corps and the armed forces), the force found itself selecting applicants from the whole of the British Isles. This was because recruiting from the London area failed to meet the Met's annual requirements. For example, between January and December 1966, out of 838 men recruited, only 327 came from the Greater London area.[35] A significant number of recruits were drawn from those parts of the country where there was no black community. Many of these officers, often drawn from rural areas, had little or no experience of immigrant communities, or of the difficulties of life for black people in London, when they began to police areas with a sizeable number of black residents. A former police officer who left his home in Lancashire in 1962 to become a Met cadet recalled, 'I came to London as a sixteen year old and I'd [previously] seen probably one black person.'[36] The Met knew that by seeking to recruit applicants from traditional sources it would attract those who were likely to stay once they joined. Accordingly, there appears to have been little desire to spend valuable advertising revenue on those from sections of society that had traditionally shown little interest in a police career. As such, black and Asian men were largely overlooked as potential recruits in favour of tried-and-trusted sections of the labour market.

For the black person who not only applied but was accepted by the Met, the battle was far from won. Problems would very likely be encountered from one or more of three directions. The downward spiral in relations between the Met and the Caribbean community, which had begun in the 1950s, continued throughout the following decade. Many black people would have seen an application by a member of their community to join the Met as siding with the opposition. As one Met officer of the period put it:

> It is fair to say that recruiting black West Indians was a failure. They fell foul of the whites because they were black, and they were despised [by other blacks] because they betrayed the brothers. You were, therefore, as a black copper caught at home, at play and at work: a no, no, no win situation. You were a traitor.[37]

Successful black applicants also had to contend with the prejudices of the British public, as was the case with London's first black policewoman,

Sislin Fay Allen, when she began her career in 1968. Every branch of the media was in attendance when she was presented to the press on her first day at the police training school. However, within days she became the target of hate mail that was simultaneously racist and sexist; the following being an extract from one of many unsigned letters received:

> I would refuse to be interrogated by a black alien policewoman or man, nor would I be interrogated by one. It is monstrous that the white English of these islands should be subjected to any form of control by foreign settlers whom we bitterly resent. You have a country of your own ... you have a young child for whom you should be caring [it was reported in the press that Mrs Allen had a young child], and there must be many in the police force who object to working with you.[38]

Black recruits also had to work with colleagues whose knowledge of their background and culture was largely based upon their own, frequently confrontational dealings with the black community. Norwell Roberts recalled his experience with his supervising sergeant when he arrived at Bow Street Police Station after completing his basic training:

> I went out on Division and I remember going to the station at Bow Street and within the first week my reporting sergeant said to me, 'Look nigger, I'll see to it that you never pass your probation.' We were all on two years probation and it was his way of saying, 'Mr Roberts, welcome to the real world, and I'll make sure that you were the first and you'll be the last.' That's what he was saying basically.[39]

A former senior police officer recalled the attitude of many of his colleagues to the recruitment of black policemen in the 1960s:

> I'm not conscious of any occasion when we sat around talking about it, but we were only involved with black people up against the law. The fact that West Indians, black people, were working on our buses, in our hospitals, or in our factories was, to some extent, lost on us. So we largely formed our opinion of black people by virtue of their coming into contact with us ... [and] such was our concept of the black person that it would never have been considered as a serious probability. They were just not suited.[40]

It was largely for these reasons, and the growing mistrust of the police among the West Indian community, that the plan to recruit the most able black men, and black youths to the cadet corps, was such a spectacular failure.

Where ignorance is bliss: race relations training in the Met

Training in racial awareness for Metropolitan Police officers gradually evolved in the 1960s. However, much of it foundered on the rocks of credibility and attitude. On 21 May 1959 a meeting was held at the Colonial Office at which the Acting Secretary of the Migrant Services Division of the WIF, Mr Fraser, informed the Met's Assistant Commissioner 'A' Department (ACA) of areas of concern regarding police policy towards the West Indian community. He suggested that, as he had already addressed an audience of women police, it might be helpful if he were to talk to male officers at Brixton, Notting Hill and Paddington. The ACA consulted with his female colleagues and reported Fraser's offer to the Commissioner in less than enthusiastic terms:

> He [Fraser] is inclined to get people's backs up (particularly a police audience) and was not well received. He was not asked to address the last course . . . to allow him to address PCs etc. at Notting Hill for example, would cause trouble I think. If he has anything to say he should say it to us.[41]

On 3 June 1959 Fraser was at a meeting attended by Simpson at the WIF. He again took the opportunity to suggest that relations might improve if Met officers were made aware of the difficulties faced by West Indians living in London. Simpson was not at all receptive to the idea and reported in terms that suggested he did not believe that the problem was as bad as Fraser had described:

> I explained that this was very difficult and that it would have to be for me to decide how best to carry out any agreed improvement in understanding of the problem by police. For the moment I do not propose to do more than to let them tell me . . . the sort of thing they want to get over. I can then decide how best, if at all, to get them over.[42]

On 9 September 1959 Mr Gordon, the WIF Commissioner, again informed the ACA that his staff would be willing to give talks to police, and added that he could also provide films that would enable officers to learn more about life in the Caribbean. His offer was declined and, with the subsequent demise of the West Indies Federation, any thought of raising levels of racial awareness among London's police was put to one side.

On 19 June 1963 Simpson met Mr Walker, the Welfare Counsellor at the Jamaican High Commission. The issue of talks to police was raised again and this time Simpson stated that agreement had been reached for such talks to be given to officers attending the 'A' course at the Police College.[43] As a result, he was now considering whether:

It might be possible to do something more in the Metropolitan Police District to put over at the Probationer's Refresher Courses the need for greater care in dealing with coloured people and, with that in mind, it might be possible to arrange for a talk to those of the Training School staff who supervised these courses.[44]

The first talks by representatives of the Jamaican High Commission to Metropolitan Police officers began at the end of 1964, some five years after Gordon had made his original offer to raise police awareness levels of immigrant life in London: five years during which it was commonly accepted that relations between police and Caribbean immigrants had deteriorated.

The issue of training for Metropolitan Police officers in the problems of immigrant communities was raised in the Commons in a parliamentary question to the Home Secretary on 8 July 1965.[45] The police response glossed over difficulties between Met officers and immigrants and, drawing on extracts from presentations given by Jamaican High Commission speakers, suggested that the difficulties which were now being experienced were primarily the result of problems that existed between immigrants and police in their countries of origin.

One main factor which ... was possibly the greatest source of friction between these rural immigrants and the police of our larger cities and towns ... was the prevailing customary habit of West Indian police officers making arbitrary on-the-spot decisions in matters which, in this country, are outside the scope of police work ... Thus the immigrants feel that there is some degree of prejudice when, under the same circumstances here, our police officers refuse to take sides or give any arbitrary decision and refers both parties to either the Court or their civil remedies.[46]

In the 1960s, new recruits to the Met attended training school for an initial period of 13 weeks. As well as academic instruction, drill and physical fitness were elements of the curriculum. At various stages of the initial course students would be required to pass written examinations, and failure to do so would involve the recruit studying that particular aspect of the course again. If the student was once more unsuccessful his services might be dispensed with. This meant that throughout the course students were under intense pressure to reach requisite academic standards. Talks by visiting speakers on 'social issues', such as those on immigrant life in London, did not form part of the overall assessment and recruits were not tested on these subjects. For many recruits, such talks were an opportunity to 'put their feet up' and take a break from formal class work. This state of affairs continued until race relations legislation was enacted from 1965 but, as much of this legislation dealt with issues outside the remit of the criminal courts, there was little requirement other than that officers should be aware of its existence.

The training syllabus was incorporated in the *Metropolitan Police Instruction Book* (the *IB*), a publication that was issued to every officer on joining the Met. It was the constables' training manual throughout the two-year probationary period and examinations were based on its contents. While the *IB* gave brief details of specific race relations legislation that might require police action, it did nothing to raise awareness levels of the difficulties faced by black immigrants when encountering racial discrimination. The *IB* covered legislation and procedure and was rigidly adhered to, as was *General Orders* (*G.O.*), a more detailed volume that covered procedural matters and was essentially aimed at the ranks of sergeant and above. Recruits were encouraged to learn and recite sections of the *IB*, known as 'A' reports, verbatim. An officer of the period summed up his experience of the Met's training methods and their interpretation by London officers:

> I don't think the job [the Met] bred innovative people at all. You learnt the rules at Training School and you went out and carried out the law and the rules. If you went for promotion you were guided by *G.O.* and you stuck to that. I don't remember too many reports, or reading any that actually made this job more innovative. You were very confined to what it said in those books.[47]

The training syllabus was a congested one, and both the police and Home Office were concerned that the inclusion of racial awareness as a permanent feature of police training would inevitably mean that a topic of 'equal importance' might be dropped. It was suggested that, 'race relations training must be balanced in relation to the many other equally important subjects that have to be taught'.[48] Such a view appears hard to sustain when one considers that the Home Office training curriculum for probationary constables (that applied to all police forces in England and Wales outside the Metropolitan Police District) included instruction on such apparently minor and archaic matters as how to deal with pedlars and hawkers.[49]

Training in racial awareness was relatively easy to provide for a captive audience of new recruits. However, for a police force that was seriously undermanned, training was also a drain on resources leaving fewer officers to work the streets. To make matters worse, most experienced policemen saw it as a distraction they could do without. They accepted that there would be occasions when changes in law and procedure would necessitate their re-training, such as in 1967 when the breathalyser was introduced; or 1968, when the Larceny Act was replaced by the Theft Act. But, such occasions apart, a training day would invariably result in only a small number of officers attending.

A major flaw in the provision of race relations training was that the trainers were, in the eyes of many experienced policemen, lacking in credibility.[50] Training school instructors were under pressure to get their students through examinations in policing subjects. They were not appointed for their understanding of immigrant cultures and problems. As a result, the standard of much of the race relations training in the 1960s left a great deal to be desired, as one recruit recalled:

> My introduction to ethnic minority training was a sergeant. He said, 'Well look, if it's a gang of blacks, you'll always find that one is the boss man. So find out who the boss man is and go up to him and tell him what you want the others to do and they'll do it.' That was my first and only introduction to human awareness training.[51]

Many instructors, including the head of the training school, chief superintendent Wall, had spent a period of years at the school and, as such, would have had little or no recent experience of policing immigrant communities. Such a system went against the advice contained in a paper presented to the Working Party on Police Training in Race Relations, which suggested that officers charged with providing such training should possess an intimate knowledge of the problems involved; and that poor handling of the subject by inexperienced instructors might create its own problems.[52]

In response to a parliamentary question on race relations training, chief superintendent Wall stated that multi-racial students of all creeds, colours and social standings attended Hendon to take part in the overseas courses, and went on to paint a rosy picture of life at the Met's Hendon training school: 'There has grown up a happy community whose family life has resulted in mutual understanding and respect for the customs and problems of the various countries of origin and, in addition, proved a useful aid to improve instruction.'[53] While colonial students did attend Hendon, their contact with Metropolitan Police recruits was small, due largely to the fact that students tended to socialise with others on their own particular course. It is also unlikely that any dialogue that did take place would have been helpful in improving race relations in London. When police officers from different forces came together, their conversations invariably focused on hair-raising experiences in pursuit of law-breakers (frequently exaggerated, or drawn from a well of such stories), pay, conditions of service and the difficulties of life for the police themselves. As such, policemen from the Caribbean who may have discussed their own experiences with their London counterparts would probably have confirmed views among Metropolitan officers that West Indians were a real or potential problem.

While new recruits undoubtedly regarded training school staff highly, this was not the case with experienced officers. Instructors were not considered to be 'real policemen' by their colleagues on the streets and probationer constables quickly developed this attitude when they joined their divisions. Commander Goulding, reporting in October 1970, informed the Working Party on Police Training in Race Relations of the way in which familiarity with street policing appeared to have a negative impact on police attitudes to problems faced by immigrant communities:

> With 20 months service the probationer attends a two-week final course at Hendon. This covers the wider sphere of community relations, but some time is also spent on the practical problems involving immigrants. It is at this stage that the probationers sometimes suggest that the matter is over emphasised.[54]

The Working Party on police training in race relations

In September 1969 the Home Office summoned a meeting at Sunningdale in response to concerns that were being expressed regarding police training in race relations. The meeting had been prompted by comments in *Colour and Citizenship*, a book published by the Institute of Race Relations the previous year; and by a recommendation of the Advisory Committee on Race Relations Research that there was a need to, 'evaluate the present arrangements for police training in race relations at all levels, and to identify areas for further research'.[55]

One of the academic delegates at the meeting, Professor Banton, criticised the claim of the Home Office Police Department that the police response to race relations was standard throughout the country, and argued that there were a number of reasons why divergence existed: these included the differences between immigrant communities themselves, that forces and even divisions within forces displayed different attitudes towards law enforcement, and, perhaps most significantly, that training in race relations relied to a large extent on new officers learning from their older colleagues. He put forward a number of proposals, one of which was that a working party should be created from the advisory committee, 'to study the effectiveness and objectives of police training in race relations.'[56]

The Home Office view was that racial problems varied to a greater or lesser degree from one force to another and, as a result, it would be better to deliver race relations training at individual force level, 'where account can be taken of local situations and the dominance of particular ethnic groups'.[57] Banton's criticism appears to be well founded. It is difficult to reconcile the Home Office claim that local needs must predominate in race relations training with its earlier claim that there was a uniform police response nationally to the question of race relations.

In the Metropolitan Police recruits received race relations training during the senior stage of their basic 13-week training. This consisted of a talk given by one of the police liaison officers. Arrangements would also be made for probationers to meet with a representative group from their local community to discuss racial issues during their first 20 months of service. It was found that talks by guest speakers were not well received. As part of their final course at Hendon a speaker from the Community Relations Branch A7 (1) at New Scotland Yard would give a talk on the wider aspects of immigration and associated problems.

Operational police officers saw police liaison officers and those from the Community Relations Branch in much the same light as training school staff: they were officers who were divorced from the real world of everyday policing. As such, they were unlikely to have a positive influence on the attitudes of young officers who were keen to be accepted by their older, street-wise colleagues. Race relations training for experienced officers was even less likely to be well received in view of the low esteem in which those delivering the training were held, and by the already hardened attitudes that existed among many experienced policemen. One such officer recalled his experience of race relations training:

> No training was given until the late '60s. It was given at training school to new recruits – well, a kind of training. The 'old sweats' had to go on one-day courses. To be instructed on how to what and where by someone who has never experienced what and where made such days out a real waste of time.[58]

Banton asked the Working Party to consider an article by Burton Levy entitled 'Cops in the Ghetto'.[59] Levy had studied police attitudes to blacks in Detroit, and argued that problems arose as a result of, 'a set of values and attitudes and a pattern of anti-black behaviour socialised within and reinforced by the police system'. He claimed that police forces recruited from a population (the working class) whose members are more likely than average to possess anti-black attitudes. The basic training of such recruits was unlikely to change these sentiments and, once the recruit went out on the street, he was more likely than not to have his attitudes reinforced and hardened by older policemen. The most able officers were likely to move on to promotion or specialist posts, leaving the remainder to become gradually more cynical, authoritarian and hostile towards the non-police world in general, and towards the black community in particular.[60]

A consideration of Levy's contention in the context of the Metropolitan Police reveals a number of unhealthy comparisons with the situation in the United States. Most of the Met's recruits at this time were drawn from the lower-middle and working classes. Both the Home Office and senior Metropolitan Police officers had expressed concern over the poor standard of education of those joining the service, many of whom had little or no previous knowledge of immigrant communities.[61] The over-congested recruit-training programme allowed only a brief introduction to topics related to immigrants and race relations. Even then, instructors found policemen reluctant to engage in the issues once they had acquired some street knowledge.[62] Experienced officers, whose views on the black community were based primarily on their often-confrontational dealings with them, were even less likely to adopt attitudes promulgated by speakers who they generally regarded as having no experience of the problem.

Recommendations of the Working Party were incorporated in Metropolitan Police racial awareness training from 1971, and included a general programme of sociology and liberal studies as well as additional talks on the background and cultures of the larger immigrant groups in London. However, the Home Office remained unconvinced by academic claims of the 'socialisation' of racist attitudes within the police service. Its view was that, whatever the merits of Levy's research in the context of the United States, the Working Party needed to consider how pertinent such observations were in respect of policing in Britain. It concluded that:

> To accept Mr. Levy's argument in the British context one would have to accept that our police service contains 'a strong racialist element' and that on entering the police service the recruit has his prejudices reinforced. This is not so.[63]

Reflections on race, training and recruitment

John Lambert, writing in 1970, considered the question of race relations training in the police, and argued that alterations to the content without a corresponding change to the style of training might bring about little change, and added:

> If the essential point is that policemen are normally prejudiced, and to a marked extent police work allows the extension of attitudes into

action, then it is no good to lecture and hector men that they must not allow attitudes – political, religious or racial – to affect their behaviour as policemen; and it is insufficient to expose them to addresses by community 'leaders' or race relations 'experts'. A style of training needs to develop which explores how attitudes are expressed and perceived, exactly what 'handling people' means in a multi-racial context.[64]

Such a holistic view of racial awareness training was not considered to be an option in policing circles at the time, and it was to take rioting in Brixton and elsewhere in 1981 to ignite the spark of change – at least for a little while – in police attitudes to training in multi-racial issues. For the time being, such training as there was, was subject to the limits of the training budget, the maintenance of minimum manning levels and the degree of importance placed on race relations by the Met's hierarchy. A former Assistant Commissioner believed that, at the time, the force never took the issue of race relations training seriously:

I became conscious of it when I became DAC [Deputy Assistant Commissioner]. Yes, I suppose mid-1970s was when we really thought we've got to get hold of this properly. I mean we'd paid lip service to it with all sorts of things.[65]

What is perhaps significant about the Met's race relations training in the 1960s was that, in interviews conducted with officers of the period, they either could not recall having received any, or spoke disparagingly of the quality of the training. Yet the programme was running from late 1964, operating at all levels of the service and was emphasised at each stage of training for promoted officers. A major part of the problem with police training in the 1950s and 1960s was that it was bedevilled by an insistence on rote learning and a curriculum that, in terms of its enormous content, crammed far too much into the initial course. For example, the Home Office programme for probationary constables, published in 1963, contained no fewer than 125 different subjects and associated definitions that had to be taught in the 13 weeks of initial instruction. When one considers the generally low standard of academic attainment of the majority of recruits, and that they were required to pass examinations in policing subjects at various stages of the basic course, it seems logical that one session spent discussing race relations – a subject that was not included in the examination syllabus – would have been relatively low priority in the students' overall considerations.

Metropolitan officers were trained on the *Instruction Book*, and *General Orders* (sergeants and above), and stuck rigidly to their guidelines. As one officer put it: 'I don't want to sound disrespectful but they

[*Instruction Book* and *General Orders*] were as important as the New Testament in Rome. You didn't blink unless it said you could blink in *General Orders*.'[66] There was a notable absence of directives in these publications on police involvement with any community, let alone the immigrant one; other than a vague statement in the *Instruction Book* that all law-abiding citizens, irrespective of race, colour, creed or social position should be treated with unfailing patience and courtesy.[67] Only a small handful of officers, whose work was seen as largely irrelevant by the rank-and-file, were engaged in community relations work and in developing dialogue with the black community.

The Met, by its refusal to accept the offer of talks by West Indian Federation staff for its officers, ensured that awareness levels of the difficulties of life in London faced by Caribbean immigrants remained low at a time when racial antagonism and loss of confidence in the police were on the increase. The five years that elapsed before the offer was finally accepted saw a decline in police/Caribbean relations that has continued to the present day. It should not, of course, be forgotten that senior Met officers had not themselves experienced the day-to-day policing of immigrant communities. The 1950s and 1960s witnessed the introduction of major new legislation, all of which it was essential that police officers knew, and were able to administer on a daily basis: a brief example of which would include the Prevention of Crime Act 1953, the Street Offences Act 1959, the Road Traffic Act 1960 and the Theft Act 1968. These, and the many other pieces of criminal law legislation, were the really important issues to which all training was directed.

The Metropolitan Police Commissioner, Sir Joseph Simpson, and the chief constables set different standards for black and white applicants for the police service in the 1960s. Though the Home Office encouraged dialogue on the subject, it shared the police view that black applicants would need to be of a higher standard than their white counterparts and, as such, a racist element was introduced into the selection process. It is difficult to envisage the type of black applicant who would have been acceptable in the first half of the 1960s. Clearly, he would have needed to possess impeccable credentials and be superior to white applicants, have been educated to a high standard, and, as in the case of Norwell Roberts, to possess the tolerance and dignity of a saint:

When I was there [Bow Street Police Station] during the first three years I had match-sticks in the wheels of my car, I was spat at, I was told where to park my car – and it was removed, my tyres were slashed, I had half-crowns down the side of it, I was ostracised, I had cups of tea thrown at me. This is all in the nick, and general degrading treatment like that. I used to go back to the Section House [single officers' quarters] and cry because I had no one to turn to. I'd come back for another dose next day. About nineteen-seventy-odd, it was a nice day and I was walking outside the Opera House, the area car [police instant response car] draws by – you've got the driver, the operator, and the observer – the driver winds the window down, and remember, this is a nice summer's day, he shouts out, 'You black cunt.' Now I was a little bit embarrassed at this because everybody could hear it and I felt a little bit ashamed. So I thought, 'I've had enough of this,' and so I went in and saw the Superintendent. He said, 'What can I do for you?' I related the circumstances and he said, 'Well ye', what do you want me to do about it?' It was only then that I withdrew and thought, 'Fuck it, I've lost,' because it was the first time that I'd allowed anybody to see that they'd got to me and I was more worried about my own self-respect.[68]

It is hard to imagine, therefore, what would have been the attraction to such an individual to a job that, at the time, offered pay rates that were low, and conditions of service and working hours that severely restricted the private lives of police officers. The fact, as Robert Mark pointed out, that black officers would not have been welcome anyway, would probably have been the deciding factor against a life on the beat. A former Met inspector who served at Southall for many years recalled how accurate was Mark's observation, and how an opportunity to recruit high-quality black officers was missed at an early stage:

What I regret is that the Metropolitan Police, along with other forces, didn't move quicker to [sic] recruiting ethnic people into the job. We were pitifully slow . . . It all goes down to us in the early '60s and late-'50s not recruiting these people when we could have done . . . Some of them were constables, sergeants and inspectors who could have been recruited into the job and would have made excellent police officers . . . They'd come in [to the police station] as proud as punch and show you this certificate they'd got when they retired, or decided to emigrate; and they'd got this certificate from their police force. And there we were: 'Bugger off. We don't want you.' They felt this. I found it hard going for a very long time but, coward-like, you didn't say too much because then you're: 'He likes blacks', and all that sort of thing. I can only repeat that we missed a golden opportunity . . . It's too late now. The damage is done and it's going to be with us [the police] for a long time.[69]

The Home Office, despite the meetings it initiated with chief constables and others to highlight issues of black recruitment and racial awareness in the 1960s, had little to offer in the form of practical advice on these issues. It threw its weight behind the police view, the principal architect of which was the Commissioner, that the best way to introduce black men to the police service was by means of a gradual process through the police cadet scheme. Had it been better informed on the subject, it must surely have realised that, in an ever-rising climate of antagonism and resentment between police and the immigrant communities, such a policy was most unlikely to succeed.

However, one should not forget that for all concerned these were uncharted waters: issues without precedent for which neither the police nor the Home Office had a well of knowledge or experience from which to draw comfort. New guidelines on multi-culturalism and human awareness had to be devised as knowledge and understanding gradually increased in a police service that was seriously under-strength, uninformed on issues of cultural and ethnic diversity and with a multitude of other training demands; all of which were more in keeping with its traditional roles and responsibilities.

Notes

1 Interviewed by author, 24 July 2000.
2 NAPRO HO 287/ 273 Annual Reports of the Commissioner of Police of the Metropolis: 1955–59.
3 NA MEPO 2/8614 Nationality Qualifications for Candidates for the Police Service: 1931–50, 1962–63.
4 Ibid.
5 NA HO 325/9 Racial Disturbances, Notting Hill: 1959–61.
6 NA MEPO 2/9854 Police Liaison with West Indian Community in London: 1959–68.
7 Ibid.
8 Roberts interview.
9 NA MEPO 2/9854.
10 Ibid.
11 'D' Department was responsible at the time for recruitment and training.
12 NA MEPO 2/9854.
13 NA HO 287/1458 Recruitment of 'coloured' policemen: policy.
14 A. Dummett, *A Portrait of English Racism* (1963), p.66.
15 NA HO 287/1458 Mark became Metropolitan Police Commissioner in 1972.
16 Ibid.
17 NA MEPO 2/11463 National Police Recruiting Campaign: 1962–69: Metropolitan Police participation.
18 NA HO 287/43 Commissioner's Annual Reports.
19 NA HO 287/1458.
20 Ibid.
21 NA MEPO 2/10435, Commissioner's Conferences 1966.

22 Ibid. This was because in the first two years of service one in every two direct entrants resigned, whereas only one in ten of those entering via the cadet scheme resigned.

23 The minimum height requirement for men had previously been 5'8", and 5'4" for women.

24 Entry could now be gained by passing a written or oral examination in reading, writing and simple arithmetic; or a higher standard as prescribed by the chief officer of police.

25 NA HO 377/76 Recruiting Survey 1969 This referred to a suggestion that sixth-formers with two 'A' levels be recruited to the Cadet Scheme with the offer of time being allocated to complete a higher education course.

26 Ibid.

27 Ibid.

28 NA HO 287/1454.

29 Ibid.

30 Ibid. The writer was a Mr Stotebury.

31 NA HO 287/1458.

32 NA HO 376/135 Police/Immigrants 1965–67. Meeting held 17 January 1966.

33 Roberts interview.

34 NA MEPO 2./10834 Police Federation Outlining Deficiencies in Manpower: 1964–66.

35 NA MEPO 2/11463 National Police Recruiting.

36 Ex chief inspector D. Collinson, interviewed by author, 23 November 2000.

37 Ex police constable D. King, letter to author, 13 December 2000.

38 NA MEPO 2/11283 First Black Policewoman: Press Interest and Racist Correspondence.

39 Roberts interview.

40 Ex chief superintendent S. Higgins, interviewed by author, 21 November 2000.

41 NA HO 287/43 Commissioner's Reports 1955–59.

42 NA MEPO 2/9854.

43 The Police College at Bramshill in Hampshire provides higher-level training for selected officers from all police forces in England and Wales.

44 Ibid.

45 *Parliamentary Debates (Commons)* (8 July 1965), Vol.715, Col.149.

46 NA MEPO 2/9730 Police Training: Methods Employed Concerning the Problems of Immigrant Communities 1965.

47 Sergeant M. English, instructor at the Met's Hendon Training College, interviewed by author, 23 November 2000.

48 NA HO 287/1455 Working Party on Police Training in Race Relations, minutes: 1970.

49 NA HO 287/107 Students' lesson notes 1961 and 1963; training of probationary constables.

50 'Race relations training' was the term used in the 1960s. References to 'awareness training' were not introduced until after Judy Katz's work on the subject at the end of the decade.

51 Ex chief inspector D. Collinson, interviewed by author, 23 November 2003.

52 NA HO 287/1455 (Paper RRT (70)3 Present Arrangements for Police Training in Race Relations.
53 NA MEPO 2/9730 Police training.
54 Ibid.
55 NA HO 287/1455 Working Party on police training in race relations.
56 Ibid. His other recommendations were that there should be a comparative study of law enforcement; a study of attitudes to law and order among immigrant communities; a study of the expectations that immigrants have of the police and a study of complaints against police made by black people.
57 Ibid.
58 Ex PC D. King, letter to author, 13 December 2000.
59 NA HO 287/1455 – (RRT (70) 7) the article had originally appeared in the March–April 1968 edition of *American Behavioural Scientist*. Levy was the Director of the Community Services Division of the Michigan Civil Rights Commission.
60 Ibid.
61 NA HO 377/76 Recruiting Survey, p.13.
62 NA MEPO 2/9730 Police Training, p.25.
63 NA HO 287/1455.
64 J. Lambert, 'Police and the Community', *Race Today* (1970), pp.388–90.
65 Gerrard interview.
66 Higgins interview.
67 *Metropolitan Police Instruction Book*, Ch.1, Item 3.
68 Roberts interview.
69 Ex inspector B. Robbins, interviewed by author, 15 January 2001.

Chapter 6

Negative stereotyping: the Met and the West Indian immigrant

From the Metropolitan Police officers' perspective, post-war London was a mixture of the old and the new. The perennial problem of year-on-year rising crime rates – which would continue throughout the 1950s and 1960s – remained, as did the growth of motorised transportation, which placed an ever-increasing burden on police to keep the capital's arterial roads open and its traffic moving. Moreover, as the killings of police constables Edgar (1948) and Miles (1952) showed, in the aftermath of war, guns were readily available to the criminal classes, and they were not afraid to use them in order to commit crime and to resist arrest.

The capital's housing stock, decimated as it had been by wartime enemy action, was still massively depleted. The inevitable consequence was that more people than ever before resided in multi-occupancy housing of varying standards and degrees of overcrowding. The arrival in London from the late 1940s of growing numbers of predominantly male West Indians had an immediate impact on the life of a city that was still characterised by post-war austerity and rationing.[1] To some, their *joie de vivre* was a breath of fresh air: others considered them to be flamboyant, arrogant and a threat in the competitive market for accommodation, female partners and, later, employment.

As we have seen in previous chapters, the early ambivalence of many Londoners gave way in some sections of British society to a sense of resentment at the increasing numbers of West Indian immigrants now living in their midst. This was exemplified by the 'Keep Britain White' posters that appeared from the mid-1950s in support of right-wing activists, such as Oswald Mosley, and in the vociferously expressed views of politicians such as Norman Pannell and Cyril Osborne, who argued that their alien presence posed a threat to the traditional British way of life. Some members of the white community used racial threats and violence against West Indian immigrants, who increasingly met force with force in order to defend themselves.[2] It fell upon the Metropolitan Police to quell the disturbances that occurred and this resulted in London's West Indian community coming more and more under the Met's spotlight. The increasing presence of people from different parts of the Caribbean in many of London's poorer and most overcrowded districts, and their relations with the indigenous population, presented the Metropolitan Police with problems of racial discrimination and racially motivated crime on a scale that it had not encountered since the 1930s.

It would be difficult to identify any period that might be described as a 'golden age' in relations between London's West Indians and the Met. What is undoubtedly true, however, is that a climate developed during this period in which both sides began to view the other in an increasingly negative manner. The stereotypical policeman was biased, uncaring, prone to use excessive force and willing to lie on oath to obtain convictions: while his West Indian counterpart was considered to be truculent, likely to make unwarranted and unfounded complaints, and to be possessed of violent criminal tendencies and low moral standards. As we will see, one thing that they had in common was that each saw themselves as victims of society.

Police concerns regarding the activities of the West Indian community in the early years of large-scale migration were centred less on traditional crime matters than on public order and morality-based problems related to social inclusion and exclusion. Social inclusion was related to the difficulties that arose from the sharing of housing facilities and the growth of black enclaves, and to the romantic and sexual relationships that crossed the 'colour line'. As the vast majority of West Indians living in London in the early 1950s were male, it followed that their female companions would invariably be white. Hostility to such relationships had as much to do with attitudes on both sides to the dominant and subordinate extremes of the colonial and cultural heritage they shared as it did with general ignorance and misinformation. Social exclusion acted on the West Indian community so as to discourage, and frequently prevent, casual and informal interaction with whites in certain places of public resort, such as pubs and clubs. The operation of a 'colour bar' in these and other premises effectively limited the range of entertainment facilities on offer to West Indians. This invariably resulted in their gathering together socially in each other's homes, often to the annoyance of their white neighbours.

Inter-racial sexual relationships and the social habits of West Indians were interpreted by police and some in white society as symbolic of the alien, deviant influence of black men, and of the threat they posed to law and order. Such considerations coincided with the debate on sexual norms and practices that was current in the 1950s. Police negativity towards West Indians, though certainly not affecting all officers, developed from a combination of adverse personal experience and the experience of colleagues; and can best be described as occupational 'folklore'. Such attitudes were largely the result of an inward-looking culture in which law enforcement was central to the policing ethos. This was allied to the Met's philosophy of what it regarded as acceptable standards of behaviour: standards which at all levels of the police service accorded with the prejudices and values of white society.

Key factors in determining the Met's attitude towards the West Indian community were its self-perception and its view of the general public at a time when notions of community policing were unknown, and the fact that it fulfilled a role within the criminal justice system as both prosecutor and witness for the prosecution. At the same time, many black people were coming to believe that the court system and judiciary legitimised and supported police malpractice. During this period there were many police officers who believed that their value to society was for the most part unrecognised, largely because police officers were poorly paid, police work was low in status and their conditions of service were extremely demanding. In addition, junior-ranking officers lacked the leadership and guidance they were entitled to expect from senior officers. Each of these problems, when added together, made it far less likely that the Met's rank-and-file would have had the inclination to empathise with the plight of alienated groups, such as the West Indian community, ahead of their own worries and frustrations.

In the 1950s and 1960s the force was hidebound by rigidity in thought and deed, factors that prevented an open and imaginative discourse with West Indian immigrants and would ultimately lead to mutual mistrust, resentment and alienation. Unquestionably, the Met's failings from the 1970s onwards in race and diversity matters stemmed from policies and attitudes that were prevalent throughout this period; and included a desire to always put its own interests first, a reluctance to accept criticism from outside its own organisation, and an inability to accept that community and race relations was anything more than the preserve of social workers.

Civil remedies – even-handedness – but no solutions

In January 1952, the town clerk of Kensington Borough Council produced a report entitled, 'The Coloured Population of London'[3] It referred to difficulties that had worsened or had been created by the arrival in London of black immigrants. The writer argued that immigrants, accustomed to much lower standards of hygiene and health, were exacerbating the acute housing shortage and inhibiting the social aspirations of British people for an improved standard of living. He continued:

> The absence of coloured women subjects the coloured immigrant to the temptation of associating with undesirable white women, and there is ample evidence of considerable numbers of coloured men living with convicted prostitutes. In some cases there are grounds for thinking that the men may be living on the immoral earnings of their associates.[4]

The report added that the use of marijuana and Indian hemp appeared to be in common use among some of the immigrant community.

The Met responded by conducting its own inquiries into the claims. The Commander of Number 1 Area stated that, while he agreed on the specific issues raised, he was encouraged by statistical information, which suggested that in routine crime matters black people did not present a problem:

> It is probable that a large number of these coloured men, whose moral standard is very different to ours, would continue to live on prostitution even if there were more coloured women in this country. Although their ethical conduct is deplorably low, the same cannot be said of their honesty. Generally speaking the percentage of convictions for dishonesty among the coloured population is no higher than among white people.[5]

The acting Commander of Number 2 Area (Paddington Green) submitted his own observations in October 1954 in a report entitled 'Coloured People'. Referring to housing difficulties and attitudes to mixed-race relationships, he claimed that some blacks were purchasing poor-class property and seeking to drive out white tenants in order to accommodate black tenants. Other, less affluent blacks, were, he claimed, prone to, 'accept any type of accommodation and herd themselves into small rooms', much to the annoyance of their white neighbours. He believed that there was a certain type of white girl who was attracted to the 'coloured man', and that a number of white people believed that blacks were immoral and that they sought to seduce white women.[6]

The Met's involvement in housing and domestic matters in areas of West Indian settlement was generally confined to dealing with minor assaults and disturbances resulting from disagreements between tenants. This invariably resulted in the police, in the absence of more serious offences being disclosed, referring aggrieved parties to their 'civil remedy'; in other words, courts, solicitors and rent tribunals. Neighbour disputes and common assaults were the so-called 'civil matters' or 'domestics' that the Met had traditionally sought to distance itself from: arguing that as it had no power to prosecute in such cases it should refer complainants to others who might be able to help. Many West Indian immigrants, accustomed as they had been in their homelands to obtaining and acting upon the advice of police in such matters, interpreted what appeared to them to be an unwillingness to help on the part of the Met as a distinct lack of interest in their wellbeing. Sir Peter Imbert, former Metropolitan Police Commissioner, recalled the Met's practice in this regard when asked if it was commonly adhered to: 'Domestic issues. Yes, you're absolutely right. I don't think it was a written down policy. I think it was just the actual [police] culture.'[7]

The culture to which Imbert referred was one in which generations of Met officers had assisted complainants to obtain a summons or bring a charge against another party – for example, a wife bringing proceedings against a bullying husband for assault, or an incident between neigh-bours – only to find that when the matter came to court the complainant had decided not to proceed with the allegation or, as happened in many cases, the complainant failed to turn up. As a result, it became ingrained in the Met's culture that 'domestics' were to be avoided at all costs as they were considered to be a waste of police time. Many West Indians saw such a policy as an act of discrimination against them, especially if they had been the initial victim of an assault or threat.

Throughout the 1950s, and for much of the following decade, the focus of negative attention by police and others on the West Indian community was based upon their alleged ability to corrupt accepted social values, stemming mainly from their liaisons with, and alleged control of, white women; as well as their reputed fondness for drugs and their control of illegal drinking and gaming clubs. How did such negative imagery develop, and how was it to affect relations between the Met and black Londoners? Statements made by senior politicians and police in the 1950s tended to reflect the view that social malaise, rather than racism, lay at the heart of difficulties between blacks and whites. Their comments were also notable for the way in which they implied that black immigration itself had brought about something that was both alien and threatening to Britain's cultural heritage: dangers that were only averted by the inherent qualities of British decency and fair play. We see this in the address to the ACPO Conference in June 1959 by the then Home Secretary, R.A. Butler, whose linguistic signifiers clearly highlight and extol the virtues of 'us', the British, in contrast to the problems that have been introduced to society by 'them', the West Indian community. Speaking of racial tensions in Notting Hill, Butler pointed out that they were, 'entirely foreign to our long traditions', and that such incidents, 'threw into relief the essential normality of our society' in which, 'law and order are taken for granted'. He praised the Met for its handling of the Notting Hill disturbances and reflected how, in areas where black and white had settled down peacefully together, the good sense of the British people could be seen to overcome problems.[8] It is interesting to note that he made no mention of the good sense of the black immigrants.

The evidence suggests that during this period the Met was seriously concerned about the role of West Indian men in the vice trade. It was also determined to keep a firm control on black social clubs, a number of which were unlicensed and had sprung up in various parts of the capital. A former Met senior officer recalled that vice flourished in clubs in the Notting Hill area in the late-1950s:

> You could raid a club and the doorman's got one [a gun] in the shoulder holster, that sort of thing. Ultimately this was all brought under control, but the people who were running the clubs were people with long criminal records and prostitution was rife as well. Vice was the number one priority of the day at Notting Hill because we realised that if we could control vice we could control the area. But it took two-and-a-half years.[9]

Such a perception of the criminal tendencies of West Indians in the 1950s may have been an accurate depiction of a small local problem, but this is difficult to reconcile with what appears to have been the case generally.[10] Members of the Cabinet Committee on Colonial Immigrants (who would have had full access to police reports) at their meeting on 6 June 1957 concurred that immigrants generally conducted themselves well and that their presence did not cause problems of public order. The Committee also noted that, while a minority displayed a tendency to engage in brothel-keeping and living on immoral earnings, the numbers were in themselves quite small.[11]

In 1960 the Met carried out a study of relations between 'white and coloured persons'. Reports on the Brixton sub-division indicated that there was a low risk of racial tension in the area. However, police were closely monitoring the activities of 'coloured clubs', which they frequently raided and made a number of successful applications to the local magistrates court for club licences to be revoked. The Brixton chief superintendent's strategy for combating racial tension included targeted patrols of black areas – including the use of police dogs – and the dispersal of all groups of black or white people from the streets. Though there were not more than half-a-dozen pubs used by black men in the area, these premises were carefully watched. He added:

> The coloured population in Brixton, apart from their club and gaming activities (a small percentage only are involved), are fairly well behaved, and provided we can keep the younger irresponsible

white element away from the coloured areas racial disorder will be prevented.[12]

A notable omission from this report by the head of the Brixton sub-division is any mention of brothel-keeping or living on immoral earnings in his list of illegal black activities.

The study also looked at what were described as 'disturbances involving coloured persons'. One might be forgiven for assuming from the title that there would be some information relating to acts of aggression or other misconduct by members of the black community. However, the incidents referred to are, almost without exception, reports detailing incidents in which black people were the victims of assault or threats of assault. One case in particular is worthy of note. It concerned a middle-aged Jamaican woman who, while standing on the pavement in Notting Hill, was twice spat upon by a white motorist who said, 'You darkie. Why don't you get back to your jungle, you bastard?' The registered keeper of the vehicle was found to be a member of Oswald Mosley's Union Movement. The incident was clearly an offence for which police could themselves have taken action, coming as it did under Section 5 of the Public Order Act 1936 (using threatening, abusive or insulting words or behaviour in a public place); yet acting superintendent Gilbert Kelland (later an assistant commissioner in the Met) declined to take action because, 'from past experience it is known that no assistance would be forthcoming [from the Union Movement] and these persons would no doubt allege that police were again showing bias in favour of coloured persons.'[13]

The study raises a number of issues of concern regarding the Met's policy towards the West Indian community at this time. It is difficult to comprehend why it was that, in an area (Brixton) where the Met's most senior officer admitted that there was a low risk of racial tension, there should be such a concentration of police activity focused on a community that the Met itself described as 'fairly well behaved'. At this time a number of pubs and clubs operated a colour bar, while many other licensees barely disguised their reluctance to entertain black customers. Pilkington's example of a Jamaican who had fought in the British army was typical of the experiences of many:

> When he entered one pub alone he was told that single black men were not allowed in, so he returned with a group of white friends; this time he was told they didn't serve black men in the company of white women.[14]

It would be logical to assume that in such an unwelcome climate, people from the Caribbean would naturally seek the warmth and companionship of other West Indians. The Met's strategy of carrying out regular raids on black clubs, frequented as they were by patrons with virtually nowhere else to go, was almost guaranteed to provoke hostility. The Met's policy in this area was often compounded by vindictiveness and an apparent desire to pin something on those in charge of such premises even when they were not found to be breaking the criminal law. As former Assistant Commissioner Gerrard recalled:

> One of the best cop-outs you could do was if you raided [West Indian] premises and you couldn't do them criminally was to tell the Inland Revenue about them because they didn't know they existed. The Inland Revenue was a very useful backdrop if all else failed.[15]

The Met did not differentiate between young whites seeking confrontation, and black men who – as was their tradition – congregated on street corners to hang out with their friends. If, as the Met claimed, racial disorder could be prevented by keeping the younger irresponsible white element away from the coloured areas, it is highly likely that a tactic of moving along 'well-behaved' blacks from their own areas and subjecting them to the same treatment as young whites on the lookout for trouble was a recipe for resentment. The Met's policy of subjecting the West Indian community to aggressive and discriminatory policing methods in order to 'protect' them from white racists suggests that the Met, in common with many in society, regarded the West Indian presence as the source of the problem. Sir Peter Imbert believed that the Met's tactics in dealing with West Indians was largely the result of ignorance:

> It's often been said that the young Caribbean youth had a street culture whereas the indigenous youth didn't have a street culture in quite the same way. I think that we in the police didn't understand that. When we saw black youth hanging around street corners we couldn't understand why. We automatically thought – quite wrongly of course – on every occasion that they were up to no good. But that was because of a lack of understanding of their culture and their way of life.[16]

This is not to imply that West Indians were without their share of criminals and anti-social types, but rather that the Met's policies in dealing with them helped to focus unjustified and negative attention on the black residents of areas such as Brixton and Notting Hill. At the same time, it laid the foundation for an uncompromising policing methodology in which the illegal activities of a small minority stigmatised many law-abiding West Indians as potential law-breakers in the eyes of the police.

Kelland's fearfulness that the extreme right might accuse the Met of showing bias towards black people is, along with the rest of the report, particularly significant for what it tells us; not only of the Met's heavy-handed and unimaginative tactics, but also of the force's inability to see that its policy of not taking sides in incidents motivated by white racism would inevitably erode black confidence in the police still further. Bulpitt has argued that social modifications in pluralist or capitalists societies are inevitably translated into the political area, and goes on to say that:

> It is generally admitted that racial (and ethnic) political conflicts are awkward to manage because they often assume a zero-sum character – the demands of one group can only be granted by rejecting the demands of other rival groups.[17]

The Met's problem was that it upheld the values of white society. Even the Home Office believed that it was an extremely conservative organisation that was reluctant to change. Yet its frontline role brought it into direct contact with those considered to be black outsiders; people who frequently sought the Met's help in their quest to challenge the very values that the police embodied and embraced. The Met was also a young force, many of its officers having served in the military and in the colonies. Prior to 1964, only a tiny minority of its officers had received any training in West Indian cultures and customs. It was highly unlikely, therefore, that the Met's officers would understand and empathise with the problems encountered by the West Indian community on a daily basis.

A strong case can unquestionably be made against Metropolitan Police senior officers who never appreciated the potential goodwill that would have resulted had they taken action to deal with the divisive effects of racially motivated verbal and physical attacks on black immigrants, particularly in the 1950s, a period before black disillusionment with the police had firmly taken hold. The Met stuck rigidly to its time-honoured practice of telling victims of 'minor' assaults to instigate their own proceedings. Such unhelpfulness tended to confirm black attitudes that police were an integral part of a white, racist society. Blinkered by its 'we've always done things this way' attitude, the Met took exception to complaints from black people that it was ignoring their concerns and did not accept that its procedures were in need of revision. To Scotland Yard the situation was clear. Allegations of common assault had always been dealt with by advising complainants to pursue their own legal remedies. Blacks were getting the same advice as whites when making such allegations and so it logically followed that they were being treated in exactly the same way as everyone else. What the Met failed to comprehend, or chose to ignore, was the significance of racial motivation in the vast majority of such assaults; the aggravating dimension that this introduced to the particular crime; and the detrimental effect that police inactivity would have on the support and confidence of the West Indian community.

Looked at from the Met's perspective, however, one might argue that such criticism of the force at this time ignores the fact that at least some West Indian immigrants may have had unrealistic expectations of the police role in Britain. A Special Branch report of May 1959 described the majority of West Indian immigrants as, 'simple-minded people, extremely naïve; sadly misinformed and ill-equipped to start a new life in this country'.[18] While these observations were clearly patronising and dismissive, it cannot be denied that prior to 1964, when the Met began producing information booklets for Jamaican immigrants,[19] West Indians would have had little or no knowledge of Metropolitan Police procedures. Given the structure of the Met at the time, and the absence of specific legislation to deal with racial discrimination prior to 1965, it may well have been unrealistic to expect the Met to deal with black victims of crime – who represented a tiny minority of the capital's population – in a different manner to the way it dealt with victims generally.

'Oh white woman in the nude, working hard for the black man's food'[20]

The issue of sexual relations between black men and white women became part of the ongoing moral dilemma over sex and criminality that was to continue throughout the 1950s and early 1960s. Opposition to inter-racial sex was considerable, not only among many in the host community but also among a number of black women; some of whom argued that such liaisons were a waste of a black man.[21] Richmond, in his study of colour prejudice in Liverpool over a ten-year period from 1951, noted the twin effects of these relationships.[22] Firstly, it provoked intense prejudice against West Indian men involved in sexual relations with white women; secondly, it stigmatised the women concerned in the eyes of those who considered themselves to be respectable. The chairman of the WISC endorsed this view, and described his own experiences of indigenous attitudes to mixed-race relationships in London in the 1960s:

> If you had a white girlfriend, a white woman with a black man, she was a prostitute. She had to be a prostitute. No decent white woman would ever go to bed with a black man, or could ever love a black man. She had to be a prostitute. At that time it was the whole concept . . . She had no moral fortitude at all.[23]

Such concerns were at the heart of what was considered to be the role of women in the patriarchal climate of the 1950s and 1960s Britain; and were perceived as an external corrupting threat to white male hegemony, and to accepted standards of decency, morality and behaviour. Sexual relations between black men and white women, whether resulting from affection and love, or the lure of the new, the forbidden and the exotic, became a paradigmatic reference during the period for women who had turned their backs on respectability, and were seen as being over-sexed, of low moral standards or 'on the game'. Referring to such relationships, Gilroy observed that:

> Race was thus fixed in a matrix of squalor and that of sordid sexuality. In this context, miscegenation, which captured the descent of white womanhood and recast it as a signifier of the social problems associated with the black presence emerged ahead of crime as a theme in the popular politics of immigration control.[24]

There existed a double standard in sexual morality in which women were the perennial guilty party in carnal indiscretions and alleged immorality between the sexes. Thus, while the Home Secretary, R.A. Butler, was able to inform the Commons in 1959 that over the preceding two years there had been no fewer than 12,000 cases brought against women in the Met's West End Central Division for soliciting, he could not produce any figures for offences contrary to Section 32 Sexual Offences Act 1956, which related to men importuning women.[25] As Sydney Silverman MP tersely remarked when the Bill to remove prostitutes from the streets was debated in the Commons, 'It is accepted as a crime to offer for sale what it is not a crime to buy.'[26]

But how extensive was the black involvement in controlling prostitutes and living off their immoral earnings? Addressing the Commons on 30 January 1954, the Home Secretary, Sir David Maxwell-Fyfe, had little doubt that black men were involved in significant numbers:

> Figures I have obtained from the Metropolitan Police do show that the number of coloured men convicted for this offence is out of all proportion to the total number of coloured men in London and the police say that the practice is much more widespread than the number of convictions would appear to indicate.[27]

However, a somewhat different picture emerges of West Indian involvement in the vice trade when we consider the statistical information provided by Norman Pannell MP, a man not renowned for his fondness of the black community, during the Street Offences Bill debate in January 1959. Pannell produced figures to show that for the year 1956:

There were 106 convictions in the Metropolitan Police area for the offence of living on immoral earnings, 74 of which – or 70 per cent – concerned immigrants from the Republic of Ireland or Colonial or Commonwealth countries. There were 11 from the Republic of Ireland; 37 from Malta; 18 from West Africa and 5 from the West Indies.[28]

One might conclude that Maxwell-Fyfe's reference to 'coloured men' was no more than usage of a common term of the period to describe all those who could not be classified as white British. Although Pannell's figures implied that West Indians were less of a problem than other immigrant groups, statistics given at the Metropolitan Police Commissioner's conference on 8 October 1963 revealed that in the previous year there had been 194 convictions for living on immoral earnings, of which 43 were described as West Indian, 27 were Maltese and 19 came from the Irish Republic.[29]

A significant number of Metropolitan officers from the 1950s and 1960s have suggested that West Indian involvement in prostitution was large-scale and organised. In all probability, West Indian participation in vice varied over time. This would account both for Maxwell-Fyfe's 1954 assertion that it was 'out of all proportion', and for 1956 figures showing only five convictions that year. West Indian pimps may have also been convicted of offences for which a prison term took them, if only temporarily, out of the equation. Additionally, from 1 July 1962, the courts began to use powers contained in the Commonwealth Immigrants Act to deport men convicted of living on immoral earnings. Black ponces may have been few in number but they did incalculable harm to the image of black society in general and West Indian men in particular; especially in the eyes of the police, who increasingly came to see the West Indian community in terms of its perceived criminal predisposition. Norwell Roberts provided a different view of the relative roles of police and black men in the West End vice trade of the 1960s, when asked who was controlling prostitution at the time:

> Bent coppers of course: Superintendent [name withheld] and a few others who were getting loads of money. These people, as I know now in retrospect, had black pimps who were paying the coppers . . . the black pimps were under the control of the people on vice, the PCs.[30]

But if decent, law-abiding West Indians believed that they were being falsely maligned by a society that was prejudiced, this was nothing in comparison to the extent to which police officers had come to see themselves as the real victims of both the community at large and the police service itself.

Society's disaffected minority: the Metropolitan Police

There can be little doubt that in the 1950s and 1960s one alienated group, London's West Indian community, was policed by another alienated group, the Metropolitan Police. Between October 1967 and January 1968 the Home Office conducted a survey among 3,075 police officers from constable to chief superintendent rank in England, Scotland and Wales. Part of the survey is reproduced in Tables 6.1 and 6.2.

Table 6.1 Survey of police officers who had seriously considered resigning from the police service

Home Office Table 123
'Have you at any time seriously considered resigning from the police service?'[31]

| | | Satisfaction Score | |
	Satisfied %	Fairly dissatisfied %	Very dissatisfied %
Has seriously considered resigning	18	47	81
Has never seriously considered resigning	82	53	19
	100	100	100
BASES All constables and sergeants (before weighting)	520	1,505	620

Table 6.2 Survey of police officers who thought they would stay in the police service until they were eligible for pension

Home Office Table 124
'Do you think you will stay in the police service until you are eligible for a pension?'[32]

| | | Satisfaction Score | |
	Satisfied %	Fairly dissatisfied %	Very dissatisfied %
Will probably stay till eligible	98	93	75
Will probably leave	1	5	19
Unable to say at present	1	2	5
Already eligible for a pension	–	–	1
	100	100	100
BASES All constables and sergeants (before weighting)	520	1,505	620

The figures show that almost one officer in five of those constables and sergeants who expressed satisfaction with the job had seriously considered resigning from the police service. Almost 50 per cent of those who were fairly dissatisfied, and over 80 per cent of those who stated that they were very dissatisfied, had seriously considered leaving the police. Despite such high levels of dissatisfaction, over 90 per cent of those who were fairly dissatisfied, and 75 per cent of constables and sergeants who were very dissatisfied with police work, added that they would probably remain in the police until they could collect their pensions. One sees, therefore, that a great many police officers felt unfulfilled in their chosen career but were prepared to soldier on for pensionable purposes. This begs the question: how would such dissatisfied individuals, possessed as they were of powers to arrest and prosecute, behave towards the community they policed; particularly in confrontational and challenging situations?

Also in 1967 the Home Office conducted a survey in Liverpool and Manchester on the question of premature wastage from the police.[33] Though constables enjoyed their work, their major concerns were that senior officers were out of touch with the problems faced by men on the beat; there were insufficient free weekends; there was too much petty discipline; too little was spent on modern equipment; and the police service was obsessed with tradition.[34] Problems did not end, however, when a policeman went home. In many cases alienation from the community continued in the officer's off-duty time. As one observer noted:

> Policemen are an identifiable minority and are to some extent shunned by the non-police public. This is particularly true when police houses are grouped together, and certainly for single policemen living in Section Houses ... the police are also expected to set an example in their private life for the rest of the community and the police disciplinary code reinforces this in encompassing their off-duty behaviour. And so the policeman is set apart from the rest of the community, yet is expected to be well integrated with that community to carry out a major part of his role.[35]

In spite of the bond that existed between the junior ranks of the police service and their enjoyment of police work, other factors came into play that made policing in the Met a less than attractive option. Pay rates were low and the three-month shift pattern (two months of day duties and one month of night duty), which included compulsory worked rest days, was decidedly unattractive.[36] This was made even worse by the requirement that night duty arresting officers had to attend court the following morning with overnight charges, followed later that day by another tour of night duty. Not surprisingly, wastage rates were extremely high. In his annual report for 1965, Simpson noted that:

> At a time of full employment, the turnover rate in any job or profession is at its highest; there is no exception in the police service. In 1965 the wastage of men resigning before qualifying for pension, mostly in the first few years of service, maintained the average of recent years at a figure of 495 which represents over 40 per cent of the annual intake of recruits.[37]

An added irritant for Metropolitan officers was the fact that they were always likely to have their few weekends off disrupted by one or more of the Met's numerous public order commitments, which regularly included sporting events, political demonstrations and marches. Low rates of pay ensured that many officers and their families lived in police houses or flats, some in matrimonial quarters above police stations. This practice tended to ensure that both on- and off-duty time was spent in a police environment in which the men, their wives and children lived and socialised together. Other factors limiting an officer's freedom of choice included a requirement that they refrain from taking an active part in politics; and the obligations not only to obtain permission to live at premises that were not provided by the police, but also to marry the partner of one's choice. The London weighting allowance in the mid-1960s of £20 per year did nothing to aid recruitment to the Met, or to prevent Met officers opting to further deplete the capital's policing establishment by transferring to forces in more pleasant parts of the country.[38]

The junior ranks of the police service unquestionably saw themselves as a body that performed an extremely difficult, often tedious and dangerous job that set them apart from the rest of society, and for which they received meagre financial remuneration. These feelings of alienation could be, and often were, directed also at the higher ranks of the police; particularly those who no longer worked anti-social hours, and who, as the survey in Liverpool and Manchester showed, were considered to inhabit 'ivory towers'.[39] As such, divisions could, and did, occur within the police as well as between the police and the community.

In February 1965, the Deputy Commander of the Met's Research and Planning Unit, George Howlett, presented the results of his study into the supervision by duty officers [inspectors] and sergeants of police constables.[40] Howlett's terms of reference were to:

(i)   Enquire into the extent to which duty officers and section sergeants have become engaged on paperwork to the detriment of supervision,

(ii)   Establish whether this work is essential and, if so, whether it is susceptible to rationalisation, and

(iii) In the event that a serious situation should disclose itself, to seek a means of redirecting the various ranks concerned to their primary functions.[41]

Howlett found that the amount of time spent dealing with paperwork by duty officers and sergeants had increased dramatically over the course of the preceding 10 to 15 years. Some 75 per cent of the augmentation could be accounted for by the increase in summonses for motoring offences, double those of the years preceding the Second World War. When looking at the role of superintendents and chief inspectors, Howlett found that they also tended to spend much of their time tied to their desks:

> When a process section has been authorised and was led by an inspector ... it was evident that a reasonable amount of time was available to these officers [superintendents and chief inspectors] for purposes other than paperwork but elsewhere a situation seemed to exist where they were preoccupied with paperwork, often of a routine nature, to the exclusion of personal supervision, proper contact with the men and the conception of fresh ideas and plans for combating the problems of their area.[42]

Howlett noted that many constables had complained that they rarely saw their superintendents after they had completed their probationary period. More than half of each working day was being spent by supervisory officers inside the police station, rather than, 'in the direction, advice and encouragement so necessary to the efficient performance of street duty and to the morale of constables'.[43]

   Howlett's report was considered by the Assistant Commissioner 'D' Department (ACD) who submitted his own observations in a memorandum of 22 February 1965 to the Assistant Commissioner. In it he made reference to the use of 'Book 92', a book in which Met officers were required to record visits to, and time spent in the police station. Constables could be dealt with as defaulters if they failed to record their visits or if they remained in the station for too long. ACD noted that:

> They [constables] know full well that the officers who are supposed to be supervising them are quite deliberately making false entries in the Duty Books in regard to their own visits to the stations, and are frequently not recording them at all. This leads to bad discipline and a serious deterioration in officer/man relationships. In a word, it is another example of extremely bad man-management.[44]

He went on to suggest that senior officers in the Met were obsessed with paperwork, adding that: 'every piece of paper submitted . . . to *CO [Commissioner's Office] has to be checked two or three times at various levels for fear of submitting something which may contain a mistake. It has become almost a fetish.'[45]

One sees here a situation in which Metropolitan Police constables were receiving precious little in the way of leadership, support and encouragement from practically every supervisory level from sergeant to chief superintendent, the vast majority of whom appeared to spend much of their time shuffling paperwork; most of which was of a routine or trivial nature. There can be little wonder, therefore, that at a time when the Met was seriously undermanned and wastage rates were extremely high, those officers who remained developed a resentment of senior officers who were seen to be out of touch with the difficulties that were being encountered at street level. In the absence of quality leadership and supervision, it was perhaps inevitable that police deficiencies and malpractices would increasingly come to light. Nonetheless, camaraderie among the lower ranks remained strong, as one officer of the period recalled: 'If a cock up was discovered the PBs [pocket books] and OBs [Occurrence Books] were rewritten "to close the gates".'[46]

Given such resentment and alienation, one might well wonder why more officers did not opt to leave the Met. There were a number of reasons why those who remained did so. Firstly, while senior officers gave little in the way of leadership to their men, they were also individuals who had gone through the system and had themselves experienced the hardships of life on the beat. As a result, they often compensated for inadequacies in leadership and supervision by a generosity in welfare matters. An officer recalled the prevailing attitude to welfare in the Met when he was seriously assaulted on duty:

> When I was originally injured the superintendent had my wife brought to the hospital. She had a car each time she wanted to visit me. Anything she wanted she phoned the nick and she had the ear of the duty officer. Nothing was ever too much trouble. I was raised in the job to work and play hard. If the wheel came off then up went the defensive walls from the top down. Comradeship was paramount. The job came first.[47]

Secondly, senior officers turned something of a blind eye to certain longstanding malpractices. These involved what might be termed cases of low-level corruption, and included such time-honoured procedures as the 'golden hook',[48] 'mumping' and 'blagging'.[49] The third saving grace from the constables' perspective was the way in which only a minority of complaints were ever substantiated by senior officers who, in the absence of overwhelming proof, would always side with their junior colleagues rather than a complainant. Thus, in an atmosphere where comradeship was paramount and indiscretions went largely un-punished, constables generally believed that they had licence to operate as they saw fit. In consequence, and in spite of the shortcomings of life in the police, there were opportunities for the unscrupulous to take advantage of their position in cash and kind.

How then was the disaffection of the men on the beat displayed in their dealings with the public, particularly the Caribbean community? Police disillusionment had bred a culture in which officers increasingly referred to themselves as victims. They protected society from its worst vices, in some cases paying the ultimate price for doing so, yet while right-minded people regarded them as the world's finest, they also faced malicious and unfounded complaints (especially, they argued, from the West Indian community), and accusations of lying on oath. On 1 September 1968, *The Observer*, in an article entitled 'Police brush up their race relations', noted that police were complaining that discrimination was working in favour of immigrants because police were fearful of complaints of racial harassment. According to one officer:

> So many actions you take as a police officer have to be selective . . . you can't stop everyone for speeding. These days if you are a coloured man you may be less likely to be stopped. The officer doesn't want the risk of a complaint.[50]

Such fears, however, had little factual basis. Of 127 complaints made by black people against the Met in the 12-month period from 1 April 1961 to 31 March 1962, only six were substantiated.[51] General complaint figures for 1968 revealed that of 909 allegations of offences committed by Metropolitan officers (excluding traffic offences), only 12 were substan-tiated;[52] and in the case of specific allegations of racial discrimination by Met officers in 1969, of 41 complaints, none were substantiated.[53] A former sergeant at West Ham police station recalled a telephone conversation with his area commander in the 1970s concerning the possibility of a complaint ensuing from the death of an Asian man in police custody:

> I had a telephone call from the Commander asking for a bit more detail about it. He asked me, 'What colour was he?' I said that he was an Asian. He said, 'Well don't worry then.' He didn't realise that I was an Asian.[54]

The police view that they were hard done by became progressively more significant as pressure for greater political control grew from the mid-1950s. In 1960 the *Police Review*, in apparent exasperation, began an article entitled 'Who is the prisoner?' by suggesting that, 'The number of policemen who step down from the witness box feeling uncertain whether it is they or the prisoner in the dock who is on trial is increasing.'[55] Such feelings of frustration and indignation shaped police attitudes towards the community. The result was that people from the Caribbean living in London could expect little in the way of empathy for the difficulties they encountered from a police force that at the top was determined to steer its own independent course; whose middle-ranking officers were largely preoccupied with paperwork and thoughts of enhancing their own careers; and policemen on the beat who lacked adequate guidance and support from supervisory officers, and whose minds were firmly focused on their own problems. As a former chief superintendent recalled:

> There was no conception at all of customer care. When people came to the counter they waited. Anything and everything that came across the counter was yours, and sergeants were having break-downs ... They [the public] weren't customers. They were people with problems and you had more than enough problems to deal with.[56]

Sir Peter Imbert concurred with the observation that police officers believed they were taken advantage of by society, when asked if the police felt hard done by at this time:

> Yes. I wouldn't disagree with you. Because the police were not paid properly and they needed to hold their head up in the community, I think a lot of them felt that because they couldn't afford decent homes or cars, that they were doing the menial tasks ... I'm sure they did at times, yes. They have done throughout this whole time.[57]

Two decades on: from bad to worse

Two issues become immediately apparent when we consider the way in which the Metropolitan Police dealt with the Caribbean community in this period. Firstly, the crimes of the individual came to be seen as the crimes of the community; and secondly, the police response to black crime was uncompromising firmness in which the end was not infre-quently seen to justify the means. A collective imagery developed in which each side viewed the other in increasingly negative terms. As one officer put it, 'the police at times were being very judgemental. If they saw a black person then that black person must be up to no good, especially if he was a young person.'[58] The same officer described the way in which some members of the West Indian community set out to tarnish the Met's reputation:

The more fringe elements of the West Indians complained about being arrested, taken to a police station and beaten up. They used to talk about being beaten up almost as though night follows day. It became part of the language of the media and it was a throwaway line, 'beaten up'. They hadn't been arrested, so there was dirty play on both sides.[59]

There are a number of reasons that can be advanced to explain why such an unhealthy relationship developed between the Met and London's West Indians at a time when police inadequacies were beginning to attract attention and racial discrimination was increasingly prompting calls for government action. Firstly, the Met viewed 'community relations' as little more than the means by which it could obtain better criminal intelligence from the public, and as an early warning system that would enable the Commissioner to forestall or respond positively to criticism of his force.

Secondly, the Met's promotion system inhibited the chances of developing long-term strategies to address particular problems, such as community relations. The important thing for those seeking promotion was to convince a Promotion Board that the individual had acquired a varied range of skills and experiences, both at divisional level and in specialist posts.[60] This often meant that, in order to 'catch the eye', those seeking promotion would invariable seek a posting to whatever was currently fashionable with the Met's hierarchy.[61] As a result, some officers would – not infrequently with the help of friends in higher places – seek postings to specialist departments, such as community relations, to which their skills were not always suited. In addition, when an officer left a specialist post it was invariably the case that the new incumbent, keen to impress with his own stamp of authority and initiative, would quickly set about dismantling the work of his predecessor so that his own distinctive contribution would be evident and recognised. Succession planning, therefore, was, and remained for many years, virtually nonexistent and the good work of one officer could be instantly destroyed by his successor. We see this in the Met's response to accusations of deteriorating relations between the organisation and the Caribbean community, which were raised at a Colonial Office meeting in December 1961. In answer to the claim, made by Mr De Souza of the WIF, it was noted that the police liaison officer, 'believed that recent movements of senior police officers in some of the areas concerned might account for possible changes of attitude'.[62]

Perhaps more importantly, by its failure to include the public in developing its policing strategy, the Met merely enforced the law and its own priorities and took no account of Caribbean cultural differences and social problems. The fact that the judicial system appeared to support the police added to the sense of frustration and alienation felt by many in the West Indian community. Police prosecutions in the 1950s and 1960s differed markedly from the system in operation today. There was no Crown Prosecution Service (CPS), and the Metropolitan Police Solicitors' Department (MPSD) conducted the majority of prosecutions in the Met. In magistrates' courts it was not uncommon for prosecutions – including the cross-examination of witnesses – to be conducted by police officers themselves. There was no concept of police as the 'independent investigator'. The police function in criminal investigations today is to investigate and impartially weigh the evidence, interview witnesses and suspects, and present their findings to the CPS, where the ultimate decision on whether or not the case should proceed to trial is made. In the period under consideration, police officers saw their role entirely differently.

In the 1950s and 1960s police investigations were, to a large extent, suspect based. This meant that if a person was arrested for an alleged crime, the police saw it as their role to prove the case against that individual. The surest way to do this was by means of a written statement of admission by the accused, or by way of a 'verbal' admission of guilt. Both of these practices were widely criticised by defendants and the legal profession.[63] An officer of the period described the way in which criminal investigations were conducted:

> We had no concept of the independent investigator. The police would say, 'You've done it', and they would work the evidence around the fact that they had done it. That's why you're getting so many cases coming to the surface. If you were a really wicked so-and-so and you had an envelope from a witness who said, 'He couldn't have done the murder because he was in Blackpool with me', if that wasn't part of your case you'd put it over there [to one side] because there was no requirement in those days to disclose [evidence]. But you've got to bear in mind; it was thirty or forty years ago.[64]

Many in the West Indian community regarded the criminal courts, especially the magistrates' courts, as endorsing what they believe was an unfair system of justice. Indeed, the magistrates' courts were, as if to emphasise the power of the police, colloquially known as the 'police courts'. The chairman of the WISC described the way in which magistrates tended to view accusations by West Indian defendants that police had lied or acted improperly:

When you went to court and you explained to the magistrate he would tell you straight up, 'A British officer would never do such a thing.' The magistrate would not believe it. We used to call it the police court because you had no say, absolutely no say. It was a waste of time saying 'Not Guilty'. The magistrates were out of the same mould and had the same philosophy.[65]

The Commissioner and his senior colleagues knew that relations between the Met and London's West Indians were deteriorating. The problem was how to improve them. The Met had a simple answer. West Indians should start behaving like everybody else: obey the law and stop complaining, because policemen had enough problems to deal with.

Though Scotland Yard's Community Relations Branch was up and running from 1968, it failed to establish a constructive dialogue with the West Indian community for two basic reasons. First, in the 1960s neither liaison with the wider community nor the specific subject of race relations was sufficiently high on the Met's list of priorities to convince those at Scotland Yard that the force needed to change. Secondly, though community liaison officers made welcoming noises, their efforts were not backed up at street level, the place where it really mattered. Race relations meant something different to the men on the beat, who were not averse to incorporating the term into what can only be described as police humour. A good example of which was the 'Marples Marble', so called after Ernest Marples, a minister of transport of the period:

Each area car in Brixton had a supply of glass marbles. On finding an excellent piece of driving by a black driver, when stopped he would be congratulated and given a 'Marples Marble'. He was told that when he had collected three marbles he was to take them in to Streatham nick [police station] and collect his good driving prize. This idea improved the driving habits in the district for months. Sadly, some actually got three marbles and took them to Streatham [where they] did not know about the scheme and didn't have any prizes. Race relations, '60s style.[66]

Between November 1969 and March 1970 internal research was conducted into the work of the Met's Community Relations Branch.[67] The authors of the report conducted interviews with a number of police officers on the specific subject of race relations. The majority view was that black people were the architects of their own misfortune in their dealings with police because of their tendency to behave awkwardly and aggressively when approached. In conclusion, the authors stated that the concept of community/police relations was poorly understood – if not misunderstood – by many officers. The problem was compounded by a lack of knowledge of the subject by police officers; there was a reluctance to change; a fear of dealing with issues for which they, 'did not have a great deal of sympathy or understanding'; there was a blinkered view of community relations in which the police function was seen purely in terms of law enforcement; and there was a reluctance to see any benefit in what were regarded as social work matters like community relations.[68]

The 1985 Policy Studies Institute (PSI) research into relations between the Met and the people of London referred to a time (ten years previously – 1975) 'when CLOs were despised by "operational" police officers, and regarded as soft-centred do-gooders or public relations men'.[69] If this was the case in the mid-1970s, one might assume that the attitude of 'operational' police officers to CLOs in the preceding decades would have been even less accommodating. Senior Met officers simply failed to grasp the importance of positive relations with London's minority ethnic communities and, when investigating complaints by black people against its officers, merely demonstrated their support and endorsement of the activities of the junior ranks. Dick Taverne remembered his talks with police officers in Brixton and elsewhere during his time as a Home Office Minister in the mid-1960s:

> A lot of the ordinary police were very reactionary. A lot of them said, 'Well, we've got to deal with these criminals. What we should do is beat them on the soles of their feet', that kind of attitude . . . Of course, a lot of the crime in mixed areas would be black crime . . . those who lost on the swings lost on the roundabouts as well. Their [the police's] natural reaction was that there were far more blacks committing crimes proportionately than whites, and we've just got to deal with them. It became a sort of prejudice against blacks. There was no doubt that a lot of police had racist views, racist views and reactionary views.[70]

Throughout the period under consideration, the Met's approach to the public it served was largely confrontational, centred on a 'them and us' outlook in which rules and regulations were enforced on a community that the Met, as an organisation, was set apart from. The problem was compounded by the acute awareness among the junior ranks of their own difficulties, poor wages and low status. As one officer put it, 'when the law was enforced police were respected and the policeman felt that he was the "governor" '.[71] A former chief superintendent's observation of policing in London's West End in the 1960s shows how alienated the Met was from the community it 'served':

> Thinking back, it was almost as though we were at war. Providing the public behaved itself and didn't come into contact with us then

by and large that was OK. But if they did come into contact with us then woe betide them. Nobody actually escaped the police in those days. We would report hundreds, if not thousands, of motorists; and, at night, certainly Friday and Saturday nights, we'd be out hunting youngsters who'd had a few pints.[72]

It was indeed unfortunate in this period that, in response to the ever-worsening nature of its relationship with the capital's West Indian community, a lack of interest, a blinkered view and a reluctance to change remained the order of the day for the Metropolitan Police.

Notes

1 It was not until the early to mid-1950s that West Indian women migrated to Britain in substantial numbers.
2 Mosley had been the leader of the pre-war British Union of Fascists. After the war he led the Union Movement, a political party with a racist agenda. Paul, *Whitewashing Britain*, (p.139) refers to black/white clashes taking place in Camden Town in 1954 and at Deptford in 1949, as well as the more widely publicised disturbances at Notting Hill in 1958.
3 NA MEPO 2/9047 Reports on settlement of 'coloured' Commonwealth immigrants in London Boroughs: 1949–52.
4 Ibid. See also NA MEPO 2/10432 Commissioner's Conferences notes and minutes 1963.
5 NA MEPO 2/9047 Report dated 28 March 1952.
6 NA MEPO 2/9563 Reports on settlement of 'coloured' Commonwealth immigrants in London Boroughs: 1949–52.
7 Imbert interview.
8 NA HO 287/43.
9 Gerrard interview.
10 Many of those with long criminal records who operated such clubs were, in fact, white British.
11 NA CAB 134/1466 Section 30 Sexual Offences Act 1956 made it an offence for a man to live wholly or in part on the earnings of prostitution.
12 NA MEPO 2/9992 Disturbances involving 'coloured' person in London. Metropolitan Police reports on incidents: 1960–61.
13 Ibid.
14 E. Pilkington, 'The West Indian community and the Notting Hill riots of 1958', in E. Panayi (ed.) *Racial Violence in Britain in the Nineteenth and Twentieth Centuries* (Leicester: 1996), p.174.
15 Gerrard interview.
16 Imbert Interview.
17 J. Bulpitt, 'Continuity, Autonomy and Peripheralisation: the Anatomy of the Centre's Race Statecraft in England', in Z. Layton-Henry and P.B. Rich (eds.) *Race, Government and Politics in Britain* (1986), p.19.

163

18 NA HO 325/9.
19 See Appendix II.
20 The start of the second verse to a 1950s racist song based on Harry Belafonte's *Island in the Sun*. See page 20.
21 An observation made by a Trinidadian lady who arrived in Britain in the 1960s, in conversation with the author, 2002.
22 Richmond, *Colour Prejudice* (1954), p.77.
23 Thompson interview.
24 Gilroy, *Union Jack* (1987), p.80.
25 Parliamentary Debates (Commons) (29 June 1959), Vol.598, Cols.1282–84: during the debate on the Street Offences Bill.
26 Ibid. Col.1301.
27 Quoted in Gilroy, *Union Jack*, p.79.
28 *Parliamentary Debates (Commons)* (29 January 1959), Vol.598, Col.1317.
29 NA MEPO 2/10432 Commissioner's Conferences, 1963.
30 Roberts interview (former Metropolitan Police detective sergeant and London's first black policeman).
31 NA HO 377/85. Man Management Survey by the Home Office Police Planning Organisation – January 1970.
32 Ibid.
33 NA HO 377/43 Pilot experiment on premature wastage of officers from the police service 1967.
34 Ibid.
35 N. Deakin, *Colour, Citizenship and British Society*, pp.349–50.
36 Day duties comprised early (6 a.m.–2 p.m.) and late (2 p.m.–10 p.m.) shifts, as well as a spare 8-hour shift covering office hours or late evening and early morning (6 p.m.–2 a.m.). Night duty was from 10 p.m.–6 a.m.
37 NA MEPO 4/213 *Report of the Commissioner of Police of the Metropolis 1965*, p.8.
38 London weighting was raised to £50 per annum in April 1966. See Ascoli, *The Queen's Peace*, pp.293–4.
39 NA HO 377/43.
40 NA MEPO 2/10434 Commissioner's Conferences 1965.
41 Ibid.
42 Ibid. Process sections were administrative offices, largely staffed by non-police personnel dealing with the paperwork side of traffic matters. An inspector or chief inspector invariably headed each unit.
43 Ibid.
44 Ibid. Book 92 was subsequently abolished.
45 Ibid.
46 Ex PC D. King, letter to author, 3 January 2001. The OB was effectively a station diary of notable events occurring over a 24-hour period.
47 Ibid.
48 In which an officer called to deal with an accident, as a result of which one or more vehicles had to be towed from the scene, would call a local garage to remove the vehicle(s) and would received a cash sum by way of thanks from the garage.
49 'Mumping' and 'blagging' were expressions used for the practice of obtaining goods or services for nothing, or at greatly reduced price, because the

individual was a policeman. The most successful mumpers and blaggers were considered to be home beat officers and the CID.

50 *The Observer* (1 September 1968).
51 NA MEPO 2/9854.
52 NA MEPO 2/10790.
53 NA MEPO 2/10791.
54 Bhamra interview.
55 *Police Review*, No.3503, Vol.43 (4 March 1960), p.173.
56 Higgins interview.
57 Imbert interview.
58 Higgins interview.
59 Ibid.
60 Command areas within London are now based on borough boundaries and the term 'Division' is no longer in use.
61 In the late 1980s the author was offered a job on the Met's PLUS team and was told that such a posting would virtually guarantee promotion to the next rank.
62 NA CO 1032/331 Immigration into the United Kingdom from the West Indies: 1960–62.
63 The oral admission was widely known as a 'verbal' and there were two differing definitions. The defence version was that a 'verbal' was a statement of admission concocted by the police in order to incriminate the accused. The police version was that the 'verbal' was an admission of guilt made by the accused, but which he later wished to deny after advice from his solicitor.
64 Higgins interview.
65 Thompson interview.
66 Ex PC D. King, letter to author, 12 December 2000.
67 NA MEPO 28/9.
68 Ibid.
69 D.J. Smith and J. Gray, *Police and the People of London* (1985), p.427.
70 Taverne interview.
71 NA MEPO 2/10435 Commissioner's Conference with chief superintendents, 11 January 1966.
72 Higgins interview.

Chapter 7

Lack of commitment, lessons that went unheeded and the dawn of a new era

In previous chapters we looked at why it was that the downward spiral in the Metropolitan Police's relationship with London's West Indian community, which began in the 1950s, continued in the following decade. As we have seen, difficulties in the relationship were largely a reflection of the unwillingness of many in the host community to embrace the concept of multi-racial Britain, coupled with a desire to maintain racial inequalities in all aspects of economic and social life. Successive British governments must shoulder much of the blame for this state of affairs. Inertia and indecision were ever-present factors, particularly from the early 1950s, when the government failed to deal with escalating social problems resulting from large-scale West Indian immigration. A major impediment to integration/assimilation was the failure of governments to educate and inform the host community why such immigration was occurring. Whitehall severely underestimated the likely numbers of Caribbean immigrants who would come to Britain from the late 1940s onwards and kept no accurate figures on numbers arriving during the peak years of migration. The duplicitous scheming of Conservative governments in the 1950s: arguing, on the one hand, that it was the right of all Commonwealth citizens to settle in the 'mother country' while all the time looking for ways to end black migration from the Caribbean and elsewhere, virtually guaranteed that the road to multi-racial Britain would be beset with difficulties.

Police attitudes were generally in keeping with those of the wider society, and were based upon colour prejudice; ignorance of, and an unwillingness to understand Caribbean cultures and lifestyles; and a self-perception in which Britain's one-time superior status *vis-à-vis* the territories that had comprised its vast empire continued unabated in the minds of many British people. The Commonwealth may have replaced the empire, but there were few who did not regard it as the 'British Commonwealth'. The Metropolitan Police Commissioner and his senior colleagues continually sought to maintain their *de facto* independence from political control, aided always by the inability of its police authority, the Home Secretary, to effectively influence operational policing priorities. Aspects of the Commissioner's wide-ranging independence were observed in his rejection of overtures from West Indian community leaders – during a period of racial tension in London' Notting Hill in the late 1950s – to provide training for his officers in West Indian cultures, and in the way in which the Met dragged its heels in the mid-1960s when the Home Secretary, Roy Jenkins, urged police forces to begin the process of recruiting black policemen.

The commencement of race relations training in 1964, followed four years later by the setting up of the Met's Community Relations Branch A7 (1), were positive moves but they had little impact on changing entrenched attitudes. As a service, the Met was still steeped in its own history. Its priorities were the same in 1969 as they had been when the force was established in 1829: the prevention and detection of crime, and the prosecution of offenders against the peace. Added to this was the all-pervasive police culture – or rather, police cultures – that acted as a barrier, not only between police and public, but also between different ranks and departments of the police service. Above all, the Met believed that if problems existed in its relationship with the West Indian community, it was incumbent on that community to toe the line and fit in with everybody else. It saw little need at this time to consider a revision of its own policies and strategies.

In this chapter we will consider developments in the Met's relationship with black Londoners from 1970 to the present. One issue that has continued to be of major importance is the Met's Community and Race Relations (CRR) training programme. The Scarman Inquiry into the disturbances at Brixton in 1981, could, and should have been the turning point in developing better understanding between the Met and the black community. Although the Met initiated a revised training syllabus in light of Scarman's recommendations, the gulf in trust and confidence grew ever wider. The Met's CRR training foundered largely as a result of a lack of commitment at the highest levels of the force. In addition, many rank-and-file officers were unenthusiastic about the concept of CRR training; a number sharing the belief that it was low priority, while others claimed that black youths were possessed of criminal tendencies that required firm handling rather than empathy and understanding. All this took place at a time when the children of West Indian immigrants could clearly see that many aspects of social and economic life in Britain were blighted by an increasingly covert form of racism. As a result, the police – the physical manifestation of state authority and indigenous prejudice – were placed in the unenviable position of being white society's scapegoat and black society's arch-villain.

The political fallout engendered by Peter Griffiths' election victory at Smethwick in 1964 heralded a period in which there was broad parliamentary consensus on the perceived need to control immigration, particularly black Commonwealth immigration. This was fuelled by the rhetoric of Enoch Powell and the activities of the National Front, an umbrella organisation made up of a number of right-wing political groups.[1] Playing the 'race card', an activity that was – especially at election times – used to drum up support for viewpoints that were detrimental to the interests of the black community, became a prominent feature of the extreme political right. However, the 'race card' was not the exclusive property of white racists. From the 1970s it was increasingly a weapon deployed by representatives of minority ethnic communities to highlight problems of policing and social and economic inequality, as well as by those seeking control of the Met; a number of whom saw political advantage in publicising the difficulties then existing between the force and London's black community. They were, of course, helped immeasurably by the Met's use of Section 4 Vagrancy Act 1824, otherwise known as the 'sus' law; and by discriminatory stop-and-search tactics.[2] Indeed, one might argue that the Met played into the hands of such groups as a result of political naivety at a time when policing was increasingly coming under scrutiny from politicians and the media. On the other hand, the suggestion could be made with equal justification that there were those in society who had a vested interest in derailing the Met's attempts to improve relations with the black community. Elements of each will be found in our examination of problems in the relationship, particularly in the 1970s and 1980s.

The widely publicised corruption scandals of the 1960s and 1970s prompted the Met Police Commissioner, Sir Robert Mark, to encourage a more professional standard amongst his officers; a campaign that was taken up in the 1980s by two of his successors, Sir Kenneth Newman and Sir Peter Imbert. Despite their efforts, a massive investment in training and a host of community liaison initiatives, the Met still found great difficulty in establishing a rapport with black Londoners. One explanation for this is to be found in the Macpherson Inquiry's conclusion that the Met was 'institutionally racist': a verdict that was, as the evidence of previous chapters clearly shows, both well founded and long overdue. The chapter concludes with a consideration of the way in which the cultures and sub-cultures within the Met have often worked against efforts to develop a positive attitude towards the community; an explanation why it was that the Met finally lost its unique status and succumbed to the control of a democratically elected police authority for London; and a detailed critique of the barriers that still restrict the Met's efforts to respond positively to the policing needs of the capital's diverse community.

Community and race relations training in the Met in the post-Scarman era

Community and race relations training for Metropolitan officers continued, despite short-term initiatives that invariably emerged in the aftermath of public disorder and media interest, to be of secondary importance in the force's list of priorities almost to the end of the twentieth century. In the 1970s, the *Metropolitan Police Instruction Book (IB)*[3] (the training manual for constables) made no reference to community relations, merely listing police enforcement powers under relevant legislation. Indeed, an examination of Metropolitan *Police Orders* from 1970 to 1980 reveals that references to race or immigration invariably focused upon the powers of police and immigration officers to detain, arrest and recommend for deportation offenders under certain provisions of the Commonwealth Immigrants Act 1962, and the Immigration Act 1971.[4]

Her Majesty's Inspector of Constabulary (HMIC) referred to the problems encountered by the black community in his annual report for 1971, and went on to state that:

> The training police officers as a whole receive in race relations training is vital. The subject is included at both national and local level and consideration is now being given to the recommendations in the report of the Working Party on Police Training in Race Relations.[5]

In his annual report for 1973, HMIC emphasised the importance of good relations between 'coloured' people and the police. He pointed out that considerable effort was being made in police training to broaden police officers' understanding of society and the different groups in it, and added that, 'The aim is to ensure that police officers react sensitively to the variety of situations they encounter.'[6] Thereafter, HMIC's annual reports described the advances made by the police service in community relations training. Despite this, his report for 1978, while acknowledging the 'very considerable amount of hard work which is being put in by the police', admitted that:

> Relations between the police and the ethnic minority communities continued . . . to be a major preoccupation in 1978. It would be futile

to deny that there is a problem, and that relations are not as good as they might be in some parts of the country.[8]

The image created in HMIC's annual reports is one of a police service wholly committed to improving relations with minority ethnic communities, and that community awareness training for operational police officers was an essential element in the process. Why then did relations deteriorate; and why did the police's community relations training fail to bring about improved trust and understanding between police and minority ethnic communities?

An internal survey carried out by the Met revealed that as late as January 1983, traditional serious shortcomings in the quality of on-the-job training still existed.[9] These included the fact that junior officers were under pressure to report minor offences, success often being measured by the quantity of process they produced rather than by its quality.[10] There was a lack of standardisation in procedures, which adversely affected morale and made staff reluctant to make decisions in case they were countermanded. It was common for probationers and others to receive an almost total lack of help, both with operational matters and when compiling reports. The introduction of personal radios in 1967 had led to advice being given by radio when the supervisor should have attended the scene of the incident. The result was that subordinates had to make on-the-spot decisions that they were not competent to make. Many sergeants failed to understand their training role and fell into the trap of acting as a critic, rather than a coach.[11] One sees, therefore, that young police officers were pressured to report as many offenders as possible, often for minor matters, by supervisory officers who gave little effective support and who were inclined to be critical if mistakes were made. Such a policy, aimed almost exclusively at law enforcement, was hardly conducive to the development of policies aimed at embracing cultural diversity and promoting greater sensitivity towards minority ethnic communities.

The Scarman Inquiry Report, which followed serious public disorder at Brixton in 1981, reviewed the state of relations between the Met and black Londoners. On the subject of training in community relations, the report recommended the establishment of:

> Training courses designed to develop an appreciation that good community relations were essential to effective policing ... these courses should be part of a continuous and compulsory training programme for all officers up to the rank of superintendent.[12]

In January 1982, following Scarman's report, the Police Training Council (PTC) appointed a working party to review community relations training for the police service. Its report, appropriately entitled *Community and Race Relations Training for the Police*, was published in February 1983. It is from the recommendations of this report that all subsequent community and race relations training for police officers evolved.[13] The rationale of the training programme was to encourage police officers – from constable to chief inspector rank – to take a subjective look through a range of techniques, including role-play, at the way in which policing impacted on the public. This was radically different to traditional police training, which had been based on a simple formula: this is the law, these are your powers, and this is what you do when someone disobeys the law.[14] The results of the initial training programme were published in 1984.[15]

It was commonly found that police officers on the courses rejected the 'awareness' approach in favour of an information-giving style. They were more inclined to want facts, and were less prepared to, 'acknowledge emotions, feelings and perceptions as facts'.[16] The author of the report was forced to admit that:

> It may be difficult for some to realise just how much effort it can take to 'sell' the idea of Racism Awareness Training (RAT) to some police officers ... There is a real danger that if they perceive racial awareness training as part of such a crusade it will be rejected.[17]

It was also noted that unless RAT-trained officers were supported at senior management level, it would be unlikely that lessons learned would be put into practice when the officer returned to her or his police force. Scarman had proposed the creation of a national community and race relations specialist support-training unit for the police service.[18] The aim was to train and develop specially selected police staff who could manage and deliver CRR training to their own forces. It was envisaged that a national strategy would enable CRR training to become integrated into the curriculum of all police training, and that consistency would be provided as a result of the standardised nature of the instruction given to those attending the courses. In his report, *Winning the Race, Policing Plural Communities*, published in 1996–97, HMIC conducted a thematic inspection of CRR training in London.

HMIC concluded that the Met had failed to develop a CRR training strategy tailored to meet its own needs; neither had it used its training course graduates in either managerial or training roles. There was no standard force-wide selection procedure, some officers being sent on CRR trainers' courses merely because they asked to go. It was noted that:

> The inspection team did not meet training staff who have graduated from Turvey [the national training centre from 1989–98] who are

talented, committed trainers and training managers who are utilising the skills they had gained to good effect.[19]

Though the Met invested some £780,000 in CRR training between 1989 and 1998, it had no accurate figures on the number of its officers who had received training. Furthermore, feedback reports from Met officers who had attended trainers' courses suggested that CRR training in the Met suffered from, 'poor leadership, lack of co-ordination, lack of support, lack of commitment and failure to use [trained officers'] skills'. HMIC found that:

> The inspection process has been unable to find a policy, strategy or plan which outlines the MPS's [Metropolitan Police Service's] commitment to CRR training covering the period 1989–98. There was no substantive evidence of a cohesive and co-ordinated training plan, nor evidence of training packages or modules designed for delivery to the entire workforce of the MPS as part of a 'cascade approach'.[20]

The MPS annual training catalogue, which outlined all of the centrally provided training to be delivered at the Hendon training college in the year April 1998 to March 1999, listed 293 separate courses. However, not one of the 351,000 allocated student training days at Hendon was set aside for centrally delivered CRR courses.[21] The obvious conclusion, and one drawn by HMIC, was that CRR training in the Met was of low priority, and that, at best, it was being provided at local (area or borough) level only, by trainers who were personally committed to the concept of CRR training. In his report, HMIC emphasised both the failure of the Met's hierarchy to accord CRR training the priority it deserved, and the way in which such failure was likely to exacerbate the Met's already difficult relationship with minority ethnic communities:

> Despite guidance given in the Thematic Reports *Winning the Race* (1997) and *Developing Diversity in the Police Service* (1995), in the past the MPS at Policy Board level has not given sufficient priority within the training programme for community and race relations training. The lack of training may well have affected the ability of some members of staff to carry out their duties and responsibilities effectively. Where this lack of training results in a negative experience for a member of the public during an interaction with the MPS, this in turn may well lead to or reinforce the lack of confidence and trust that some communities have in the service they receive.[22]

What conclusions might one draw from these observations on the Met's response to CRR training in the aftermath of the Brixton riots and the Scarman recommendations? It appears obvious that the Met failed to recognise the importance of CRR. The evidence would suggest that from the 1980s onwards CRR training was, despite the lessons of the urban riots in 1981, low on the Met's list of priorities. This view is endorsed by Nadine Peppard, a senior member of Equality Associates (the organisation that provided CRR training to the police over a ten-year period from 1989), who recalled that: 'I edited the quarterly journal called the *Newsletter*. We thought, optimistically, that its main item would be "News from the Forces", only to discover that they had no news to offer, as they weren't doing anything.'[23] It seems clear that the lip-service approach of the 1970s, referred to by former Assistant Commissioner Gerrard, was still the order of the day in the 1990s. The author's experience as a former training manager in the Met was that policy on diversity training was invariably the product of, and a response to, a particular problem or event, such as the findings of Scarman. However, once initial anxieties over the particular problem had subsided and related concerns about policing had ceased to be headline news, be it Brixton or Broadwater Farm, it generally transpired that new legislation and operationally based training demands – such as public order or officer safety training – assumed greater priority, and CRR was consigned to the margins once more. An excellent example of this is to be found in the Met's *Special Police Order* 'Policing policy and serious public disorder', of 30 June 1986.

The order stated that, 'greater emphasis has been placed on race awareness and interpersonal skills in our training programme since 1981'.[24] Such training, known as 'policing skills', was reported to account for 22 per cent of the initial 20-week recruit-training programme.[25] A condensed version of the training had been introduced for all Met officers in September 1984. However, the order continued, 'unfortunately because of the need for training in new procedures prior to the introduction of the Police and Criminal Evidence Act, the "policing skills" training had to be suspended'.[26] When one considers how serious the outbreaks of public disorder at Brixton and elsewhere had been in 1981, and their destructive impact on relations between police and the black community, it is tempting to suggest that the Met's claim that 'greater emphasis' was being placed on racial awareness and interpersonal skills training is difficult to justify; particularly when it could be so easily put on hold within months of antagonism between police and the black community escalating into serious disorder and the murder of PC Blakelock at Tottenham in 1985.

An allied problem was the Met's long-held belief that when an officer had attended a training course on a particular subject, the force had fulfilled its obligation both to society and the officer. There was no concept of continuing needs assessment, ongoing training or evaluation.[27] It was one thing for a captive audience of new recruits to receive policing skills training as part of a diversity programme; where the Met failed was in its lack of commitment to the provision of high-quality training and leadership to experienced officers, those who would inevitably influence the approach of new recruits towards black Londoners in the real world of policing. An example of this was the author's attendance at an inspectors' promotion course at the Hendon Police College in October 1987. Officers attending the course were provided with an *Inspectors Initial Course* handbook. Apart from a brief explanation of the work of CLOs, the subject of community and race relations was not mentioned, either in the handbook or during the course, both of which were intended to cover all aspects of supervision for inspectors in the Metropolitan Police. The Met's lack of consistency and uniformity in its approach to CRR training was highlighted by Robin Oakley, an advisor to the Met on CRR, who recalled that projects on which he was engaged at both Tottenham and Hendon in 1990 were terminated when there was a change in senior police personnel.

Oakley pointed out what he believed were the differing attitudes to police training that he encountered among officers in Britain and the USA, and suggested that the concept of 'professionalism' had different connotations for British and American officers:

Up to the present time the police service simply hasn't made the journey towards recognising what kind of a profession it is and the skills and abilities that are required of it ... When I meet police officers at John Jay College (USA) I just think, 'gosh, they're so different.' They are reflective, they want to learn, they believe that things like knowledge and research can help them do their job: being literate and knowing that they have got a knowledge-based profession like doctors, nurses and teachers. It's hard to find anyone here who has that concept. They still see it as a craft type of job, and professionalism is about technical efficiency in driving cars, or shooting guns, or doing forensic investigations or whatever.[28]

The cultural watershed in the Met's approach to CRR training would seem to have been provided by the findings of the Macpherson Inquiry Report into the death of Stephen Lawrence, which was published in February 1999, though little progress appeared to have been made prior to that time in the period following the Lawrence murder in 1993. Despite Macpherson, concerns remained that the errors and omissions of the past, a philosophy in which the latest problem was always the greatest problem, might be repeated. An officer from the Met's Racial and Violent Crime Task Force expressed his fears about police training priorities:

Stephen Lawrence was at the top of the political agenda for two or three years. Now it's gone down a bit because what we're now focusing on is 'safer streets'. The danger is to think that the two things aren't connected.[29]

Though the Met's senior ranks only appear to have viewed cultural and ethnic diversity training for police officers as an immediate and short-term response to a particular problem which might be put to one side when new problems arose, there were others who saw the continuing difficulties in the Met's relationship with the black community as an opportunity to elevate the subject of policing and control of the Met to the centre stage of political debate.

Playing politics: mixed messages and control of the Metropolitan Police

At the end of 1966 it appeared that the relationship between the Met and its police authority, the Home Secretary, which had existed since 1829, was secure for the foreseeable future. An internal Home Office note of 23 December 1966 stated that:

> Firm ground was reached on fundamental constitutional aspects of the position of the Metropolitan Police as a result of the deliberations of the Royal Commission on London government and the police: the position of the Home Secretary as police authority, with special responsibilities for and powers over the force and answerable to Parliament – which had assumed larger proportions with the formation of the Greater London Council – was probably laid for good.[30]

Such complacency would prove to be misguided, and in the following decades the campaign for political control of the Met was taken up with vigour. The basis of the case against the police – the Met in particular – was that from the early 1970s successive commissioners (and an assortment of chief police officers)[31] strode the political stage in an increasingly imposing and outspoken manner; and, in so doing, championed new policing strategies which were, it was alleged, an intrusion into the lives of the general public.

From the early 1970s the Commissioner's *de facto* independence from political control was all the time more challenged. It must be borne in mind that many of the Met's critics were seeking to advance their own political agendas and that the alleged politicisation of the role of the police had as much to do with the 'state of the nation' debate and the role of government, as it did with the way in which the Metropolitan Police carried out its function. It was frequently alleged that Sir Robert Mark and his successors, as well as organisations such as the Police Federation and the Superintendents' Association, increasingly high-lighted perceived problems of law and order in their attempt to extend the boundaries of policing; masked always in such a way that it appeared as though the police's desire was merely to serve the public interest: a 'public' defined by critics such as Martin Kettle as, 'some . . . [make-believe] public of whose collective opinion the police claim unique knowledge'.[32] Gilroy described, 'the emergence of the Police Federation on to the stage of national politics' during this period, and argued that its 'Law and Order' campaign in the autumn of 1975, in which black crime was highlighted, 'may have provided common ground between the force's developing rank and file and the views of its senior officers'.[33]

There is a fundamental flaw in the argument of critics who assert that the role of the Metropolitan Police Commissioner and the Police Federation became ever more politicised in the 1970s. Neither had ever been apolitical. Bob Morris, the Home Office liaison officer with the Met (1971–73) contends that politics had always been part of the Commissioner's role since the time of Sir Richard Mayne, the Met's first Commissioner in 1829; and that from the 1970s:

> What perhaps people were fastening on was the greater public prominence of certain chief officers . . . Robert Mark was capable of thinking for himself and speaking for himself, and there were a number of issues around at that time that he wanted to speak about. But chief officers have always done this to a greater or lesser extent . . . There's never been a period when policing hasn't been political. It's naïve to imagine that it ever was apolitical. What it might have been at times was relatively uncontroversial.[34]

The Police Federation's opposition to the Home Affairs Committee's proposal to introduce a specific police discipline offence of racial discrimination in 1968 (seven years before Gilroy claims that the Federation began dabbling in politics) forced the then Home Secretary, James Callaghan, to abandon the proposal.[35] Branches of the police service had for many years been represented on an assortment of Home Office committees and prior consultation with police (the Met in particular) on proposed legislation having a policing dimension was standard procedure: as was the case, for example, at the discussion stage of the Race Relations Act 1965.[36] In short, it was not that policing had become politicised at this time, but that the 1970s and 1980s, character-ised as the period was by industrial and urban unrest,[37] heralded a change in the nature and behaviour of the policed population, in which its use of violence in furtherance of collective objectives became an increasing feature of British life at that time. It was society that became politicised, not the already politicised police service. This view is endorsed by Bridges, who argues that the riots of 1981 were an opportunity that was seized on by, 'more radical elements in Labour-controlled local authorities, such as the Greater London Council (GLC)' to politicise the role of the Met in order to further their own political objectives: namely, to assume control of the force, and, 'to re-open the debate on police powers and the RCCP [Royal Commission on Criminal Procedure] proposals.'[38]

HMIC's annual reports from 1970 onwards clearly show that, at the highest levels of the service, there was recognition that community relations were an essential aspect of policing. The problem, it was claimed, was that police fulfilled a dual responsibility to society: their social function and their enforcement role. The latter was often seen to nullify the positive effects of the former. One also sees in HMIC's annual report for 1970 an attitude expressed that appears closer to a Baldwines-que view of national life in the 1930s than that of multi-ethnic Britain in the age of space exploration:

> Before the car and motorcycle became common, when people generally worked and found their leisure in their own towns and villages, there was a closer sense of local community. With no traffic offences, the average citizen rarely fell foul of the law ... the local policeman used once to know, and be known by, everyone in the neighbourhood he served. With a shortage of police manpower, and the requirement for greater mobility this is now more difficult.[39]

HMIC's report for the following year drew attention to the problems of immigrant communities and, despite the efforts police were making to improve relations in this area, he claimed that the police service was being held to account for the failings of others:

> Social change and improvement in the situation of immigrants depends on general matters over which the police have no control, such as housing, education, employment and opportunities for recreation. But it is the police who often have to bear the brunt of the resentment generated by inadequacies in these fields and they can suffer directly when dissatisfaction results from social grievances and racial discrimination.[40]

In 1972, the House of Commons Select Committee on Race Relations chose to consider relations between police and 'coloured' people as the topic of its third inquiry. Their report, 'expressed a feeling that there was a widespread belief that police/immigrant relations are deteriorating, and that this belief is nearly as important as the actual state of the relationship'.[41] It was noted that in the seven years that had elapsed since the appointment of the first black police officer, there were still only 39 black officers (including five female officers) in England and Wales.[42] Subsequent reports revealed a growing sense that the police service was being forced to take responsibility for the nation's failure to address the problems that were leading to immigrants, 'suffering disproportionately from the difficulties facing our society'.[43] While progress had been made in developing links with immigrant community leaders, predominantly among those coming from the Indian subcontinent, it was found to be more difficult to foster contact with young Britons of West Indian descent who had spent all their lives in the United Kingdom, and for whom the concept of community leaders had no meaning.

In his annual report for 1974, HMIC reaffirmed his belief that the police were the unwitting victims of society's failings:

> Until coloured people are treated as equal in our society, and feel themselves to be equal – until colour is genuinely no more than a physical distinction, and not one on which judgements of worth and ability are made – race relations will remain an important matter for the police. It is the police who are exposed to the reactions to which society's injustices give rise. The police do not, however, have the power to change society. They can only strive to act impartially towards all groups within the existing framework . . . social poverty and crime call for greater resources, yet these are the areas where manpower is at its shortest.[44]

What HMIC failed to mention is that the very people who were most likely to use colour as a determinant of a black person's worth at this time were police officers themselves. A former chief superintendent recalled that, having given a résumé of a discussion paper he had prepared on relations between police in Notting Hill and the West Indian community, he was approached by an assistant commissioner who retorted, ' "Well, they're at it, aren't they?" Meaning that they [West Indians] were largely focused on committing crime, "they", this generalisation.'[45]

From the mid-1970s, those arguing for an end to the Home Secretary's role as police authority for the Met premised their case on the belief that the Met had failed to develop a constructive dialogue with its community, and that this could only be remedied by an elected assembly to replace the Home Secretary. They also argued that public confidence in the Met suffered because the police disciplinary system, in which police

officers sat in behind-closed-doors tribunals to judge their own colleagues, was neither impartial nor transparent and that, increasingly, the
Met failed to give sufficient priority to the investigation of alleged
offences that were aggravated by racism. On 11 March 1980, Jack Straw
MP introduced a Bill in the Commons that, though ultimately unsuccessful, contained measures to reorganise the Metropolitan Police; to create
a National Police Agency and a Greater London police force; to establish
a Greater London Police Authority and to create a separate police
investigation agency for England and Wales. Straw argued that:

> Experience has shown that in the Metropolitan area there is
> insufficient contact between police officers and the community and
> that there is insufficient accountability by the police through local
> representatives. That can only be remedied by having a Greater
> London police force responsible to a local and democratically
> elected police authority.[46]

In 1981 the Labour Party acquired a working majority in the GLC
elections and established its own Police Committee for London. Although this body had no statutory powers, the GLC encouraged and
funded the creation of police monitoring groups in a number of London
Boroughs. When, following Scarman's recommendations, the Met introduced a process of public consultation through its Police and Community Consultative Groups (PCCGs) in the mid-1980s, it soon became
apparent that the rationale of monitoring groups was to undermine the
concept of PCCGs: arguing that such assemblies were both undemocratic
and unrepresentative. However, for the time being at least, the aspirations of Jack Straw and the GLC were doomed to failure: firstly, because
the Met fulfilled a number of functions at the time – the Criminal Record
Office being one – that were national in character and therefore could not
be hived off to a local authority to manage; secondly, in a period of
industrial and social unrest, it would have been unimaginable to think
that the government of Margaret Thatcher would hand control of the
Met, by far and away the largest police force in the country, to a radical
left-wing council.

Allegations persisted that from the early-1980s the Met, through its use
of PCCGs and Neighbourhood Watch schemes, spied on the people of
London in order to gain intelligence. Such claims lack credibility on two
counts. Firstly, although there was undoubtedly an intelligence-gather-
ing aspect to both, critics ignore the fact that intelligence was invariably
provided by participating members of the community because they
wanted police officers attending the meetings to deal with local problems. It was far less common for police to use such meetings to seek
information. Secondly, Neighbourhood Watch tended to thrive in the

more affluent areas where local residents were likely to be conservative-minded homeowners who generally supported the police. The Met found it extremely difficult to establish such schemes on housing estates, or in the less affluent parts of inner London: the very areas one might have expected the Met's critics to have had in mind in opposing the idea of consultation with the Met.

What then were the factors that led to the demise of a system of supervision of the Met that had existed for over 170 years? Michael O'Byrne suggests that:

> Up until the 1980s the police service had an enviable reputation for carrying out its responsibilities with an impartiality which was unusual, even in the developed west. In the 1980s the perception grew that the police were no longer impartial but actively supported the political stance being taken by the Conservative government.[47]

To an extent, Mark and his successors, the Police Federation and the Superintendents' Association were hoist by their own petard in seeking to highlight issues of rising crime and 'law and order' in the mid-1970s. The Superintendents' Association's edicts on the problem of rising crime bearing all the hallmarks of a moral panic:

> The widest support should be given . . . in combating violence and reinforcing values of what as a nation we had believed for many years, namely, a free society and the right of freedom. Without due care the all too common attitude of self preservation and the growing general acceptance of permissiveness to do as one pleased without fear of retribution would . . . lead the country to anarchy.[48]

The problem for the police was that eventually politicians and public alike would, and ultimately did, demand to know what it was that the police were doing about crime and disorder. Policing thus emerged as a topic that transcended local matters and became a key aspect of the national political debate. Closer scrutiny of performance revealed that the Met's success rates in tackling crime were less than impressive. In view of this, and the implications for the government of the day, it was hardly surprising that the traditional triumvirate of police authority, chief police officer and the Home Secretary became increasingly dominated by the latter.

Despite the progression to a more centralised form of direction for the police, it would appear that the concept of an elected Metropolitan Police Authority began to be viewed more favourably by the Conservative government in the early 1990s. Morris recalled that when Michael Howard was Home Secretary (1993–97):

Michael Howard set up an advisory committee, which in retrospect can be seen as a nascent or shadow authority and therefore the writing was on the wall. However, setting up an independent authority was not something that would have been easy for, or was at any time positively sought by, a Conservative government. Nonetheless, that initiative and other changes which progressively transferred 'national' functions from the Met to new bodies like NCIS can be seen as paving the way for the change actually made later by the Labour government.[49]

The great problem the Home Office had always faced in its dealings with the Met was that the Commissioner of Police was too high profile an individual to treat in the same manner as it might, for example, treat a prison governor. As Morris recalled, 'You had in the Commissioner, in a way, an over-mighty subject.'[50] It might well have been considered an attractive option after 1997 for the new Labour government and the Home Office to hive off the management of the Met to the Greater London Assembly, particularly when one considers the impending fallout from the Macpherson Inquiry Report. The trials and tribulations that went hand in hand with the Home Secretary's position as supervisor of his 'over-mighty subject' would cease to be his direct responsibility while, at the same time, the Home Office would maintain a position of increasing influence over the Met's activities through its ever more influential circulars and directives, best value and key performance indicators. Ceding control to the Greater London Assembly placed the Home Office in a no-lose situation.

The process by which the Met became accountable to London's electorate had been long and often painful. It was, however, a relatively smooth transition when compared with the enormity of the task required to bring about more positive police attitudes to the community.

Progression and regression: the Met's cultural millstones and the need for change

In our earlier analysis of the Met's performance form 1950 to 1970 we saw the way in which the force's reluctance to embrace change was accompanied by an inability to develop and maintain positive community initiatives: problems that were compounded by its conviction that it had nothing to learn from those outside of its own organisation. As Robert Mark recalled, 'The Met had long felt itself pre-eminent in police affairs and resented comment or criticism from outsiders.'[51] This was especially the case in the field of community relations, particularly when it came to West Indians and other visible ethnic minorities. The chapter now continues with an examination of the Met's record in the field of community and race relations to the time of the publication of the Lawrence Inquiry Report in 1999.

The Met was sufficiently concerned at the state of relations between its officers and the people of London that, in March 1970, it announced that it had appointed Dr W.A. Belson to undertake a series of research studies into the relationship between the public and the Metropolitan Police.[52] The aim was to provide authoritative and practical information to help to promote the best possible co-operation between police and public. One thousand Met officers took part in the study. The findings of the police survey revealed that, at a time when the police service was being accused of taking an increasingly active part in politics, 90 per cent of officers questioned believed that the police view should be presented more forcefully in order to change laws that police thought unfair or unenforceable.[53] Almost two-thirds of officers (62%) believed that there was no need for an independent element in police complaint procedures.[54] Asked if different sub-groups produced problems for the police, officers identified West Indians (53%), and Africans (43%) as the most problematic.[55] When asked about the adequacy of police powers in relation to stop-and-search procedures, making arrests and searching suspects' homes, most officers in each category (82%, 72% and 70% respectively) believed that powers were adequate; while the remainder (18%, 28% and 30% respectively) felt that police needed more powers.[56] Just over half of the officers (51%) agreed that a minority of people were dedicated to the overthrow of society.[57] When asked if immigrants should be obliged to adopt the British way of life, two-thirds (66%) of officers believed that they should; and almost one-third (32%) of officers were of the belief that 'coloured' people were less intelligent than whites.[58]

HMIC's reports suggested that morale was low in the police service in the 1970s, and that it was made worse in the Met by the eternal problems of under-manning and the lurid press stories of corrupt practices. Perhaps in order to address these issues, Sir Robert Mark, the Met's Commissioner (1972–76), encouraged the concept of policing as a profession, arguing that:

> The time has come when the police are abandoning their artisan status and are achieving, by our ever increasing variety of services, our integrity, our accountability and our dedication to the public good, a status no less admirable than that of the most learned and distinguished professions.[59]

In April 1985, Mark's initial steps to inculcate a professional ethos within the service were developed by another Commissioner of the Met, Sir Kenneth Newman, in his book, *The Metropolitan Police*: *The Principles of*

Policing and Guidance for Professional Behaviour. The book was distributed to all serving Met officers and, because of its cover, quickly became known as 'the blue book'. In its foreword, Newman, though extolling the principles on which the Met was founded in 1829, pointed out that many aspects of society had changed and that it was incumbent on the Met to adapt in order to meet the present-day needs of its community. The main aims of the book were to encourage the extension of policing principles so as, 'to blend [policing's] traditionally British character with the new requirements of a vibrant democracy',[60] and to persuade Met officers of the potential advantages to the service in, 'moving from a profession which has been comparatively inward-looking to one which is more attuned to other people's needs'.[61]

In his book, Newman made a number of references to the Scarman Inquiry Report, and clearly had the Brixton riots of 1981 in mind when he noted that:

> The Queen's Peace will be endangered if citizens perceive police action to be inconsistent with the fundamental values of British society. These values emphasise a just balance between order and freedom . . . the British ideal is that policing should be shaped by the consent of the population.[62]

Writing in the mid-1980s, Gilroy picked up on such value systems and their depiction of inherited qualities that were essentially white and could only be threatened by the black presence:

> It is precisely this unified national culture articulated around the theme of legality and . . . constitution which black criminality is alleged to violate, thus jeopardising both the state and civilization. Crime in general and black crime in particular disrupts the reverence for law which has been accepted by left and right as a fundamental compound of Englishness.[63]

Newman's policy for potential public-order flashpoints was to think first in terms of mediation. He recognised the potential for disorder among some black youngsters, especially those of West Indian origin, but acknowledged that:

> There is an uncritical readiness in some of us [police] to think poorly of the black community, not only the young. There is an over-generalised assumption on occasions, of their involvement in crime; deceit and collaboration in avoiding detection and rescuing lawfully detained prisoners, lack of intelligence and the ability to articulate and absence of the motivation to work.[64]

The disturbances at Brixton and Tottenham in the 1980s echoed a number of the findings of the National Advisory Commission on Civil Disorders (the Kerner Report), which investigated rioting in cities in the United States in 1967.[65] Kerner found that disorder was not the result of a single 'triggering' or 'precipitating' incident. Instead, it was generated out of an increasingly disturbed social atmosphere, in which typically a series of tension-heightening incidents over a period of weeks or months became linked in the minds of many in the black community with a shared network of underlying grievances; as was the case with the Met's 'Swamp '81' campaign in Brixton, and in the unrest in the Tottenham area prior to the outbreak of rioting at Broadwater Farm. A study of the aftermath of disorder led to disturbing conclusions that were, once again, paralleled in London. It was found that, despite the institution of some post-riot programmes, there was little basic change in the conditions underlying the outbreak of the disorder. Actions to ameliorate black grievances had been limited and sporadic; with few exceptions, they had not significantly reduced tensions; and, crucially, the principal official response in several cities had been to train and equip police with more sophisticated weapons.[66]

A comparison with the British experience at locations such as Brixton and Toxteth would suggest that the post-riot experiences of the black communities were very similar, as were the measures taken to improve police riot-control capability. Scarman concluded that Brixton's eruption in 1981 was largely the result of social deprivation and intensive and unimaginative policing; yet only four years later, in the aftermath of rioting at Broadwater Farm, these findings appeared not to suit the prevailing mood. As O'Byrne noted:

Black youth involved were described as being clearly criminal, and the . . . riots were depicted as being part of a concerted attempt to keep the police out of the area in order to allow criminal activities, especially drug dealing, to take place. Almost all the commentary ignored the possibility that the actions of the youth may have been caused by their ghettoisation, frustration caused by high unemployment, alienation and what they saw as police harassment. It was almost as though Lord Scarman's inquiry had never happened.[67]

It is hardly surprising that the black community bore much of the blame for the events at Broadwater Farm: firstly, because the government made much of the fact that it had invested heavily in the deprived urban areas – such as Brixton and Toxteth – that had witnessed the worst of the rioting in 1981; and because the horrific murder of Police Constable Blakelock during the rioting led to massive public support and sympathy for the police. There was, therefore, nobody else left at which the media's finger of blame could be pointed.

In his book, Newman saw the Met's camaraderie as one of its strengths, and looked to the supervisory ranks to, 'arrange our organisations and our policies so that their combined effect is to create and sustain such a spirit'.[68] However, the Met's camaraderie had a darker side which, as Imbert observed, could, and did at times, work against Newman's objectives:

> You know we have a camaraderie within the police service. We wear uniform, we go to Hendon, we go into class together, we do first aid and we do sport together. We have a great camaraderie and that should be cherished. But it can become a force for evil.[69]

The 'blue book' was a praiseworthy effort by a Commissioner who recognised the Met's deficiencies in professionalism and in its inability to look beyond what it saw as its own priorities. However, it largely failed to bring about the changes hoped for. Its initial failure, and one that was something of an own-goal in terms of lack of professionalism, was the way in which the book was marketed to the workforce. The vast majority of officers, the author included, found that the book suddenly appeared in their correspondence pigeonholes. One simply chose to read it, or, as was the case with many officers who believed that they needed no lectures on how to do their job, disposed of it. Though the book's intention was to develop a corporate approach, it contained a get-out clause for those officers intent on pursuing their own policing priorities. Under the heading, 'The importance of discretion', the book stated that:

> A constable, though he must obey lawful and reasonable orders from any senior rank, does not hold his office and exercise his powers at the behest of a more senior officer, who in any case, whatever his title, is constitutionally a constable also. Nor is he answerable to any government official, or to the Home Office or Parliament. He is answerable to the law and holds his office independently of anyone else.[70]

Reminding police officers, the majority of whom saw no need for change, that they possessed almost unbridled discretionary powers was hardly the way to persuade them to conform to a new philosophy of policing with which many were ill at ease. Old habits remained, along with the belief that community-based initiatives had little in common with real police work. An example of this can be seen in the Met's twice-weekly publication, *Police Orders*; which frequently contained a section entitled, 'Commendations and awards'. While one would regularly read of commendations being awarded for courage and determination in the arrest of a violent offender, or for outstanding detective ability in a complex case of fraud, an examination of *Police Orders* over a 12-year period from 1970 to 1982 revealed that no commendations or awards were ever made to officers who developed positive links with the community. The reason why physical courage and crime arrests were held in such high regard in comparison to other aspects of policing were, as O'Byrne astutely observed:

> [Because] it's what we all joined the job to do. I think a lot of people forget that fact. Police officers like helping people. There's no problem about that and they go out of their way to be helpful. But we actually joined the job as nineteen or twenty-year-olds to get in fast cars, and have blue lights, and get out and get into a bit of a scrum, and nick a few people, and get into the excitement of police work and the excitement of investigation. Social workers joined the social services, and if you wanted to become a teacher, in the main, you became a teacher.[71]

In the late 1980s, Imbert followed Newman's initiative when he introduced the PLUS programme. This was a largely internal scheme that was intended to address longstanding deficiencies in the relationship between police officers and non-police members of staff. Imbert's frustration with his police colleagues was clearly evident in his explanation of the rationale of PLUS:

> I felt that we had to change the [police] culture. We were not even treating our own civil staff correctly. Their complaint, and it was justified, was that they were being treated as second-class citizens, and, indeed, that was true. There was a fear [among police officers] that the civil staff were taking over, and they were going to tell us – the real police – what to do.[72]

As with his predecessor's initiatives, Imbert's programme was only marginally successful in its effort to change police attitudes. The problem, as ever, was that middle-ranking officers (inspector to superintendent) tended to share the belief of the junior ranks that the whole thing was a passing fancy, which would eventually fade away. Most officers adapted to changes in legislation and associated procedures. What many were not prepared to do was go along with changes that required a more open attitude, and a greater willingness to see both the community and non-police members of the Met as equals. As O'Byrne points out, lip service was often the order of the day when policies such as PLUS and CRR were introduced:

The actual behaviour of the leadership shows that they share the same values as the rest of the organisation and have developed policies due to political necessity rather than personal belief: an implicit signal that the organisation can ignore them if operational necessity dictates.[73]

In *Policing London*, reference was made to the Met's diversity strategy, 'Protect and respect', which described the force's intention to involve the community in its decision-making process: 'We want to involve the community in our work in order to have a genuine understanding of their expectations and aspirations and to make full use of their experience and expertise.'[74] The inspection by HMIC found, however, that:

The written determination to consult with the diverse community of London was not always matched by internal vocal support. Indeed, HMIC found evidence that some cultural change is required, often at a senior level, to enable a truly consultative organisation to flourish.[75]

Many, if not all, of the shortcomings in the Met's performance since the 1950s that have been considered here were also referred to in the conclusions and summary of the Macpherson Inquiry team's final report into the death of Stephen Lawrence, published in 1999. The inquiry found that, 'the investigation was marred by a combination of professional incompetence, institutional racism and a failure of leadership by senior officers'.[76] On the question of police racism, the inquiry concluded that, 'At its most stark the case against the police was that racism infected the MPS and that the catalogue of errors could only be accounted for by something more than incompetence.'[77] It was noted that racism awareness training was almost nonexistent at every level. The inquiry determined that:

First and foremost and fundamentally we believe that there must be a change so that there is genuine partnership between the police and all sections of the community. This cannot be achieved by the police alone. The onus is upon them to start the process . . . Co-operation must be genuine and vigorous. Strategies to be delivered under the new Crime & Disorder Act will provide an opportunity in this respect. Training will play its part. The active involvement of people from diverse ethnic groups is essential. Otherwise there will be no acceptance of change, and policing by consent may be the victim.[78]

The Inquiry team's findings will surely come as no surprise to the reader of this chapter and those that have preceded it. It appears clear that, after some 35 years of race relations training in the Met, racist attitudes persisted at all levels of the service. There were many reasons for this; perhaps the most crucial of which was that, despite stirring pronouncements to the contrary from successive commissioners and inspectors of constabulary, community and racial relations training was only given any real attention when political expediency demanded it. Allied to this was the fact that community relations had always been low in the pecking order of a police culture that saw success in terms of criminal investigation and detection, and the maintenance of public order, and gave scant regard to the work of the many individual officers whose efforts to develop positive links with the public went unrecognised and unrewarded.

The Macpherson Report highlighted the failures of senior officers to adequately supervise and direct their subordinates in the Lawrence case; a failure that was identified more than 30 years earlier by Deputy-Commander Howlett in his condemnatory report of 1965, in which he concluded that those in the sergeant to superintendent ranks were largely failing to give sufficient guidance, supervision and support to constables. As Howlett also identified, self-promotion for many seeking higher rank became of greater relevance than the service that was being provided. The Met was essentially a collection of individuals and sub-groups, each of whom, though committed to the general principles the force strove to uphold, pursued their own aims, in their own ways, with their own end-products in mind. The Met's ultimate failing was its complacency: a state of mind that had developed out of the wide latitude allowed by successive home secretaries as a result of their inability to adequately manage the Metropolitan Police. Out of complacency grew an arrogance, which, as Mark identified, was borne of a belief that the Met was the police force *par excellence* and that it had nothing to learn from 'outsiders'.[79] In consequence, the Met only ever took cultural and ethnic diversity seriously when political and public disquiet demanded it. The lack of commitment to change ensured that, once the dust had settled, good intentions were always short-lived.

No room for complacency: the Met and the Police Service in the twenty-first century

The findings and recommendations set out in the Macpherson Inquiry Report had a profound impact on the Metropolitan Police.[80] The readiness with which the then Commissioner, Sir Paul Condon, and his successor, Sir John Stephens, accepted its findings and recommendations was, however, not always matched by other officers, a number of whom believed that the accusation of 'institutional racism' was a personal affront – rather than, as was intended, a considered observation on the failings of the organisation. Since the Report there have been a number of changes, both to the management structure of the Met and to its approach to CRR; measures which, if successful, offer the prospect of improved performance in race and diversity matters. A more positive and open attitude to public scrutiny now appears to exist at all levels of the Met, and one senses an almost tangible willingness to learn from the mistakes and shortcomings of the past. However, despite the efforts that are being made, doubts remain as to the Met's ability to make real progress in gaining the trust and confidence of minority ethnic communities. In this final section we will consider positive and negative aspects of the measures now being taken by the police to meet the needs of multi-ethnic Britain in the twenty-first century.

The Met's first success in the aftermath of the Lawrence case was its acceptance that, henceforth, diversity was to be a central pillar of its strategies, both internally and at the point of service delivery. At the same time, there was a widespread acknowledgement within the MPS hierarchy that CRR training, which had been introduced in the aftermath of the Scarman Inquiry Report in 1981, had never really been prioritised. In the late 1990s, a pilot CRR training programme was launched at Lambeth, and was subsequently implemented throughout the MPS. All members of the MPS now receive race and diversity training. The original scheme is being developed to provide second-phase training (CRR2), which builds on the first course and examines ways of behaving in the workplace; focusing particularly on attitudes towards what has been described as the 'gender agenda' and non-police members of staff.

There appears to be a greater willingness since the Lawrence case for the Met to accept external criticism; and, more importantly, to respond positively to recommendations emanating from outside the service on ways in which improvements can be made. This may be due in no small part to the establishment of the Metropolitan Police Authority, which replaced the Home Secretary as police authority for the Met on 3 July 2000. From that date, and for the first time, the Met became directly accountable – through their elected representatives – to the people of London. In addition, the MPA's strategy for the MPS has placed high priority on the requirement of the Race Relations (Amendment) Act 2000, that public authorities must, 'have due regard to the need to tackle racial discrimination, promote equality of opportunity and promote good race relations'.[81] The Met is now achieving notable success in actively recruiting a workforce that more accurately reflects London's diverse population. Scrutiny of all police forces is greater than ever before; and HMIC, ACPO and the Police Training and Development Board (PTDB)[82] strive to ensure that training standards are continually monitored and improved.[83] The Met unquestionably wishes to put its house in order on race and diversity issues. Unfortunately, much of the positive work now being done is in danger of being undermined.

There is at present no national corporate structure to CRR training despite the fact that, following the Scarman Report in 1981, the Police Training Council (PTC) set up a national training scheme in 1983. In the 2003 report, *Diversity Matters*, HMIC looked at the PTC's recommendations on CRR training,[84] and reported that, 'This inspection concludes that after 20 years, none of the above has been adequately encompassed in training programmes.'[85] HMIC also argued that, 'underpinning [the critical success factors of race and diversity] is a requirement for effective and sustained leadership at every level (not only within the training function but also in the wider workplace'.[86] However, in the same report, it was admitted that:

> The overall strategy for training and development ... lacks clarity, direction and unified commitment ... ineffective supervision/line management undermines any message that is contained within training ... there is insufficient community involvement in all aspects of the training cycle.[87]

When one looks at these issues in the context of the Metropolitan Police, it appears clear that, as an inspector at its Hendon Training College suggests, serious difficulties still exist in providing adequate supervision to young and inexperienced constables at street level: the very officers who interact with the public on a daily basis, and who form the front line in the delivery of its policies on race and diversity:

> Seventy per cent of the shifts are probationers. You've got a massive crisis in the Metropolitan Police with junior leadership. They cannot get enough sergeants. I think they're something like three hundred and fifty short. A lot of the sergeants out there are acting sergeants ... therefore there's no junior leaders ... you've got senior PCs – probably with three years service – taking the sergeant's role on and leading junior PCs, probably of two years service and less in street duties at the sharp end ... Probation as a concept of training is laughable. In the Met now I'm looking at Performance Development Reviews (PDRs) they're just not getting done. It's lip service because they can't. The sergeants cannot do it. They're too busy ... My perception is that people now see street duty as the lowest form of known life, and, despite every effort of the Met to say you will only get promoted from a street position, it's still seen as the one thing you have to get away from ... That's where all the bad duties are, poor transport, you get all the rough jobs, you're stressed, overworked, too few officers, poor supervision. After a while you become

dysfunctional because you start to take it out on the people. There's quite a refreshing lack of cynicism because the officers are so young. They're still flushed with enthusiasm. By and large the probationers still want to get out there and do the job. There's a huge desire to want to do the job in the first two or three years: then the reality kicks in.[88]

The inspector's observation endorses the findings of HMIC, who, in his 2002 report, *Training Matters*; stated:

As a consequence of current demands and resources, first-line supervisors are too often assigned to other duties . . . thus resulting in: insufficient assessment interaction between probationer and supervisor; [and] inadequate support being provided to potentially vulnerable new officers.[89]

Compounding the problem of inadequate supervision is the finding of the MPS Scrutiny Report (2003) that 'turnover [of MPS] staff appeared embedded in the MPS culture';[90] as one CDRP partner observed, 'we have had five borough commanders and three BLOs in five years'.[91] The poor quality of leadership and supervision of probationary constables, the desire of the latter to leave frontline policing at the earliest opportunity to join various squads or seek promotion (thereby ensuring an almost constant round of new, inexperienced and poorly led officers to replace them), and the expectation of senior officers at borough level to enhance their career prospects by moving onwards and upwards at the earliest opportunity, ensures that the development of good relations with the community,[92] and gaining their trust and confidence are tasks that are always going to be difficult to achieve under present arrangements. A senior member of the MPA staff has suggested that lack of supervision throughout the Met is a major cause for concern:

It's an unsupervised, unmanaged police force at every level. The questions are not only being asked at the front line but also at the borough level. We're seeing huge discrepancies in stop and search rates by borough. Borough commanders aren't being supervised. Nobody's managing the police at every level.[93]

Metropolitan Police culture, an enduring view of police and society in which the Met has always placed great value on its *de facto* independence from external operational control, remains one of the biggest hurdles to be overcome if its race and diversity policies are to succeed. To whom do the Met see themselves as being accountable? Newman's 'blue book'[94] emphasised the police officer's independence and his accountability to the law, rather than to any superior ranking authority. Such a viewpoint makes the MPA's management function extremely difficult. As one observer put it:

> They're [the Met] accountable to the Crown, to the Queen, to the laws of the land and to their own organisation. They're not accountable to the public. That's not to whom they see where their accountability lies ... the MPA is unique in terms of the national situation because we're only three years old ... why are we [the MPA] right next door to Scotland Yard: why aren't we closer to the GLA? The MPA, trying to assert its own mandate, its own responsibilities as the civilian oversight body, and its not sure how far it can go in asserting that governance over the police. We're hamstrung, because they [the Met] run to the Home Office ... and it's this constant struggle of finding out what they do, this sort of reactive process; and they won't tell you any more than what you've asked for. So this tiny little office over here is trying to figure out what that massive organisation over there is doing. They don't tell you if you don't ask.[95]

Peter Bottomley MP has suggested that, 'the time when the police treat the public fairly will come only when police treat their own colleagues fairly'.[96] Sir Peter Imbert's PLUS programme of the late 1980s was, as we have seen, intended to address the negative attitudes of many police officers towards their civilian colleagues. How little the situation has improved can be gleaned from the observations of a former Met inspector, now a civilian instructor at one of the Met's training centres:

> There is still a serious problem with the way in which police officers regard civilian members of the organisation. If you are a civilian you are still regarded as being 'not in the club.' If I don't tell them [police officers undergoing training] that I'm an ex-police officer when I'm instructing, I can tell there is an attitude of, 'what does he know about policing?' This is a deep-rooted cultural problem.[97]

This observation is supported by the most recent evaluation on training within the Met, carried out on behalf of the MPA. Researchers were 'taken aback' by the stark difference in police response to police and non-police instructors: officers giving far more credence to police instructors.[98]

The problem with the Met's current CRR training is that it begins by considering the Brixton riots of 1981 and the Scarman Report that followed. As such, those receiving training have no understanding or knowledge of the way in which, from the early 1950s, the Met mirrored the racist prejudices of an unenlightened British public. This results in police officers having no conception of crucial developments that shaped the Met's relationship with minority ethnic communities during the first 30 years of large-scale black immigration. The result is that, while people who are black or Asian are often acutely aware of the prejudices and obstacles that were traditionally placed in the way of their parents and grandparents, police officers have a distorted view of the history of police/immigrant relations, and little idea of why black resentment and mistrust of the police developed. Such a problem was highlighted when the MPA organised a one-on-one meeting of 15 young black people and 15 police officers in Hackney:

> One of the aspects of the training was the young people explaining to the officers why they feel they are not being properly policed, and a lot of it was to do with the history. They were able to say, 'Our parents told us about this, our grandparents told us, we've seen it on television.' . . . They had come to this training with history. Many of the police officers were saying, 'Well, it's nothing to do with us. We weren't there. So why are you expecting us to know what attitude you are coming with?' . . . It took the officers a very long time, and I was not sure that they left hearing these very clear messages of how current policing is informed by the history. And, of course, the CRR training doesn't deal with that.[99]

The positive intent now being shown by the Commissioner and his senior colleagues to the question of race and diversity is doomed to fail if supremacist attitudes in the workplace (identified in the 1980s by Sir Peter Imbert) are not eradicated; if the democratically elected MPA is not allowed to properly manage the MPS (as was the complaint of the Home Office Police Department in respect of its own supervision of the Met some 40 years earlier); if the failings in supervision and leadership (identified by Deputy Commander Howlett as far back as 1965) are not put right; and if attitudes to the development of good community relations and partnership (concepts that the evidence would suggest the MPS is yet to truly comprehend) are not immediately given the highest priority. Admittedly, ACPO, HMIC and the Home Office have now identified such problems. But they were identified 20 years earlier and they still exist today. As HMIC Robin Field-Smith admitted, it is the need for cultural change that lies at the heart of the problem:[100] a view that was endorsed by the MPA's Head of Consultation and Diversity:

> The [MPS] culture is not an evaluating culture; it's not a thinking culture; it's not a reflector organisation. It's an activist; and so the

activist constantly acts, and that's why it's actually very difficult for the policies to effect any lasting change ... the core organisation remains unchanged.[101]

There is clearly much to be done if the Met's aspirations in race and diversity are to be realised. The task will for ever be hampered if the 'bobby on the beat', the physical representation of the police service at street level, is inexperienced; frustrated and wants out; lacks understanding of the community he/she serves; is periodically traded in for even more inexperienced replacements; is poorly led and is largely unsupervised. Real improvement will only come with cultural change and the realisation that the priorities of the people of London matter more than what the Met regards as its own priorities. Only then will London's police service be truly accountable. Traditional responses to problems of action and reaction must now find new allies in thought, reflection and a genuine willingness to embrace change.

Notes

1 These included the British National Party (BNP) and the League of Empire Loyalists (LEL). Bowling, *Violent Racism*, pp.39–40.

2 'Sus' was an offence that consisted of acts that were preparatory to the commission of a more substantive offence. For example, a police officer might allege that an accused had been seen to try a number of car doors when stopped: the implication being that such actions were preparatory to the commission of the substantive offence of taking a conveyance or stealing something from the vehicle.

3 The *IB* was replaced in the 1980s by a series of 'white notes' that covered various training issues, one aspect of which did include information on community and race relations.

4 *Police Orders* were published twice weekly, with periodic *Special Police Orders* that dealt with major policy changes or new legislation. The title was later changed to *Police Notices*. There were, however, occasional references to travelling bursaries organised by the Community Relations Commission for senior officers. See *Police Orders* 9, November 1971, Item 11.

5 *Annual Report of Her Majesty's Inspector of Constabulary* (1971), p.63.

6 *HMIC Annual Report* (1973), p.57. The use of the term 'coloured' was still in common usage in official reports at this time.

7 See *HMIC Annual Reports* (1974), p.59; (1975–76), p.61 and (1978), p.67.

8 HMIC Annual Report (1978), p.66.

9 It was partly to address this failing that a system of street duty training was introduced in the early 1980s for probationer constables on leaving Hendon and joining divisions.

10 The term 'process' was used in the Met to refer to the procedure whereby an alleged offender was informed by a police officer that he was to be

reported for an alleged offence, and was particularly used to deal with motoring offences.

11 *Metropolitan Police Inspectors' Initial Course Handbook*, Revised Edition, Section 16, 16 January 1983.

12 *The Brixton Disorders 10–12 April 1981*, Cmnd 8427.

13 HMIC, *Policing London 'Winning Consent'*, A Review of Murder Investigation and Community and Race Relations in the Metropolitan Police (2000), Ch.4.5.

14 See *HMIC Annual Report* (1979), p.90. It is hardly surprising that such a simplistic teaching philosophy was in still in use in the early 1980s. Official figures for educational qualifications of recruits joining the service in England and Wales (excluding the Met) for 1979 revealed that almost 30% of male recruits had no 'O' level (CSE 1) passes. This was an improvement on previous figures. For example, in 1973 and 1974 the percentage of officers joining the service without educational qualifications was 50% of the total. See *HMIC Annual Report* (1974), p.20.

15 P. Southgate, *Home Office Research and Planning Unit, Paper 29, Racism Awareness Training for the Police*, (1984).

16 Ibid. pp.6–7.

17 Ibid. p.7.

18 Policing London, Ch.4.7. The unit was initially based at Brunel University, but from 1989 to 1998 Equality Associates, based in Turvey, Bedfordshire provided training. Though community relations and race relations are clearly divisible issues, the nature of the Met's relationship with West Indians and their descendants was such that, at this time, both terms effectively referred to racial matters.

19 Ibid. Ch.4.19.

20 Ibid. Ch.4.30.

21 Ibid. Ch.4.39.

22 Ibid. Ch.4.47.

23 N. Peppard, letter to author, 25 October 2002.

24 *Special Police Order*, 30 June 1986, p.2.

25 The initial training course is currently of 18 weeks' duration.

26 Special Police Order, 30 June 1986, p.3.

27 Exceptions included advanced driving, firearms training and, in more recent years, public order training; all of which required an officer to undergo periodic reassessment.

28 Dr R. Oakley, interviewed by author, 21 November 2002.

29 Detective chief inspector D. Tucker, interviewed by author, 8 August 2002.

30 NA HO 287/25 The Metropolitan Police and powers of the Secretary of State.

31 Most notably Sir Robert Mark, Commissioner of the Met 1972–76, and James Anderton, Chief Constable of Greater Manchester Police.

32 M. Kettle, 'The Politics of Policing and the Policing of Politics', *Policing the Police*, Vol.2 (1980), p.24.

33 Gilroy, *Union Jack*, p.95.

34 B. Morris interviewed by author, 11 November 2002. Morris was Principal Private Secretary to the Home Secretary 1976–78.

35 See Ch.4 'A New Home Secretary, the Power of the Police Federation and Let's Not Rock the Boat'.

36 The government had originally included a criminal sanction for racial discrimination in the draft of the Race Relations Bill. The proposal was dropped after receipt of advice from police and others that the sanction would be unenforceable.

37 See Weight, *Patriots*, pp.536–39.

38 L. Bridges, 'Policing the urban wasteland', *Race & Class*, No.2 (Autumn 1983), p.163.

39 *HMIC Report* (1970), p.5.

40 *HMIC Report* (1971), p.63.

41 *HMIC Report* (1972), p.63.

42 Ibid.

43 *HMIC Report* (1973), p.57.

44 HMIC Report (1974), p.59.

45 Higgins interview.

46 *Parliamentary Debates (Commons)* (11 March 1980), Vol.980, Cols.1153–57.

47 O'Byrne, *Changing Policing*, p.24. O'Byrne is a former chief constable of Bedfordshire who served in the Met from constable to chief inspector rank.

48 *HMIC Report* (1975), 'The Police Superintendents' Association of England and Wales', p.3.

49 Morris interview. NCIS is the abbreviation for the National Criminal Intelligence Service.

50 Ibid.

51 R. Mark, *In the Office of Constable* (1978), p.87.

52 *Police Orders*, 24 March 1970.

53 W.A. Belson, *The Public and the Police* (1975), p.20.

54 Ibid.

55 Ibid. p.28.

56 Ibid. p.37 Significantly, none of the officers believed that police powers were too extensive.

57 Ibid. p.39.

58 Ibid. p.42.

59 Mark, *Office of Constable*, p.42.

60 K. Newman, The Metropolitan Police: *The Principles of Policing and Guidance for Professional Behaviour* (1985), p.6.

61 Ibid.

62 Ibid. p.12.

63 Gilroy, Union Jack, p.76.

64 Newman, *Principles*, p.48.

65 Report of the National Advisory Commission on Civil Disorders (Washington, DC, 1968).

66 NA CK 2/2 Amendments to the 1965 Race Relations Act.

67 O'Byrne, *Changing Policing*, pp.17–18.

68 Newman, *Principles*, p.54.

69 Imbert interview.

70 Newman, *Principles*, p.21.

71 M. O'Byrne, interviewed by author, 30 October 2002.

72 Imbert interview.
73 O'Byrne, *Changing Policing*, p.96.
74 *Policing London*, Ch.2.4.
75 Ibid. Ch.2.7.
76 *The Stephen Lawrence Inquiry Report*, 1999, Cmnd 4262 – I, Ch.46.1.
77 Ibid. Ch.46.26.
78 Ibid. Ch.46.4.
79 Mark, *Office of Constable*, p.87.
80 The full report was published in February 1999, though some of the recommendations were widely known in the police service before publication.
81 MPA, *Race Equality Scheme*, (n.d.), p.7.
82 Also known as CENTREX and the body which replaced the Police Training Council.
83 See particularly HMIC reports, *Training Matters* (January 2002), and *Diversity Matters* (March 2003).
84 HMIC, *Diversity Matters* (2003), 1.41 These related to probationer training, supervision, the need for a varied approach to training and selection of trainers, individual assessment, training evaluation and recognition that training should ensure effectiveness of operational performance.
85 Ibid.
86 Ibid. 1.31.
87 Ibid. 1.52.
88 Inspector D. Lewis, interviewed by author, 18 December 2003.
89 HMIC, *Training Matters* (2002), 2.35.
90 MPA, *MPS Scrutiny Report: Crime and Disorder Reduction Partnerships* (January, 2003), 2.3.1.
91 Ibid. 2.3.
92 In *Training Matters*, 4.19, HMIC noted that, 'this inspection found that few probationers possessed an adequate understanding of the community.'
93 T. Rees, Policy MPA Development Officer, interviewed by author, 13 January 2004. Robin Field-Smith, HMIC, has argued that supervision of borough commanders is a two-way process. Those supervising them must ensure that they are allowed to get on with the job, while borough commanders often feel they do not need to be supervised. Interviewed by author, 15 January 2004.
94 Newman, *Principles of Policing*, p.71.
95 Rees interview.
96 Quoted in *Training Matters*, 2.24. 8 November 2001.
97 Mr. E. Driscoll, interviewed by author, 29 December 2003.
98 J. Smith, MPA Head of Consultation and Diversity, interviewed by author, 13 January 2004.
99 Smith (MPA) interview.
100 Field-Smith interview.
101 Smith (MPA) interview.

Appendix I

List of interviewees

Name	Position	Date
Banton, Professor Michael	Author of multiple texts on the sociology of policing and relations with immigrant communities. Original member of the Police Working Party on Race Relations in 1969	17.4.2001
Barrow, Dame Jocelyn	Former member of the Campaign Against Racial Discrimination [CARD] and equal rights activist	9.11.2001
Bhamra, Gurdial	Former Inspector, Metropolitan Police	20.11.2001
Collinson, David	Former Chief Inspector, Metropolitan Police	23.11.2000
Dholakia, Navnit	Leader of the Liberal Democrats in the House of Lords	2.5.2001
Driscoll, Edmund	Former Inspector, Metropolitan Police	29.12.2003
English, Michael	Sergeant, Metropolitan Police	23.11.2000
Field-Smith, Robin	Her Majesty's Inspector of Constabulary	15.1.2004
Gerrard, John	Former Assistant Commissioner, Metropolitan Police	24.7.2000
Hall, Dr Trevor	Former Home Office Advisor on race relations	30.1.2002
Higgins, Stewart	Former Chief Superintendent, Metropolitan Police	21.11.2000

Howard-Drake, Jack	Senior civil servant at the Cabinet Office and the Home Office in the 1960s	15.5.2001
Imbert, Sir Peter	Former Commissioner, Metropolitan Police	20.2.2002
Jones, Jack	Former General Secretary of the Trades Union Congress and President of the Transport and General Workers Union	14.1.2002
Kuya, Dorothy	Instructor to police officers on diversity and equal opportunities, equal rights campaigner	3.5.2001
Ladha, Amin	Former member of the GLC-funded Ealing Police Monitoring Group	12.12.2000
Lewis, David	Inspector, Metropolitan Police	18.12.2003
Linge, Frederick	Former Police Constable, Metropolitan Police	7.1.2001
Mangar, Harold	Former member of the Community Relations Commission and actively involved in police training. Equal rights activist	30.4.2001
Morris, Bob	Former senior civil servant at the Home Office and Home Office liaison officer with the Metropolitan Police	11.11.2002
Nicholls, Harry	Former Metropolitan Police Special Branch Chief Superintendent	23.7.2002
Oakley, Dr Robin	Consultant to the Metropolitan Police on diversity training and former training advisor on the Turvey Training Programme	21.11.2002
O'Byrne, Michael	Former Chief Constable, Bedfordshire Police and ex Metropolitan Police Officer	30.10.2002
Peppard, Nadine	Former Secretary of the National Committee for Commonwealth Immigrants and its successor, the Community Relations Commission	12.2.2001
Rees, Tim	Policy Development Officer, Metropolitan Police Authority	13.1.2004

Reid, Gladstone	West Indian immigrant to Britain and former police officer in Guyana	17.10.2000
Robbins, Brian	Former Inspector, Metropolitan Police	15.1.2001
Roberts, Norwell QPM	Former Detective Sergeant, Metropolitan Police	2.4.2002
Smith, Julia	Head of Consultation and Diversity, Metropolitan Police Authority	13.1.2004
Taverne, Dick	Member of the Liberal Democrats in the House of Lords, and former Labour Home Office Minister in the 1960s	9.2.2001
Thompson, Clarence	Chairman, West Indian Standing Conference	9.10.2001
Tucker, David	Detective Chief Inspector, Metropolitan Police Diversity Directorate	8.8.2002

The Policeman

RELEASE FOLLOWING ARREST

The question of releasing a person who has been arrested is a matter for the officer in charge of the Police Station to which the person was taken. After he has been charged with the offence for which he was arrested the person will, unless the circumstances are unusual, generally be released provided he gives a personal guarantee to attend the Magistrates' Court the following day. If this undertaking is broken the person may suffer financial penalty. For serious offences it may be necessary for the person to find some friends who will give their own personal guarantees that he will attend court as directed.

FACILITIES

If you wish to visit a person who is held at a Police Station the officer in charge will decide whether this can be arranged.

If a person kept at a Police Station is charged with an offence he will be given a form which will tell him how he may obtain release of the circumstances allow, and how arrangements can be made for him to get in touch with his solicitor or friends, or for them to visit him at the Police Station.

NOTE

This leaflet sets out very briefly certain basic facts about a policeman's duty which will bring him into direct contact with the general public. It does not pretend to cover every situation and if in any difficulty or doubt you are advised to call at a Police Station. In many parts of London Police Liaison Officers have been specially appointed to help immigrants in their dealings with Police.

NA HO287/1456 *The Policeman*, an advice leaflet for immigrants to Britain on the role of the police. Courtesy: The National Archive.

LONDON'S METROPOLITAN POLICE

The object of this leaflet is to provide newcomers to this country, and to London in particular, with a brief outline and so a better understanding of the policeman's role in society.

The Police, both men and women, are there to help you and will always do so whenever they can, even if it is only to tell you the right person to go to see in the case of problems with which they cannot deal. You may contact the Police by calling at any Police Station or, in the case of an emergency, by dialling "999" from any telephone. Naturally, if you see a policeman in the street you can always seek his assistance.

WHERE POLICE CAN HELP

Police can help you in many ways. If young people or children are missing from home, or older people have left without warning and it is feared that they may have come to some harm, you should tell the Police. In the case of adults who have left home, however, even if they have not told anyone they are leaving, Police can only help if the person missing is believed to be ill or may have come to some harm.

If some offence against the law has or may seem to have been committed against you, you should not hesitate to report the matter. Police will ask for your help in looking into the facts and you should be prepared to give this help.

WHERE POLICE CANNOT HELP

Unlike other countries, the policeman in London cannot act like a judge in such things as a quarrel between husband and wife, or between a landlord and tenant. His duty, by law, is limited to keeping order and calm and to advise the people concerned who can help them. It is not a question of his not wishing to help or that he is not interested in your problem, but he would be acting beyond his powers if he took any other course.

POWER OF POLICE WHEN A CRIME IS COMMITTED

When a policeman is trying to find out who has committed an offence he has to question any person who may be able to help in tracing the offender and it is the duty of every citizen to assist him in this task.

In London and other large cities, if a policeman has reason to believe that someone has stolen goods with him, he has the power to stop that person, question him and generally to satisfy himself whether a crime has been committed or not. This will sometimes mean that a private person will be stopped in the street and asked to open say a suitcase, bag, parcel or the boot of a car, etc., and if that person does not do this the policeman may have to take him to a Police Station. Such powers are used tactfully and the policeman will not keep you longer than is necessary, provided a satisfactory explanation is given quickly.

KEEPING PUBLIC ORDER

The policeman, besides being responsible for preventing crime and helping to protect people and their property, also has the duty of keeping order in the streets and other public places. The roads and pavements are for the free use of all persons and it may be necessary for a policeman to ask people to move if he considers they are causing an obstruction.

ARREST

It should be clearly understood that the Police do not make the laws, but it is their duty to carry them out. To help them to do this Parliament has given the Police certain powers, and these include the power of arrest in particular circumstances. If a person is arrested he must go with the policeman to a Police Station. He should not offer resistance because this means that the policeman may then have to use force to overcome such resistance and no policeman likes doing this if he can avoid it.

As proof that he may act as a policeman every officer who is not wearing uniform carries a "Warrant Card" giving his name and proof of his authority which he must produce if you ask him. If you have doubts you should ask for a uniformed officer to be called or go to the nearest Police Station.

Appendix III

Take pride in doing a man's job- join London's Police

Maintaining law and order in a city as big as London is a man's job. As a London policeman you're right in the centre of things. It's a job which commands respect and demands integrity and the ability to take decisions.

Pay is good, too. For a Constable it starts at £780 (£880 if 22 or over) and rises to £1,155 after nine years' service. You get free housing or a generous tax-free rent allowance of up to £6.10.0 a week - and full job security. And, if you have the will to get ahead, promotion can come fast.

You can apply to join if you are 5'8' or over, between 19 and 30, and have good health and normal eyesight (men who wear glasses or contact lenses within certain minimum standards are eligible). Fill in the coupon below for full information.

To Recruiting Officer, Dept xxx, New Scotland Yard, London, S.W.1

NAME

ADDRESS

AGE

E. Take pride in doing a man's job

NA MEPO2/11463 Metropolitan Police recruiting advertisement: National Police Recruiting Campaign 1962–69. Courtesy: The National Archive.

Bibliography

Official records (unpublished)

National Archive, Kew

Cabinet minutes and memoranda

CAB124/1191   Proposal to restrict the right of British subjects from overseas to enter and remain in UK 1954 (Jan–Dec)

CAB124/1192   Proposal to restrict the right of British subjects from overseas to enter and remain in UK 1955 Jan–1965 Feb

CAB134/1466   Cabinet meeting 1957

CAB124/1515   Report on the projection of the Commonwealth in the United Kingdom

Race Relations Board

CK2/2   Amendments to Race Relations Act

CK2/16   Race Relations Board – Chairman's correspondence with the Home Secretary

CK2/572   Race Relations Board. Singh v Police: case outside scope of Act 1969

Colonial Office

CO1032/331   Immigration into the United Kingdom from the West Indies

CO1037/2   Colonial Office working party on the position of police forces in the later stages of constitutional development 1953–1954

CO1037/80   Saint Vincent Statutory Rules and Orders 1948, No. 110

CO318/399/3   Movements of Marcus Garvey 1930

CO318/427/11 Trinidad and Barbados riots 1937: West Indian repercussions

Home Office

HMIC	*Annual Reports 1971–85*
HMIC	*Training Matters*, 2002
HMIC	*Diversity Matters*, 2003
HO272/2	Royal Commission Report 1962
HO272/53	Commissioner's evidence to the Royal Commission on the Police
HO287/25	Metropolitan Police: relationship with Home Secretary, formation of a committee to ensure closure relationship: history of the Metropolitan Police from 1829 to date. 1961–69
HO287/85	Report of the Royal Commission on the Police
HO287/107	Students' lesson notes 1961 and 1963; training of probationary constables
HO287/250	Operational control of colonial police forces: policy on policing in the colonies 1956
HO287/273	Metropolitan Police reports for 1955–59
HO287/274	Annual report of the Commissioner of Police for the Metropolis, 1959
HO287/1453	Home Office view on whether it should urge police forces to recruit from ethnic minorities 1965–69
HO287/1455	Working Party on police training in race relations: minutes 1970
HO287/1456	Working Party on police training in race relations: research 1971
HO287/1458	Recruitment of 'coloured' policemen: policy
HO287/1459	Police and Colour Recruitment
HO287/1466	(PAB (68) 2) Proposed amendment to the Police Discipline Code 1968–69
HO287/1468	Suggested exchange arrangements between British and West Indian police forces 1965
HO307/150	The first annual report of the Race Relations Board
HO325/9	Racial disturbances in Notting Hill, activities of extreme organisations: deputation of MPs to see the Secretary of State 1951–61
HO344/11	'Immigration of British subjects into the United Kingdom', Report by *ad hoc* Committee of Ministers, 1950–52
HO344/12	Working party to consider restriction of right of British subjects from overseas to enter and remain in the UK, report and statistics 1953–58
HO344/27	Explanation of government policy in light of anxiety of Commonwealth Committee of Conservative Back-

benchers about unrestricted immigration from the Commonwealth 1958

HO344/100 Coloured people from British colonial territories: draft Cabinet memorandum 1950

HO344/106 Chief Constables' replies to questionnaires on numbers and conduct of coloured people in their area, 1953

HO344/117 Information from Chief Constables 1955–56

HO344/122 March 1957 review of reports from chief constables on the social and economic problems caused by immigration. Insight into the spread of immigrants throughout the country and attitudes towards them

HO344/238 The appointment of 'coloured' policemen and magistrates

HO376/65 Consideration of the future structure of the Race Relations Board and National Committee for Commonwealth Immigrants 1967

HO376/81 Security implications 1968

HO376/128 Social and economic effects of coloured immigration 1963–64

HO376/135 Relations between police and immigrants

HO376/140 Ministerial Committee on Immigration and Assimilation

HO376/147 Race Relations Research: public attitudes to immigrants and the Race Relations Act

HO376/150 Extract from the PEP Report on Racial Discrimination

HO376/159 Select Committee on Race Relations and Immigration Part III of the White Paper 'Immigration from the Commonwealth' (Cmnd 2739, August 1965)

HO377/43 Pilot experiment on premature wastage of officers from the police service 1967

HO377/72 Report No.8/69 An assessment of the promotion prospects for the period 1969–78 with special reference to the effect of the graduate entry scheme and the special course

HO377/76 Recruiting survey 1969

HO377/85 Man Management Survey by the Home Office Police Planning Organisation – January 1970

HO377/88 Report of the Home Office Police Scientific Development Branch

Metropolitan Police Authority

MPA *Race Equality Scheme*, 'Action Plans 2002–2005' (n.d.)

Metropolitan Police Service

MEPO2/8342	*The Blue Lamp* script
MEPO2/8614	Nationality qualifications for candidates for the police service: 1931–50, 1962–63
MEPO2/9047	Reports on settlement of 'coloured' Commonwealth immigrants in London Boroughs: 1949–52
MEPO2/9563	Reports on settlement of 'coloured' Commonwealth immigrants in London Boroughs: 1949–52
MEPO2/9730	Police training: methods employed concerning the problems of immigrant communities 1965
MEPO2/9854	Police liaison with West Indian community in London. Account of the Metropolitan Police's attempts to improve relations with the West Indian community through liaison with the West Indian Standing Conference 1959–68
MEPO2/9992	Disturbances involving 'coloured' persons in London. Metropolitan Police reports on incidents: 1960–61
MEPO2/10431	Commissioner's conferences 1962
MEPO2/10432	Commissioner's conferences, notes and minutes of meetings with senior officers 1963
MEPO2/10432	Commissioner's conferences, notes and minutes of meetings with senior officers 1964
MEPO2/10434	Commissioner's conferences 1965
MEPO2/10435	Commissioner's conference with chief superintendents 1966
MEPO2/10489	Race Relations Act 1965. Commissioner's and Solicitor's observations on the proposed Bill, amendment to Police General Orders 1965
MEPO2/10534	Commissioner's Conference with Commanders, 9 March 1965
MEPO2/10596	Mobile unit policing (Accrington scheme): implementation of scheme in the Metropolitan Police District 1966
MEPO2/10600	Fulham Unit Beat Policing scheme 1966
MEPO2/10638	Police representation on proposed Kensington and Chelsea Inter-Racial Council 1966–69
MEPO2/10790	Complaints against the Metropolitan Police in selected categories 1968
MEPO2/10791	Complaints against the Metropolitan Police in selected categories 1969
MEPO2/10834	Police Federation the problem outlining deficiencies in manpower and equipment: Response by Superintendents' Association, Commissioner's observations and liaison with Home Office 1964–66

MEPO2/11283	First black policewoman (Sislin Fay Allen): press interest and racist correspondence
MEPO2/11463	National police recruiting campaign: 1962–69: Metropolitan Police participation
MEPO4/213	Commissioner's Annual Report 1965
MEPO4/215	Report of the Commissioner of Police for the Metropolis: 1967
MEPO4/216	Report of the Commissioner of Police for the Metropolis: 1968
MEPO28/9	Community relations survey Metropolitan Police 1969–70

Stationary Office records

STAT14/3260	Report of inquiry by Mr A.E. James QC into the circumstances in which it was possible for detective sergeant Harold Gordon Challenor of the Metropolitan Police to continue on duty at a time when he appears to have been affected by the onset of mental illness
HMSO	*The Brixton Disorders 10–12 April 1981, Cmnd 8427*
HMSO	*Stephen Lawrence Inquiry Report 1999, Cmnd 4262*

Metropolitan Police publications

Met. Police	*Instruction Book.* Restricted publication issued to each Metropolitan Police officer on joining the Service. The book was withdrawn and replaced by a series of recruit lesson notes in the early 1980s
Met. Police	*Police Orders*, 24 March 1970
Met. Police	*Special Police Order*, 30 June 1986
Met. Police	*Inspectors' Initial Course Handbook*, revised edition, January 1983
Met. Police	*Scrutiny Report: Crime and Disorder Reduction Partnerships*, January 2003

Official records (published)

Parliamentary debates (Commons)

Volume 459, 10 December 1948
Volume 459, 19 July 1948
Volume 477, 12 July 1950
Volume 488, 13 June 1951
Volume 493, 8 November 1951
Volume 514, 29 April 1953

Volume 517, 2 July 1953
Volume 569, 2 May 1957
Volume 598, 29 June 1959
Volume 603, 9 April 1959
Volume 605, 7 May 1959
Volume 607, 18 June 1959
Volume 609, 20 July 1959
Volume 615, 16 December 1959
Volume 691, 12 March 1964
Volume 715, 8 July 1965
Volume 723, 4 February 1966
Volume 728, 18 May 1966
Volume 980, 11 March 1980

Published sources

Newspaper articles

Bolton Evening News 9 November 1966
Daily Express 12 January 1955
Daily Herald 20 January 1950
Evening Standard 6 October 1954
Magnet News No.1, 13 February 1965
Media Guardian 3 February 2003
New Statesman 30 April 2001
New Statesman and Nation 13 November 1954
Police Review 27 January 1950–18 July 1969
Sun 24 November 1964
The Observer 1 September 1968
The Times 9 November 1954–20 March 1978

Books and articles to 1970

(Place of publication is London, unless indicated otherwise)
Banton, M. *White and Coloured*, Jonathan Cape, 1959
Banton, M. *The Policeman in the Community*, Basic Books, 1964
Barbour, F.B. (ed.) *The Black Power Revolt*, Toronto: Collier Books, 1968
Bastide, R. 'Dusky Venus, Black Apollo', *Race*, No. 3, 1961–2, pp.10–18
Bennett, A.G. *Because They Know Not*, Phoenix Press, 1959
Bowes, S. *The Police and Civil Liberties*, Lawrence & Wishart, 1966
Butterfield, H. *The Whig Interpretation of History*, G. Bell and Sons, 1931
Constantine, L. *Colour Bar*, Stanley Paul, 1954
Deakin, N. 'Residential Segregation in Britain: A Comparative Note', *Race*, No. 6, 1964–5, pp. 18–26

Deakin, N. 'The Politics of the Commonwealth Immigrants Bill', *The Political Quarterly*, Vol. 39, No. 1, Jan–Mar 1968, pp.37–45

Deakin, N. *Colour, Citizenship and British Society*, Panther, 1970

Glass, R. *Newcomers: West Indians in London*, George Allen & Unwin, 1960

Hatch, S. 'Coloured People in School Textbooks', *Race: The Journal of the Institute of Race Relations*, Vol. 4, No. 1, November 1962, pp.63–72

Horowitz, D. 'The British Conservatives and the Racial Issue on Decolonisation', *Race*, No. 2 (October 1970), pp.169–87

Hunte, J. *Nigger Hunting in England?* West Indian Standing Conference, 1965

Hyndman, A. 'The West Indian in London', in S.K. Ruck (ed.) *The West Indian Comes to England*, Routledge & Kegan Paul, 1960, pp.65–136

Lambert, J. 'Police and the Community', *Race Today*, November 1970, pp.388–90

Lee, R. 'The Education of Immigrant Children in England', *Race*, No.2, October 1965, pp.131–45

MacInnes, C. *City of Spades*, Macgibbon & Kee, 1957

Marland, M. *Four Television Scripts*, Longman Imprint Books, 1968

Mason, P. 'The Coloured Problem in Britain as it Affects Africa and the Commonwealth', *African Affairs*, Vol. 58, No. 231, April, 1959, pp. 110–23

Merricks, F.R. 'The Development of Community Relations in the Metropolitan Police', *Police Journal*, No. 43, January, 1970, pp.29–35

Nandy, D. 'An Illusion of Competence', in A. Lester and N. Deakin (eds) *Policies for Racial Equalities*, Fabian Society, 1967

Patterson, S. *Dark Strangers*, Tavistock Publications, 1963

Patterson, S. *Immigration and Race Relations in Britain: 1960–1967*, Oxford University Press, 1969

Richmond, A.H. *Colour Prejudice in Britain*, Routledge & Kegan Paul, 1954

Rose, R. and associates *Colour and Citizenship: A Report on British Race Relations*, Oxford University Press, 1969

Ruck, S.K. (ed.)*The West Indian Comes to England*, Routledge, 1960

Books and articles from 1970

Alderson, J. *Law and Disorder*, Hamish Hamilton, 1984

Alderson, J. 'The Case for Community Policing', in D. Cowell, T. Jones and J. Young (eds), *Policing the Riots*, Junction Books, 1982, pp.135–46

Aldgate, A. and Richards, J. *Best of British: Cinema and Society from 1930 to the Present*, I.B. Tauris Publishers, 1999

Ascoli, D. *The Queen's Peace*, Hamish Hamilton, 1979

Bagley, C. and Verma, G.K. *Racial Prejudice, the Individual and Society*, Saxon House, 1979

Bailey, V. 'The Metropolitan Police, the Home Office and the Threat of Outcast London', in V. Bailey (ed.), *Policing and Punishment in Nineteenth Century Britain*, Croom Helm, 1981, pp.94–125

Banton, M. *Police Community Relations*, William Collins & Sons, 1972

Banton, M. 'The Influence of Colonial Status upon Black-White Relations in England, 1948–58', *Sociology*, Vol.17, No.4, November 1983 pp. 546–59

Banton, M. 'Progress in Ethnic and Racial Studies', *Ethnic and Racial Studies*, Vol. 24, No. 2, March 2001, pp.173–94

Barnett, C. *The Lost Victory*, Basingstoke: Macmillan, 1995

Barr, C. *Ealing Studios*, Cameron Books, 1977

Baxter, J. and Koffman, L. *Police the Constitution and the Community*, Abingdon: Professional Books, 1985

Bell, D.S. *The Conservative Government 1979–84*, Croom Helm, 1985

Belson, W.A. *The Public and the Police*, Harper & Row, 1975

Benyon, J. and Solomons, J. (eds) *The Roots of Urban Unrest*, Oxford: Pergamon, 1987

Bernasconi, R. (ed.) *Race*, Oxford: Blackwell Publishers, 2000

Billig, M. *Fascists: A Social Psychological View of the National Front*, Academic Press, 1978

Booth, A. *British Economic Policy 1931–49*, Lewes: Harvester Wheatsheaf, 1989

Bourke, J. *Working-Class Cultures in Britain 1890–1960*, Routledge, 1994

Bourne, S. *Black in the British Frame*, Cassell, 1998

Bowling, B. *Violent Racism – Victimization, Policing and Social Context*, Oxford University Press, 1998

Bowling, B. and Phillips, C. 'Policing Ethnic Minority Communities' in T. Newburn (ed.) *Handbook of Policing*, Cullompton: Willan Publishing, 2003, pp.528–55

Brewer, J. *The Police, Public Order and the State*, Basingstoke: Macmillan, 1988

Bridges, L. 'Policing the Urban Wasteland', *Race and Class*, No. 2 Autumn, 1983 pp.31–47

Brogden, M. *The Police: Autonomy and Consent*, Academic Press, 1982

Brown, A.R. *Political Languages of Race and the Politics of Exclusion*, Ashgate Publishing, 1999

Brown, J. *A Theory of Police – Immigrant Relations*, Cranfield Institute of Technology, 1974

Brown, C. *Black and White Britain*: The Third PSI Report, Heinemann, 1984

Brown, R. *Prejudice*, Oxford: Blackwell Publishers, 1995

Bulpitt, J. 'Continuity, Autonomy and Peripheralisation: the Anatomy of the Centre's Race Statecraft in England', in Z. Layton-Henry and P.B. Rich (eds) *Race, Government and Politics in Britain*, Basingstoke: Macmillan, 1986, pp.17–44

Bundred, S. Accountability and the Metropolitan Police, in D. Cowell, T. Jones and J. Young (eds) *Policing the Riots*, Junction Books, 1982

Bunyan, T. 'The Police Against the People', *Race and Class*, Nos. 2 & 3, Autumn 1981 and Winter 1982, pp.153–70

Butler, L.J. *Britain and Empire: Adjusting to a Post-Imperial World*, I.B. Tauris, 2002

Callaghan, J. *Time and Chance*, Collins, 1987

Carr-Hill, R. and Drew, D. 'Blacks, Police and Crime' in A. Bhat, R. Carr-Hill and S. Ohri (eds) *Britain's Black Population*, Aldershot: Gower, 1988

Cashmore, E. and Troyna, A. *Black Youth in Crisis*, George Allen & Unwin, 1982

Cashmore, E. and McLaughlin, E. (eds) *Out of Order? Policing Black People*, Routledge, 1991

Chase, L.A. 'West Indians and the Police', *New Community*, Vol. 3, No. 3, Summer 1984, pp.205–10

Clarke, J., Crichter, C., Jefferson, T., Lambert, J. 'The Selection of Evidence and the Avoidance of Racialism: a Critique of the Parliamentary Select Committee on Race Relations and Immigration', *New Community*, Vol. 3, No. 3, Summer 1974, pp.172–92

Colley, L. 'Britishness and Otherness: An Argument', *Journal of British Studies*, Vol. 31, 1992, pp.309–29

Collins, M. 'Pride and Prejudice: West Indian Men in Mid-Twentieth Century Britain', *Journal of British Studies*, Vol. 40, No. 3, July, 2001, pp.391–418

Collins, M. 'The Fall of the English Gentleman: the National Character in Decline, c.1918–1970', *Historical Research*, Vol. 75, No. 187, February 2002, pp.90–111

Commission for Racial Equality *Racial Harassment on Local Authority Housing Estates*, CRE, 1981

Cox, B. *Civil Liberties in Britain*, Harmondsworth: Penguin, 1975

Craig, F.W.S. *Conservative & Labour Party Conference Decisions 1945–1981*, Parliamentary Research Services, 1982

Daniels, T. and Gerson, J. (eds)*The Colour Black: Black Images in British Television*, BFI Publishing, 1989

Davis, J. 'From "Rookeries" to "Communities": Race, Poverty and Policing in London, 1850–1985', *History Workshop Journal*, No. 27, 1989, pp.66–85

Dear, G. 'Coloured Immigrant Communities and the Police', *Police Journal*, No. 45, April, 1972, pp.128–50

Department of the Environment *Department of the Environment Inner Cities Directorate (1983): Information Notes No. 2 1981 Census, Urban Deprivation*, Department of the Environment, 1983

Drummet, M. *et al. The Death of Blair Peach*, NCCL, 1980

Dummett, A. *A Portrait of English Racism,* Harmondsworth: Pelican, 1973

Eagleton, T., Jameson, F. and Said, E.W. *Nationalism, Colonialism, and Literature,* Minneapolis: University of Minnesota Press, 1990

Emsley, C. *The English Police,* Longman, 1991

Emsley, C. 'The English Bobby: An Indulgent Tradition', in R. Porter (ed.) *Myths of the English,* Cambridge: Polity Press, 1992, pp.114–35

Ferris, P. *Sex and the British,* Mandarin, 1993

Friedlander, C.P. and Mitchell, E. *The Police: Servants or Masters?,* Hart-Davis, 1974

Fryer, P. *Black People in the British Empire: An Introduction,* Pluto Press, 1988

Fryer, P. *Staying Power: The History of Black People in Britain,* Pluto, 1984

Gamble, A. *The Conservative Nation,* Routledge & Kegan Paul, 1974

Gilroy, P. *There Ain't No Black in the Union Jack,* Hutchinson, 1987

Gilroy, P. *Between Camps,* Allen Lane, 2000

GLC *Policing London,* Vol. 3, No. 16, 1985, pp.17–32

Goldstein, J. (ed.) *Foucault and the Writing of History,* Oxford: Blackwell, 1994

Goulbourne, H. *Ethnicity and Nationalism in Post-Imperial Britain,* Cambridge University Press, 1991

Grimshaw, R. and Jefferson, T. *Interpreting Police Work,* Allen & Unwin, 1987

Grant, B.K. (ed.) *Film Genre: Theory and Criticism,* Scarecrow Press, 1977

Gutzmore, C. 'Capital, "Black Youth" and Crime', *Race and Class* Vol. 25, No. 2, 1983, pp.13–30

Hain, P. (ed.) *Policing the Police,* Vol. 2, John Calder, 1980

Hall, S. *et al. Policing the Crisis,* Basingstoke, Macmillan, 1987

Hansen, P.H. 'Confetti of Empire: The Conquest of Everest in Nepal, India, Britain and New Zealand', *Comparative Studies in Society and History,* No. 2, April 2000, pp.307–32

Hartman, P. and Husband, C. *Racism and the Mass Media,* Davis Poynter, 1974

HCRC *Policing in Hackney: A Record of HCRE's Experience 1978–1982,* Hackney CRE, 1983

Hill, J. *Sex, Class and Realism: British Cinema 1956–1963,* BFI Publishing, 1986

Her Majesty's Inspector of Constabulary *Policing London 'Winning Consent', A Review of Murder Investigation and Community and Race Relations in the Metropolitan Police,* HMSO, 2000

HMSO *Chronological Table of the Statutes Part II: 1951–1990, (n.d.)*

Holdaway, S. and Barron, A.M. *Resigners? The Experience of Black and Asian Police Officers,* University of Warwick, 1997

Holdaway, S. 'Changes in Urban Policing', *British Journal of Sociology,* Vol. 28, No. 2: 1977, pp.119–35

Holdaway, S. *Inside the British Police,* Oxford: Basil Blackwell, 1983

Holdaway, S. *The Racialisation of British Policing,* Basingstoke: Macmillan, 1996

Holmes, C. *John Bull's Island – Immigration & British Society, 1871–1971,* Basingstoke: Macmillan, 1988

Hough, J.M. and Heal, K.H. *Policing Effectiveness: Some Popular Misconceptions,* Home Office Research Bulletin, No. 7, Home Office, 1979

Howell, D.W. and Morgan, K.O. (eds) *Crime, Protest and Police in Modern British Society,* Cardiff: University of Wales Press, 1999

Humphry, D. *Police Power and Black People,* Panther, 1972

Humphry, D and John, G. *Because They're Black,* Harmondsworth: Pelican, 1971

Ignatiev, N. & Garvey, Y. (eds) *Race Traitor,* New York: Routledge, 1996

James, C.L.R. *The Black Jacobins,* Allison & Busby, 1980

Jefferson, T. and Grimshaw, R. *Controlling the Constable: Police Accountability in England and Wales,* Frederick Muller Limited, 1984

Jenkins, R. *A Life at the Centre,* Pan Books, 1991

Jones, Newburn, T. and Smith, D. *Democracy and Policing,* Policy Studies Institute, 1994

Judge, A. 'Scarman: Police Responses', *New Community,* Vol. 9, No. 3, Winter 1981/Spring 1982, pp.364–5

Judge, A. 'The Police and the Coloured Communities: A Police View', *New Community,* Vol. 3, No. 3, Summer 1984, pp.199–204

Judge, A. *The Force of Persuasion,* The Police Federation, 1994

Kettle, M. 'The Politics of Policing and the Policing of Politics', in P. Hain (ed.) *Policing the Police,* Vol. 2, 1980, pp.9–62

Kettle, M. and Hodges, L. *Uprising: The Police, the People and the Riots in Britain's Cities,* Pan, 1982

Landau, S. 'Juveniles and the Police', *British Journal of Criminology,* Vol. 21, No. 1, 1981, pp.27–46

Layton-Henry, Z. & Rich, P.B. *Race, Government & Politics in Britain,* Basingstoke, Macmillan, 1986

Layton-Henry, Z. (ed.) *Conservative Party Politics,* Basingstoke, Macmillan, 1980

Lea, J. and Young, J. *What is to be Done About Law and Order?* Harmondsworth: Penguin, 1984

London Strategic Policy Unit *Policing London: Collected Reports of the LSPU Monitoring and Research Group briefing paper* No. 2, 1987

McConville, M. and Shepherd, D. *Watching Police, Watching Communities,* Routledge, 1992

McNee, D. *McNee's Law,* William Collins & Sons, 1983

Madan, R. *Coloured Minorities in Great Britain,* Aldwych Press, 1979

Mark, R. *In the Office of Constable,* Glasgow: Fontana/Collins, 1978

Mark, R. *Policing a Perplexed Society,* Allen & Unwin, 1977

Marshall, P. 'Policing: the Community Relations Aspect', *New Community*, Vol. 3, No. 3, Summer 1984, pp.193–8

Marshall, Newby, Rose and Vogler *Social Class in Modern Britain*, Hutchinson, 1988

Marwick, A. *British Society Since 1945*, Harmondsworth: Penguin, 1982

Marwick, A. *Class: Image and Reality*, Basingstoke, Macmillan, 1980

May, R. and Cohen, R. 'The Interaction between Race and Colonialism: A Case Study of the Liverpool Race Riots of 1919', *Race and Class* Vol. 16, No. 2, 1974, pp.111–16

Mayhew, H. *London Labour and the London Poor*, Harmondsworth: Penguin, 1985

Mercer, K. *Welcome to the Jungle*, Routledge, 1994

Metropolitan Police *Force Orders on Racial Incidents*, Metropolitan Police, 1978

Miles, R. 'The Riots of 1958: Notes on the Ideological Construction of "Race Relations" as a Political Issue in Britain', *Immigrants and Minorities*, No. 33, 1984, pp.252–75

Morgan, K.O. *Callaghan: A Life*, Oxford University Press, 1997

Mullard, C. *Black Britain*, George Allen & Unwin, 1973

Murphy, R. *Sixties British Cinema*, BFI Publishing, 1992

NCCL *Southall 23 April 1979*, NCCL, 1980

Newburn, T. *Permission and Regulation: Law and Morals in Post-War Britain*, Routledge, 1992

Newman, Sir K. *The Metropolitan Police: The Principles of Policing and Guidance for Professional Behaviour*, Metropolitan Police, 1985

Nugent, N. and King, R. *The British Right*, Saxon House, 1977

Obelkevich, J. 'Consumption', *Understanding Post-War British Society*, Routledge, 1994, pp.141–54

O'Byrne, M. *Changing Policing: Revolution Not Evolution*, Lyme Regis: Russell House Publishing, 2001

Oliver, I. *Police, Government and Accountability*, Basingstoke, Macmillan, 1981

Panayi, P. (ed.) *Racial Violence in Britain in the Nineteenth and Twentieth Centuries*, Leicester University Press, 1993

Parekh, B. *Rethinking Multiculturalism*, Basingstoke, Macmillan, 2000

Paul, K. *Whitewashing Britain Race and Citizenship in the Postwar Era*, New York: Cornell University Press, 1997

Paul, K. 'Communities of Britishness: Migration in the Last Gasp of Empire', in S. Ward (ed.), *British Culture and the End of Empire*, Manchester University Press, 2001, pp.180–99

Peach, C. *et al. Ethnic Segregation in Cities*, Croom Helm, 1981

Peppard, N. 'Into the Third Decade', *New Community*, Vol. 1, No. 2, January 1972, pp.93–8

Phillips, M. and Phillips, T. *Windrush: The Irresistible Rise of Multi-Racial Britain*, Harper Collins, 1999

Pilkington, A. 'Responses – The State, the Mass Media and Racial Minorities', *Race Relations in Britain*, University Tutorial Press, 1984, pp.145–73

Pilkington, E. *Beyond the Mother Country: West Indians and the Notting Hill White Riots*, I.B. Tauris, London, 1988

Pilkington, E. 'The West Indian Community and the Notting Hill Riots of 1958', in P. Panayi (ed.) *Racial Violence in Britain in the Nineteenth and Twentieth Centuries*, Leicester University Press, 1996, pp.171–83

Pines, J. (ed.) *Black and White in Colour: Black People in British Television Since 1936*, BFI Publishing, 1992

PSI *The Police and People in London*, Vols. 1–4, Policy Studies Institute, 1983

Pope, D. *Community Relations – The Police Response*, Runnymede Trust, 1976

Pulle, S. *Police-Immigrant Relations in Ealing*, Runnymede Trust, 1973

Ratcliffe, P. (ed.) *'Race', Ethnicity & Nation*, UCL Press, 1994

Reiner, R. *The Blue-Coated Worker*, Cambridge University Press, 1978

Reiner, R. *The Politics of the Police*, Lewes: Wheatsheaf Books, 1985

Reiner, R. *Chief Constables*, Oxford University Press, 1991

Richards, J. 'Basil Dearden at Ealing', in A. Burton, T. O'Sullivan and P. Wells (eds), *Liberal Directions. Basil Dearden and the Postwar British Film Culture*, 1997, Flicks Books, pp.14–35

Richards, J. 'Imperial Heroes for a Post-Imperial Age: Films and the End of Empire', in S. Ward (ed.), *British Culture and the End of Empire*, Manchester University Press, 2001, pp.128–44

Roach, L. 'The Metropolitan Police Community Relations Branch', *Police Studies*, September, 1978

Rush, A.S. 'Imperial Identity in Colonial Minds: Harold Moody and the League of Coloured Peoples, 1931–50', *Twentieth Century British History*, Vol. 13, No. 4, 2002, pp.356–83

Said, E. *Orientalism*, Harmondsworth: Penguin, 1979

Schaffer, E. *Community Policing*, Croom Helm, 1980

Schwarz, B. (ed.) *The Expansion of England*, Routledge, 1992

Scarman Lord *The Brixton Disorders 10–12 April 1981*: Official Report, 1981

Scraton, P. *The State of the Police*, Pluto, 1985

Scraton, P. (ed.) *Community Policing: Towards the Police State?* Milton Keynes: Open University Press, 1987

Sivanandan, A. 'Race, Class and the State: The Black Experience in Britain, *Race and Class*, No. 1, Institute of Race Relations, 1976

Sivanandan, A. 'From Resistance to Rebellion: Asian and Afro-Caribbean Struggles in Britain', *Race & Class*, No. 23, 1981–82, pp.111–70

Small, S. *Policing and People in London: Vol. II – 'A Group of Young Black People'*, Policy Studies Institute, 1983

Smith, A.M. *New Right Discourse on Race & Sexuality*, Cambridge University Press, 1994

Smith, D.J. *Police and People in London, Vol. 1, 'A Survey of Londoners, Police and People in London'*, Policy Studies Institute, 1983

Smith, D.J. *Police and People in London, Vol.3, 'A Survey of Police Officers'*, Policy Studies Institute, 1983

Smith, D.J. and Gray, J. *Police and People in London*, Policy Studies Institute, 1985

Smith, M.C. 'Ethnic and Cultural Pluralism in the British Caribbean', in M. Bulmer and J. Solomos (eds), *Race*, Oxford University Press, 1999, pp.99–106

Smythe, T. 'The Police in Society', in P. Southgate, *Research and Planning Unit Paper 29*, Home Office, 1984, pp.26–7

Southgate, P. *Research and Planning Unit Paper 29*, Home Office, 1984

Solomos, J. *Black Youth, Racism and the State: The Politics of Ideology and Policy*, Cambridge University Press, 1988

Spencer, S. *Called to Account: The Case for Police Accountability in England & Wales*, National Council for Civil Liberties, 1985

Spicer, A. 'Typical Men', in S. Chibnall and R. Murphy (eds) *British Crime Cinema*, I.B. Tauris Publishers, 2001, pp.75–96

Stenson, K. 'Community Policing as a Government Technology', *Economy and Society* Vol. 22, No. 3, pp. 373–89 [n.d.]

Stevens, P. and Willis, C. *'Race, Crime and Arrests'*, Home Office Research Study No. 58, HMSO, 1979

Storch, R. 'The Policeman as Domestic Missionary', *Journal of Social History* Vol. 9, No. 4, 1976, pp.481–510

Studlar, P. 'Political Culture and Race Policy in Britain', in R. Rose and Associates, *Studies in British Politics: a Reader in Political Sociology*, Basingstoke: Macmillan, 1976, pp.105–14

Thornton, P. *Decade of Decline: Civil Liberties in the 1980s*, NCCL, 1989

Torres, R.D., Mirón, L.F. and Inda, J.X. (eds) *Race, Identity and Citizenship*, Oxford: Blackwell Publishers, 1999

Tuck, M. and Southgate, P. *Ethnic Minorities, Crime and Policing*, Home Office Research Study No. 70, HMSO, 1981

Waddington, P.A.J. 'Discretion, "Respectability" and Institutional Police Racism', *Sociological Research Online*, 1999

Walvin, J. *Passage to Britain*, Harmondsworth: Penguin Books, 1984

Wambu, O. (ed.) *Empire Windrush: Fifty Years of Writing About Black Britain*, Phoenix, 1998

Ward, S. (ed.) *British Culture and the End of Empire*, Manchester University Press, 2001

Waters, C. 'Dark Strangers in our Midst: Discourses of Race and Nation in Britain', *Journal of British Studies*, No. 36, 1997, pp.207–38

Weatheritt, M. *Innovations in Policing*, Croom Helm, 1986

Webster, W. *Imagining Home: Gender, Race and National Identity*, UCL Press, 1998

Weight, R. *Patriots: National Identity in Britain 1940–2000*, Basingstoke: Macmillan, 2002

Willis, C. *The Use, Effectiveness and Impact of Police Stop and Search Powers*, Home Office Research Unit, 1983

Young, M. *An Inside Job: Policing and Police Culture in Britain*, Oxford: Clarendon Press, 1991

Zubaida, S. (ed.) *Race and Racialism*, Tavistock Publications, 1970

Index